P9-CQQ-053

FARTHER AFIELD
See pp92–101

SOCIETY HILL AND PENN'S LANDING
See pp56–67
Street Finder maps 3 & 4

OLD CITY
See pp38–55
Street Finder maps 3 & 4

Old City

Society Hill and Penn's Landing

D e l a w a r e   R i v e r

| 0 meters | | 500 |
| 0 yards | | 500 |

6 FAMOUS ATTRACTIONS

PHILADELPHIA CityPASS

SEE IT ALL FOR LESS

SAVE 47%

The Franklin Institute

Adventure Aquarium

Phila Trolley Works Tour & The Big Bus Company

Philadelphia Zoo

Your choice of National Constitution Center or
The Academy of Natural Sciences

Your choice of Eastern State Penitentiary or
Please Touch Museum®

BUY CITYPASS AT THESE PHILADELPHIA ATTRACTIONS

SKIP MOST TICKET LINES
GOOD FOR UP TO 9 DAYS

ONLY $59 2-12 $39

CityPASS.com Atlanta Boston Chicago Hollywood Houston
New York City San Francisco Seattle Southern California Toronto 888-330-5008

Pricing and programs are subject to change.

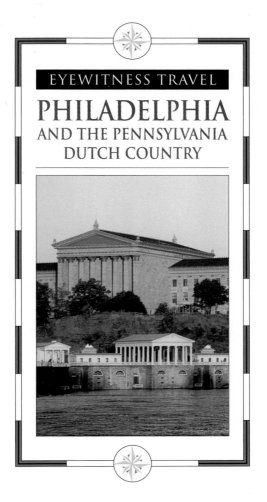

EYEWITNESS TRAVEL

PHILADELPHIA
AND THE PENNSYLVANIA
DUTCH COUNTRY

EYEWITNESS TRAVEL

PHILADELPHIA
AND THE PENNSYLVANIA DUTCH COUNTRY

MAIN CONTRIBUTOR: RICHARD VARR

DK

LONDON, NEW YORK,
MELBOURNE, MUNICH AND DELHI
www.dk.com

MANAGING EDITOR Aruna Ghose
ART EDITOR Benu Joshi
EDITORS Ankita Awasthi, Bhavna Seth Ranjan
DESIGNERS Mathew Kurien, Divya Saxena, Shruti Singhi
SENIOR CARTOGRAPHER Uma Bhattacharya
CARTOGRAPHIC RESEARCHER Suresh Kumar
PICTURE RESEARCHER Taiyaba Khatoon
DTP COORDINATOR Shailesh Sharma
DTP DESIGNER Vinod Harish

MAIN CONTRIBUTOR Richard Varr

PHOTOGRAPHER Demetrio Carrasco

ILLUSTRATORS
Arun Pottirayil, T. Gautam Trivedi, Mark Warner

Reproduced by Colourscan (Singapore)
Printed and bound in Malaysia by Vivar Printing Sdn. Bhd.

First American Edition 2005
11 12 13 14 10 9 8 7 6 5 4 3 2 1

Published in the United States by
DK Publishing, 375 Hudson Street,
New York, New York 10014

Reprinted with revisions 2007, 2009, 2011
Copyright © 2005, 2011 Dorling Kindersley Limited, London
A Penguin Company

Published in Great Britain by Dorling Kindersley Limited.

A CATALOG RECORD FOR THIS BOOK IS AVAILABLE FROM THE
LIBRARY OF CONGRESS.

ISSN: 1542-1554
ISBN: 978-0-75666-975-1

Front cover main image: Independence Hall, Philadelphia

MIX
Paper from
responsible sources
FSC
www.fsc.org   FSC™ C018179

**The information in this
DK EyeWitness Travel Guide is checked regularly.**
Every effort has been made to ensure that this book is as up-to-date
as possible at the time of going to press. Some details, however,
such as telephone numbers, opening hours, prices, gallery hanging
arrangements and travel information are liable to change. The
publishers cannot accept responsibility for any consequences arising
from the use of this book, nor for any material on third party
websites, and cannot guarantee that any website address in this
book will be a suitable source of travel information. We value the
views and suggestions of our readers very highly. Please write to:
Publisher, DK Eyewitness Travel Guides, Dorling Kindersley, 80 Strand,
London WC2R 0RL, Great Britain, or email: travelguides@dk.com.

◁ Philadelphia's skyscrapers towering over the Schuylkill River

CONTENTS

The Liberty Bell, one of the world's
greatest symbols of freedom

INTRODUCING
PHILADELPHIA
AND THE
PENNSYLVANIA
DUTCH COUNTRY

The relaxing environs of tree-
shaded Rittenhouse Square

A panoramic view of the Camden waterfront at dusk

Delicate bloom at the Magnolia Garden in Society Hill

Trademark horse and buggy in the Pennsylvania Dutch Country

The 18th-century Independence Hall

HOW TO USE THIS GUIDE

This Dorling Kindersley travel guide helps you get the most from your visit to Philadelphia. It provides detailed practical information and expert recommendations. *Introducing Philadelphia* maps the city and the region, sets it in its historical and cultural context, and describes events through the entire year. *Philadelphia at a Glance* is an overview of the city's main attractions. The main sightseeing section of the book is *Philadelphia Area by Area*, which covers all the important sights, with photographs, maps, and illustrations. *Farther Afield* suggests sights just outside the city core, while *Beyond Philadelphia* describes Dutch Country and historic Gettysburg among other areas. Information about hotels, restaurants, shopping, entertainment, and sports is found in *Travelers' Needs*. The *Survival Guide* has practical advice on everything from using Philadelphia's medical services and transport system to public telephones and post offices.

FINDING YOUR WAY AROUND THE SIGHTSEEING SECTION

Each of the four sightseeing areas in Philadelphia is color-coded for easy reference. Every chapter opens with an introduction to the area of the city it covers, describing its history and character, and has a Street-by-Street map illustrating an interesting part of that area. Finding your way around the chapter is made simple by the numbering system used throughout. Sights outside Philadelphia have a regional map.

Each area has color-coded thumb tabs.

1 Introduction to the Area
For easy reference, the sights in each area are numbered and plotted on an area map. This map also shows SEPTA subway stops and regional rail stations, as well as indicating the area covered by the Street-by-Street map. The area's key sights are listed by category.

Locator map

A locator map shows where you are in relation to other areas in the city.

A suggested route takes in some of the most interesting and attractive streets in the area.

2 Street-by-Street Map
This gives a bird's-eye view of the most interesting and important parts of each sightseeing area. The numbering of the sights ties in with the preceding area map and with the fuller descriptions of the entries on the pages that follow.

The list of star sights indicates the places that no visitor should miss.

PHILADELPHIA AREA MAP

The colored areas shown on this map *(see inside front cover)* are the four main sightseeing districts used in this guide. Each area is covered in detail in *Philadelphia Area by Area (see pp36–109)*, as are sights located outside the city center and the walks. These areas are also highlighted on other maps throughout the book. In *Philadelphia at a Glance (see pp24–31)*, for example, they help locate the top sights.

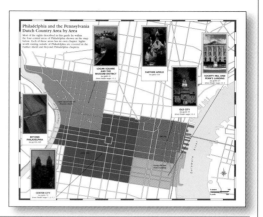

Numbers refer to each sight's position on the area map and its place in the chapter.

Practical information provides everything you need to know to visit each sight. Map references pinpoint the sight's location on the *Street Finder* maps *(see pp190–97)*.

3 Detailed Information
All the important sights in Philadelphia are described individually. They are listed in order, following the numbering on the area map at the start of the section. Practical information includes telephone numbers, opening hours, and map reference. The key to the symbols used is on the back flap.

The visitors' checklist provides all the practical information needed to plan your visit.

Story boxes provide information about historical or cultural topics relating to the sights.

4 Philadelphia's Major Sights
These are given two or more full pages in the sightseeing area where they are found. Historic buildings are dissected to reveal their interiors; color-coded floor plans in museums and galleries help you find important exhibits.

Stars recommend the features that no visitor should miss.

INTRODUCING
PHILADELPHIA
AND THE PENNSYLVANIA DUTCH COUNTRY

FOUR GREAT DAYS
IN PHILADELPHIA

You could easily spend a few weeks enjoying all the historic sights and attractions in Philadelphia, not to mention separate excursions to the Pennsylvania Dutch Country and Gettysburg. Most visitors, however, only have a few days and will want to make the most of their time. Outlined here are ideas for four separate days of sightseeing and

Grave, Christ Church Burial Ground

enjoyment – three of them in Philadelphia and one in the Pennsylvania Dutch Country. They include suggestions on what to see, where to eat, and what to do for entertainment. Of course, the suggestions are just that, and can be modified to suit your requirements. The prices are indicative of the cost of transport and admission (if any) for two adults or a family of four.

Interior of Congress Hall, adjacent to Independence Hall

HISTORIC PHILADELPHIA

- **Tour Independence Hall and National Constitution Center**
- **Lunch at Bourse Building**
- **Tour historic Old City**
- **Watch the Lights of Liberty Show**

TWO ADULTS allow at least $60

Morning
It is best to arrive at the **Independence Visitor Center** *(see p45)* when it opens at 8:30am to pick up your free, timed tickets to **Independence Hall** *(see pp42–3)*. The earlier you arrive, the better the chances of being admitted quickly. Note that tickets are usually gone by noon. Once you have your tickets the day can be planned accordingly. Visitors are first guided through the **Liberty Bell Center** *(see p44)*, and should spend the remainder of the morning visiting the **National**

Constitution Center *(see pp48–9)*. Stop for lunch at the satisfying food court in **The Bourse** *(see p145)* in Independence Mall East.

Afternoon
Start off by visiting the **Christ Church Burial Ground** *(see p46)* where Benjamin Franklin is buried. Allow 15 to 30 minutes here, and then go on to take a half-hour tour of the **Betsy Ross House** *(see p52)*. Visit the Colonial portrait gallery at the **Second Bank of the US** *(see p47)* and pass by the imposing façades of the **First Bank of the US** *(see p53)* and the **Philadelphia Merchants' Exchange** *(see p54)*. The **City Tavern** *(see p55)* is a good place to stop for some refreshment.

In the evening, take in the one-hour **Lights of Liberty Show** *(see p175)*, the premier nighttime 3D experience. It features spectacular images flashed onto historic buildings,

taking visitors on a starlit journey through Independence National Historical Park. Reservations required.

A SHOPPING DAY

- **Browse boutiques along Rittenhouse Row**
- **Lunch at Rittenhouse Square**
- **Visit King of Prussia Mall**

TWO ADULTS allow at least $60

Morning
Start by browsing through the elegant boutiques on **Rittenhouse Row** *(see p156)*, which has such high-fashion names as Jones New York and Ann Taylor. Also visit the nearby **Shops at Liberty Place** *(see p156)*. As noon approaches, check out the specialty shops at the **Bellevue Building**

Mural at Italian Market, famous for specialty foods and eateries

(see p156) and then have a quick bite at the building's upbeat food court. For restaurants with outdoor seating, head toward **Rittenhouse Square** *(see p78)*. **Pietro's Coal Oven Pizzeria**, **Devon Seafood Grill**, and **Parc** are good choices *(see p149)*.

Afternoon

Visit **The Gallery at Market East** mall *(see p156)* for some more shopping. Do not miss the nearby **Reading Terminal Market** *(see p73)*, and if you have time left over, head to the **Italian Market** *(see p99)* for coffee and Italian pastries. End your spree with a visit to the colossal **King of Prussia Mall** *(see p156)*.

The Franklin Institute in the Museum District

A FAMILY DAY

- **Visit museums around Logan Square**
- **Walk along Penn's Landing**
- **Take the RiverLink Ferry**
- **Visit the Adventure Aquarium**

FAMILY OF FOUR allow at least $175

Morning

Depending on time and budget, visit one or more of the four museums along the Benjamin Franklin Parkway – **The Franklin Institute** *(see p85)*, the **Academy of Natural Sciences** *(see p85)*, **The Barnes Foundation** *(see pp86–87)*, or the **Philadelphia Museum of Art** *(see pp90–93)*.

Break for lunch at one of the museum cafeterias before heading to the interactive **Please Touch Museum** *(see p170)* for children up to the age of seven.

Afternoon

Head over to **Penn's Landing** *(see p66)* and visit the **Independence Seaport Museum** *(see pp64–5)*. Later, take the RiverLink Ferry to the **Camden Waterfront** *(see p101)*. The ferry runs from April through mid-November. Make it a point to head to the **Adventure Aquarium** *(see p171)*, as the kids will love the aquatic life there. In the warmer months, the **Ghost Tour of Philadelphia** *(see p175)* is a great option for an evening activity. In winter, ice skate on one of the city's many rinks such as the **Blue Cross RiverRink** *(see pp168–9)*.

PENNSYLVANIA DUTCH COUNTRY

- **Tour Landis Valley Museum**
- **Have an Amish-style lunch**
- **Visit the Amish Experience**
- **Hop on board the Strasburg Railroad**

FAMILY OF FOUR allow at least $130

Morning

Arrive at **Lancaster Central Market** *(see p114)* by 8am to eat a hearty country breakfast. Only steps away are the **Lancaster Heritage Center Museum** and the **Lancaster**

The Blacksmith Shop at the Landis Valley Museum

Quilt & Textile Museum *(see p114)*. Go on to the **Landis Valley Museum** *(see pp116–17)* off Route 272 and spend some time exploring this living history village that provides an insight into the region's early farming communities. Head east on Route 340 through Bird-in-Hand and stop for a family-style lunch at the **Plain and Fancy Farm Restaurant** *(see p153)* next to the **Amish Experience** *(see p118)*.

Afternoon

Visit the Amish Experience and wander through the Country Homestead, a typical Amish home. Then watch the multimedia cultural presentation, *Jacob's Choice*, at the Amish Experience Theater. Spend the second part of the afternoon at Kitchen Kettle Village in **Intercourse** *(see p118)*, shopping for crafts and jarred foods. During the summer months, you can extend the day by hopping onto the 7pm train on the **Strasburg Railroad** *(see p119)* for the last ride through miles of farmland.

Tourists shopping for art and antiques in Lancaster

Putting Philadelphia on the Map

Located in the northeast region of the United States, Philadelphia sits on the southeastern edge of Pennsylvania along the Delaware River, which separates Pennsylvania from New Jersey. Founded by William Penn in the late 17th century, Philadelphia is now the nation's fifth largest city and the second largest on the East Coast. More than 1.5 million people live within the city's 135-sq–mile (350-sq–km) area.

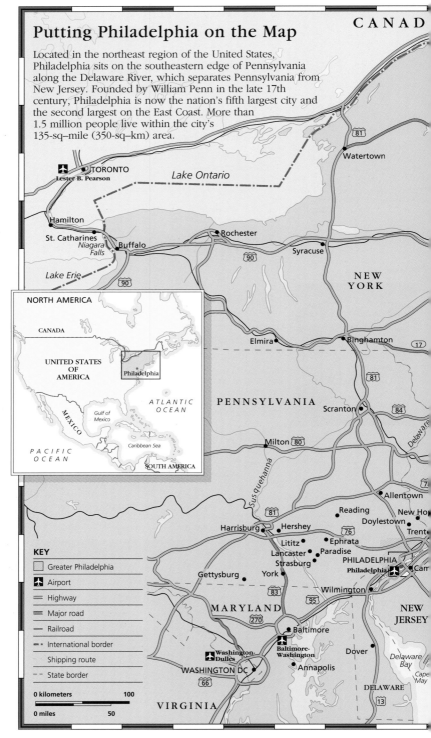

CANAD

TORONTO
Lester B. Pearson

Lake Ontario

Watertown

81

Hamilton

St. Catharines
Niagara Falls
Buffalo

Rochester

90

Syracuse

NEW YORK

NORTH AMERICA

CANADA

UNITED STATES OF AMERICA

Philadelphia

ATLANTIC OCEAN

MEXICO

Gulf of Mexico

Caribbean Sea

PACIFIC OCEAN

SOUTH AMERICA

Elmira

Binghamton

17

81

PENNSYLVANIA

Scranton

84

Delaware

Milton 80

Susquehanna

Allentown

81

Reading

New Ho

Doylestown

Trent

Harrisburg

Hershey

76

Lititz

Ephrata

Lancaster

Paradise

Strasburg

PHILADELPHIA

Philadelphia

Cam

Gettysburg

York

Wilmington

NEW JERSEY

83

95

KEY

◻ Greater Philadelphia

✈ Airport

= Highway

= Major road

— Railroad

-·- International border

Shipping route

-- State border

MARYLAND

270

Baltimore

Washington-Dulles

Baltimore-Washington

Dover

Delaware Bay

WASHINGTON DC

Annapolis

Cape May

66

DELAWARE

0 kilometers 100

0 miles 50

VIRGINIA

13

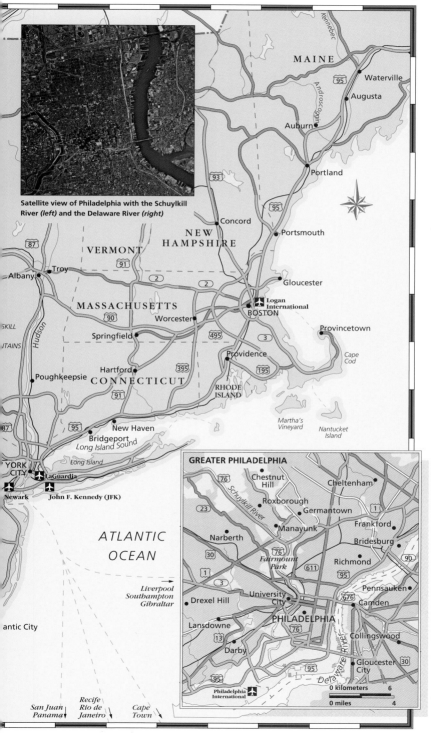

Satellite view of Philadelphia with the Schuylkill
River *(left)* and the Delaware River *(right)*

MAINE

95 Waterville
Augusta
Auburn
Portland
93
95 Portsmouth
Concord
NEW
HAMPSHIRE
VERMONT
91 Troy Gloucester
Albany 2 2
MASSACHUSETTS Logan
90 International
Worcester BOSTON
Springfield 495 Provincetown
Hartford 395 3 Cape
Poughkeepsie 91 Providence Cod
CONNECTICUT 195
RHODE
ISLAND
Hudson
KILL
TAINS
87
95 New Haven Martha's
Bridgeport Vineyard Nantucket
Long Island Sound Island
YORK
CITY LaGuardia
Long Island
Newark John F. Kennedy (JFK)

ATLANTIC
OCEAN

Liverpool
Southampton
Gibraltar

antic City

San Juan Recife Cape
Panama Rio de Town
Janeiro

GREATER PHILADELPHIA

76 Chestnut
Hill Cheltenham
23 Roxborough
Germantown 1
Schuylkill River Manayunk Frankford
Narberth Bridesburg
30 76 90
Fairmount Richmond
1 Park 611 95
3 Pennsauken
Drexel Hill University Camden
City 676
Lansdowne PHILADELPHIA
13 76 Collingswood
Darby Gloucester 30
95 City
Philadelphia
International
Delaware River

0 kilometers 6

0 miles 4

Central Philadelphia

Flanked by the Delaware and Schuylkill Rivers, central Philadelphia comprises several distinct neighborhoods, which together span more than three centuries of development. Much of the modern-day layout is based on city founder William Penn's original grid pattern – a crisscross of streets with five green squares. Four of these squares remain as pleasant, shaded parks today. The fifth, Penn's original Center Square, contains City Hall. The oldest districts are Old City and Society Hill.

Central Philadelphia
Center City (see pp68–79) skyscrapers can be seen along the Schuylkill River.

Statue of George Washington at Eakins Oval
A prominent equestrian statue pays tribute to America's founding father and first president against the backdrop of the imposing temple-like façade of the Philadelphia Museum of Art (see pp90–93).

Rittenhouse Square
One of William Penn's original five squares, this Center City park (see p78) is popular with downtown workers and residents. Extravagant high-rise buildings and upscale restaurants surround the square.

0 meters   500
0 yards   500

KEY

	Star sight
$	SEPTA subway stop
R	SEPTA regional rail station
R	PATCO rail station
T	SEPTA trolley stop
	Greyhound bus terminal
	Police station
P	Parking
+	Hospital
i	Visitor information
t	Church
	Synagogue

Old City Hall
Located next to Independence Hall (see pp42–3) in the heart of Old City, where a new nation was born in 1776, Philadelphia's Old City Hall was home to the US Supreme Court from 1791 to 1800.

Penn's Landing
This waterfront area hosts summer festivals and is home to the city's tall ships, the submarine Becuna *and the USS* Olympia. *Also located here is the Independence Seaport Museum (see pp64–5).*

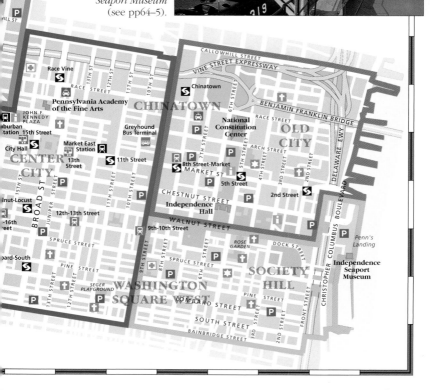

THE HISTORY OF PHILADELPHIA

William Penn first landed in the New World in 1682. Armed with a land charter, he founded a colony based on religious freedom that just a century later, would give birth to a new nation. Penn named the new city Philadelphia, derived from Greek words meaning "City of Brotherly Love."

Before William Penn's arrival, the Delaware River basin and the Schuylkill River watershed were inhabited by Algonquian-speaking Native Americans known as Lenni-Lenape. They were mostly peaceful hunters and gatherers, and many lived along the Delaware River and its tributaries. They were named "Delawares" for that reason by the first European settlers.

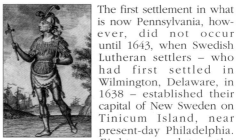

Chief Tammany, Delaware Indian chief

FIRST EUROPEAN EXPLORERS AND SETTLERS

Chartered by the Dutch East India Company, Englishman Henry Hudson's ship, the *Half Moon*, sailed into Delaware Bay in 1609 and claimed it for Holland. Dutch navigators followed shortly after: Captain Cornelius Hendricksen sailed up the Delaware in 1616 to where it meets the Schuylkill River; and in 1623, Cornelius Jacobsen explored the region further, leading to the establishment of a number of trading posts, including one on the Schuylkill in 1633.

The first settlement in what is now Pennsylvania, however, did not occur until 1643, when Swedish Lutheran settlers – who had first settled in Wilmington, Delaware, in 1638 – established their capital of New Sweden on Tinicum Island, near present-day Philadelphia. Eight years later, the Dutch, whose previous colonial efforts had been directed elsewhere, seized control and annexed the region as part of the Dutch Colony. From 1655 to 1664, the Dutch controlled the area until the English captured the Dutch colonies, calling them New York, after the Duke of York.

THE FOUNDING OF PENNSYLVANIA AND PHILADELPHIA

The son of a wealthy British admiral, William Penn was born in 1644. While attending Oxford University, Penn joined the Religious Society of Friends, the Quakers, a group who worshipped, without dogma or clergy, silently in unadorned meetinghouses. The faith was based on

TIMELINE

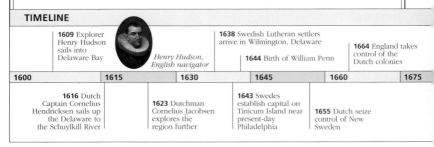

1600	1615	1630	1645	1660	1675

1609 Explorer Henry Hudson sails into Delaware Bay

Henry Hudson, English navigator

1638 Swedish Lutheran settlers arrive in Wilmington, Delaware

1644 Birth of William Penn

1664 England takes control of the Dutch colonies

1616 Dutch Captain Cornelius Hendricksen sails up the Delaware to the Schuylkill River

1623 Dutchman Cornelius Jacobsen explores the region further

1643 Swedes establish capital on Tinicum Island near present-day Philadelphia

1655 Dutch seize control of New Sweden

◁ **Detail from *Penn's Treaty with the Indians* by Edward Hicks, 1830–1840**

William Penn receiving the Charter for Pennsylvania from King Charles II of England

pacifism and equality. Expelled from university, Penn was later harassed and even imprisoned for his devotion to Quakerism. However, his wealth and social position allowed him to retain influence in the King's court.

The Charter for Pennsylvania was founded in 1681 as a result of a debt owed by King Charles II to Penn's father. The king repaid the £16,000 debt by granting the younger Penn land between Maryland and New York. In October 1682, Penn's ship, the *Welcome*, landed at New Castle in Delaware with many Quaker passengers. A few days later, Penn sailed up the Delaware to the capital of his new colony: Philadelphia.

As a Quaker, Penn espoused non-violence, and one of his first initiatives was to reach an agreement with the Delawares, thus forming treaties and enduring friendships with the Native Americans. The new colony also promised religious freedom, and was seen as a "Holy Experiment." More settlers followed, including both English and Dutch Quakers, German Mennonites, and the Amish, who settled in what is now called Pennsylvania Dutch Country.

Penn and surveyor Thomas Holmes designed Philadelphia in a grid pattern between the Delaware and Schuylkill Rivers. Their plan included five public spaces, as Penn and Holmes wanted to create a "green countrie towne." These tree-lined areas – Washington, Rittenhouse, Logan, and Franklin Squares – still remain today. City Hall now occupies the original "Center Square" at the junction of Market and Broad Streets.

Detail from *Peaceable Kingdom* by Edward Hicks (1780–1849), painted in 1826

TIMELINE

1683 Penn signs treaty with Delawares	**1684** Penn leaves Philadelphia and returns to England	**1699** Penn returns to Philadelphia	**1701** Penn grants charter to City of Philadelphia	**1718** Death of Penn in England

1680	1690	1700	1710

Gloria Dei Church

1677 Swedes establish Gloria Dei church

1682 Penn arrives in Pennsylvania and establishes Philadelphia

1701 Penn leaves America for good and returns to England

1710 Christ Church built at 2nd Street

COLONIAL EXPANSION

At the beginning of the 18th century, Philadelphia was already witnessing rapid growth. Penn had left Philadelphia in 1684 but returned in 1699 to find the population at more than 7,000. In October 1701, he granted a charter to the City of Philadelphia and left for England, never to return. As a port city, Philadelphia soon became an important center of commerce, with imports of sugar, rum, and molasses from the Caribbean. As trade flourished, so did manufacturing and shipbuilding. An increase in the number of homes led to a burgeoning community of craftsmen. The city also boasted a paper mill, furnaces, distilleries, tanneries, and a glass factory. One of its most famous residents, Benjamin Franklin *(see p53)*, arrived from Boston in 1723. His achievements as a scientist, inventor, printer, publisher, and statesman turned Philadelphia into a cultural center. In 1751, along with physician Thomas Bond, Franklin founded Pennsylvania Hospital, America's first public hospital.

Franklin, famous Philadelphia resident

The mid-1700s saw a clash between pacifist Quaker beliefs and the need to establish defenses for the colony. Pennsylvania was part of the British Empire and was involved in skirmishes against the French over land in North America. The conflicts climaxed with the French and Indian War, fought between the French and the British from 1754 to 1763, where a 21-year-old native of Virginia named George Washington received his first command. Britain was eventually victorious, but the war's end signaled a turning point for colonists, who now craved independence from Britain.

NEW NATION TAKES SHAPE

On July 4, 1776, independence from Britain was declared in Philadelphia, and in 1789, George Washington was elected the first president of the fledgling nation. The city remained the political heart of the country for a decade, serving as the capital from 1790 until 1800. During this time, America's first bank was chartered in 1791 to unify the nation's currency and to pay off war debts. The US Mint was established the following year.

In 1793, Philadelphia suffered a yellow fever epidemic, resulting in a large loss of life. Despite this, immigrants continued to flock to the city, increasing its population to nearly 70,000 by 1800, making it America's largest city at the time.

Yellow fever epidemic in Philadelphia, 1793

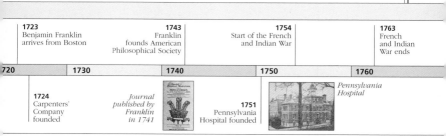

1723 Benjamin Franklin arrives from Boston	1743 Franklin founds American Philosophical Society	1754 Start of the French and Indian War	1763 French and Indian War ends

720   1730   1740   1750   1760

1724 Carpenters' Company founded	*Journal published by Franklin in 1741*	1751 Pennsylvania Hospital founded	*Pennsylvania Hospital*

Colonial Philadelphia and the American Revolution

The years leading up to, including, and after the American Revolutionary War are arguably the most important years of the history of Philadelphia. Rebellion against British rule began as early as 1765 with opposition to taxation without representation in Parliament. A decade later, the colonists elected Washington to lead their army – the Continental Army – in the war for independence. In 1776, the Declaration of Independence was signed in Philadelphia, though by 1777 the city was again occupied by British forces. Freedom was gained in 1781, and Britain at last recognized the colonies' independence with the 1783 Treaty of Paris. Five years later, the US Constitution (see pp48–9) was ratified at Independence Hall, Philadelphia.

Gunpowder casket, 1800s

George Washington
The Second Continental Congress elected Washington to lead the Continental Army against the British in 1775.

Drafting the Declaration
Thomas Jefferson wrote the first draft of the Declaration of Independence. Leaders of 13 North American colonies later ratified it at Independence Hall.

DECLARATION OF INDEPENDENCE (1776)
Delegates of the Continental Congress ratified the Declaration of Independence on July 4, 1776. This 1817 John Trumbull painting shows the presentation of the Declaration by the drafting committee. The signing of the Declaration was completed that August.

TIMELINE

1774 First Continental Congress held

1775 Second Continental Congress in Philadelphia

1776 Signing of the Declaration of Independence

1781 British surrender at Yorktown, Virginia

Postcard depicting George Washington

17 George Washingt elected natio first preside

| 1775 | 1780 | 1785 |

1777 Continental Army retreats after losing battles at Brandywine and Germantown

1776 Washington's army crosses Delaware River and defeats hired Hessian soldiers at Trenton

1783 Signing of the Treaty of Paris

1788 US Constitution ratified

Crossing the Delaware River
Washington's army crossed the Delaware River on Christmas Day in 1776, as depicted in this 1851 Emmanuel Leutze painting. They later defeated British troops at Princeton.

The Battle of Germantown (1777)
British troops barricaded themselves behind the stone walls of Cliveden, a Germantown mansion, forcing the Continental army to retreat.

Valley Forge, 1777–78
After losing the battles of Brandywine and Germantown in 1777, Washington's army lost over 2,500 men to exposure and disease during the winter encampment here.

Adoption of the Constitution (1787)
In 1787, delegates from all 13 original states, except Rhode Island, gathered at the Constitutional Convention in Philadelphia to draft and adopt a Constitution for the new nation.

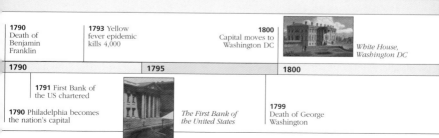

1790 Death of Benjamin Franklin

1793 Yellow fever epidemic kills 4,000

1800 Capital moves to Washington DC

White House, Washington DC

| 1790 | 1795 | 1800 |

1791 First Bank of the US chartered

The First Bank of the United States

1799 Death of George Washington

1790 Philadelphia becomes the nation's capital

The City & Port of Philadelphia (1800), engraving with watercolor by William Russell Birch

INDUSTRIALIZATION

By the 1830s, the city's financial and political prominence had begun to wane, as Washington DC, due to its location midway between the north and the south, became the nation's capital. Commercial activity and trade also diminished, as it could not compete with the more accessible port of New York City. Instead, Philadelphia turned to industry and manufacturing, becoming a regional center for textiles, iron and steel, and the shipping of coal. Shipbuilding continued along the Delaware. The city kept growing, with row houses built within the city limits and in surrounding boroughs and districts, including Germantown and Chestnut Hill. These areas soon became new neighborhoods by way of the city consolidation bill of 1854, under which they were incorporated within the city limits.

Growth also brought social clashes. For instance, there were rebellions against anti-slavery movements, and Pennsylvania Hall, the meeting place of the abolitionists, was set on fire in 1838. The 1840s saw violence against Catholics and immigrants, especially the Irish, with angry mobs burning down St. Augustine's Church, across from St. George's Church, in 1844.

POST CIVIL WAR PHILADELPHIA

The need for weapons, munitions, uniforms, and warships for the Union forces bolstered Philadelphia's economy during the Civil War years (1861–65). During the nation's centennial celebrations in 1876, the city held one of the first World Fairs and dedicated grand new buildings, some of which can be seen even today. These include Memorial Hall, a Beaux-Arts structure in Fairmount

Centennial Exhibition in 1876 at Fairmount Park, one of the oldest municipal parks in America

TIMELINE

	Burning of St. Augustine	**1844** Anti-Catholic rioters burn churches	**1856** Completion of Pennsylvania Railroad to Pittsburgh	**1876** City celebrates centennial with nation's first World Fair	**1907** First underground rail line commences	**1920s** Broad Street Subway completed	
	1840		**1860**	**1880**	**1900**		**1920**
1838 Anti-abolitionists burn Pennsylvania Hall	**1854** Surrounding boroughs incorporated	**1861** Civil War begins		*Wagons from the Civil War era*	**1890s** Electric trolleys introduced	**1914** World War I begins	

Park, and the Victorian-style Pennsylvania Academy of the Fine Arts. Politically, however, this was a time of corruption as Republican leaders controlled city contracts and thousands of jobs. Their influence only waned in the 1930s and 40s when voter support was lost due to allegations of corruption and financial mismanagement in city government.

Streetcar on 9th Street, Philadelphia, 1921

tensions mounted in the 1960s and through the mayoral terms of Frank Rizzo and W. Wilson Goode, the city's first African-American mayor, before stabilizing in the late 1980s. In 1985, during Goode's term as mayor, the controversial bombing of the headquarters of the black radical group MOVE took place, resulting in the deaths of 11 persons.

THE EARLY 20TH CENTURY

The city's infrastructure was well-established by the end of the 19th century. For instance, its streetcar system was run by electric power as early as the 1890s. There were further improvements in mass transit with the completion of its first underground rail line, the Market Street Subway, in 1907. Economic and industrial activity in Philadelphia remained brisk during World War I (1914–18), though it registered a dip during the Great Depression of the 1920s and 30s. World War II (1939–45) revived steel, chemical, and petroleum production, but Philadelphia gradually lost most of its manufacturing sector to other regions of the US.

Today, Philadelphia's economy is diversified. While some manufacturing units remain, corporate business has gained ground. Companies here specialize in technology, banking, pharmaceuticals, and insurance. Tourism is also key to the local economy. The city has more than 80 universities, colleges, medical schools, and world-class hospitals. In 2000, it hosted the Republican National Convention, which nominated George W. Bush for president, and in 2008 the city bolstered its global presence by hosting two Olympic trials ahead of the Beijing games.

MODERN PHILADELPHIA

After World War II, the city lost jobs and population to the suburbs, and then underwent political restructuring in 1951, with a new city charter that called for a stronger mayor and new city departments. It was also a time of urban preservation efforts downtown, but some neighborhoods in the city's north and west deteriorated. Racial

Celebrations at the Republican National Convention in 2000 in Philadelphia

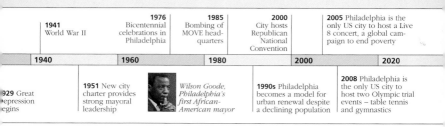

	1941 World War II	**1976** Bicentennial celebrations in Philadelphia	**1985** Bombing of MOVE head-quarters	**2000** City hosts Republican National Convention	**2005** Philadelphia is the only US city to host a Live 8 concert, a global campaign to end poverty
1940		**1960**	**1980**	**2000**	**2020**
1929 Great Depression begins	**1951** New city charter provides strong mayoral leadership	*Wilson Goode, Philadelphia's first African-American mayor*	**1990s** Philadelphia becomes a model for urban renewal despite a declining population	**2008** Philadelphia is the only US city to host two Olympic trial events – table tennis and gymnastics

PHILADELPHIA AT A GLANCE

Many of Philadelphia's most popular sights are to be found in Old City, within what's called "America's most historic square mile." They include Independence Hall *(see pp42–3)* and the iconic Liberty Bell *(see p44)*. Outstanding museums, including the Pennsylvania Academy of the Fine Arts *(see pp74–5)*, the Philadelphia Museum of Art *(see pp90–93)* and, from early 2012, the Barnes Foundation *(see pp86–7)*, are located in the city center. More than 100 places of interest are described in the *Area by Area* and *Beyond Philadelphia* sections of this book. To help you make the most of your stay, the following six pages are a guide to the best of Philadelphia, with a selection featured below.

PHILADELPHIA'S TOP TEN SIGHTS

Independence Hall
(see pp42–3)

Liberty Bell Center
(see p44)

Barnes Foundation
(see pp86–7)

Fairmount Park
(see p97)

Pennsylvania Academy of the Fine Arts
(see pp74–5)

Philadelphia Museum of Art
(see pp90–93)

National Constitution Center
(see pp48–9)

Reading Terminal Market *(see p73)*

Penn's Landing
(see p66)

Liberty Place
(see p79)

◁ Staircase and Grand Foyer of the Pennsylvania Academy of the Fine Arts *(see pp74-5)*

Philadelphia's Best: Museums

Philadelphia has several world-famous museums that reflect its cultural diversity, as well as its maritime and colonial past. Many are along the Benjamin Franklin Parkway, including The Franklin Institute, the Academy of Natural Sciences, and the Philadelphia Museum of Art, which is the third-largest fine arts museum in the country. The Rodin Museum near Logan Square houses the largest collection of sculptor Auguste Rodin's works outside Paris, while the University of Pennsylvania Museum of Archaeology and Anthropology, across the Schuylkill River, has an excellent collection of artifacts from civilizations past and present. Due to move to the Parkway's "Museum Mile" in 2012, the Barnes Foundation has an extraordinary collection of early French-modern and Postimpressionist art *(see pp86–7).*

Philadelphia Museum of Art
This museum houses over 300,000 objects, including a 12th-century stone portal from a French Augustinian abbey (see pp90–93).

Rodin Museum
The Shade *is just one of nearly 130 plaster, bronze, and marble sculptures housed in an impressive temple-like structure along the Benjamin Franklin Parkway* (see p86).

Logan Square and the Museum District

The Franklin Institute
The Giant Walk-Through Heart *is a key exhibit of this children-friendly science museum named after statesman and inventor Benjamin Franklin* (see p85).

Center City

Academy of Natural Sciences
A favorite exhibit at Philadelphia's natural history museum is Dinosaur Hall, *home to fossil constructions of the largest carnivores to ever walk the earth* (see p85).

Pennsylvania Academy of the Fine Arts
An ornate, arched foyer is the entrance to the country's oldest fine art school and museum. It was founded in 1805 with a collection of American paintings by artists such as Benjamin West and Impressionist Mary Cassatt (see pp74–5).

The African American Museum in Philadelphia
This museum celebrates important aspects of African-American history through permanent and changing exhibitions (see p51).

Philadelphia History Museum at Atwater Kent
On display here are more than 100,000 objects, including Norman Rockwell's Saturday Evening Post *covers depicting "vignettes of daily life" (see p50).*

National Museum of American Jewish History
Housed in an impressive five-story building overlooking Independence Square, this museum explores over 350 years of American Jewish history (see p46).

Old City

Society Hill and Penn's Landing

Independence Seaport Museum
A prominent seafaring museum, showcasing the submarine Becuna *and the cruiser* Olympia. *This view (right) is of the interior of the submarine* Becuna *(see pp64–5).*

| 0 meters | 500 |
| 0 yards | 500 |

Philadelphia's Architecture

Early architectural styles, derived from the colonists' native Britain, can still be seen in the older areas of Philadelphia. Colonial buildings incorporated simple Georgian and Palladian designs, which evolved into a bolder Federal style, with touches of Roman and Greek classical styles. The 19th century brought grander designs fueled by the Victorian era and the French-influenced Beaux-Arts style, which inspired many of the city's architectural wonders along the Benjamin Franklin Parkway. While modernist buildings crowd parts of Center City, it is the scattering of postmodernist skyscrapers that enliven the city skyline.

Philadelphia Merchants' Exchange, an example of the Greek Revival style

Betsy Ross House, a simple Georgian-style structure

GEORGIAN

Named after three British kings called George, this architectural style proliferated in early 18th-century Britain and soon became popular in colonial Philadelphia. Developed from the Roman Palladian style and often with columned façades, many of the early Georgian-style designs in the colonies were less elaborate than their English counterparts.

Independence Hall *(see pp42–3)* is a Georgian structure influenced by the style of English master architect Christopher Wren, while Christ Church *(see p52)* is a bold example of Georgian ecclesiastical architecture. colonial Georgian-style homes include the Deshler-Morris House, which was George Washington's summer retreat, and Cliveden, both in Germantown *(see pp106–107)*. Both houses

have columned doorways and nine front windows. A more simple home is the Betsy Ross House *(see p52)*.

FEDERAL

In Colonial America, the Georgian style quickly evolved into a more sophisticated Federal style, often with classical Greek and Roman influences. Particularly popular after the American Revolution until about 1820, this architectural style is characterized by oval and circular rooms, classical entryway detailing, rounded fanlights over doors, and Palladian windows. Also typical of this style are freestanding mansions and town houses with symmetrical brick façades and shuttered windows. Entrances are often cut from granite slabs and feature gently fluted columns. The largest and most elegant rooms of Federal houses are usually

found on the second floor. Some stately examples of such architecture are Old City Hall, Congress Hall, and the east and west wings of Independence Hall. Idyllic Fairmount Park, next to the Schuylkill River, has several mansions built with this architectural style, including Sweetbriar, Strawberry Mansion, and Lemon Hill, which has oval rooms on all three floors *(see pp108–109)*.

GREEK REVIVAL

Philadelphia's merchants' Exchange *(see p54)*, with a four-columned Corinthian portico at one end and an unusual, semi-circular portico at the other, testifies with the nation's infatuation with Greek Revival architecture in the 1830s. It was designed by the up-and-coming architect William Strickland, already noted for designing the steeple atop Indepen dence Hall. He also drafted

Strawberry Mansion, a Federal-style house in Fairmount Park

Parlor of the Victorian-style Ebenezer Maxwell House

the architectural plan for another prominent Greek Revival structure, the imposing Second Bank of the US *(see p47)*, with sturdy stone columns on its Greek temple-like façade.

A smaller Greek Revival structure, now housing the Philadelphia History Museum at Atwater Kent *(see p50)*, was designed by John Haviland, a contemporary of Strickland. This was the first home of the Franklin Institute *(see p85)*, where Strickland and other architects taught the nation's first architecture classes.

VICTORIAN

Ornate, Victorian-style façades were designed for Philadelphia buildings from the 1850s onwards.

Victorian-era architecture is influenced by various styles, such as Second

Colonnaded entrance of the Beaux-Arts style Philadelphia Museum of Art

Empire, Italianate, and Gothic Revival. For example, City Hall *(see p72)*, with its colonnades and mansard roof, is a French Second Empire design. The Academy of Music *(see p76)*, designed by prominent 19th-century architect and Philadelphia native Napoleon LeBrun, is Italianate in style, with period gas lamps on its high-windowed façade and lavish interiors. The Italianate Revival Athenaeum also has gas lamps on its walls. The city's only authentically restored Victorian home is the Ebenezer Maxwell House in Germantown *(see pp106–107)*, which is capped with a high tower, a mansard, and gable roof design.

Detail of Philadelphia Museum of Art façade

BEAUX-ARTS

American architects trained at the École des Beaux-Arts in France brought home this Greek- and Roman-influenced style of architecture, with elaborate detailing, balustrades, and prominent columns. Due to the grandiosity and size of these structures, Beaux-Arts became the favored style for court houses, government buildings, museums, and railroad terminals, and was used in many

late 19th- and early 20th-century buildings. The 1876 centennial celebration in Philadelphia ushered in Fairmount Park's Memorial Hall *(see p109)*, dotted with bronze sculptures and topped by a glass and iron dome creating a spacious atrium.

With one of the city's most splendid Corinthian porticos, 30th Street Station *(see p184)* is an example of this grand style, as is the Philadelphia Museum of Art *(see pp90–93)*. Displaying much of the same grandeur is the Free Library of Philadelphia *(see p84)*, and the similar structure next to it, both with porticos sheltering imposing colonnaded façades. On a smaller scale, the nearby temple-like Rodin Museum *(see p86)* features columns and a portico topped with a balustrade.

Philadelphia's skyscrapers, Liberty One *(left)* and Mellon Bank Center

POSTMODERNIST

The late 20th century witnessed a rebellion against the box-like glass and steel structures built after World War II. Thus was born the postmodern era in architecture, which featured sleek modernism tempered by conservative and historical design. This is evident in the twin towers of Liberty Place *(see p79)* with their pointed apexes. Also in the same style are the top floors of the Bell Atlantic Tower, while the Mellon Bank Center building is crowned with a pyramid-like dome. The latest addition to the city's skyline is the cutting edge Comcast Center.

Philadelphia's Best: Parks and Gardens

William Penn wanted his city to be "a green countrie towne" and included five squares in his original city grid. Today, four of these, Logan, Rittenhouse, Franklin, and Washington Squares, are pleasant areas with trees and park benches. Along the Schuylkill River on the outskirts of Center City is Fairmount Park. Its 9,200 acres (3,700 ha) of parkland and gardens make it America's largest urban park. The area has biking and walking paths along the river and one of its tributaries, Wissahickon Creek, which runs within a gorge. Fairmount Park includes the peaceful Shofuso Japanese House and Garden and restored historic houses that were once the homes of the colonial elite. Beyond Philadelphia, near the Delaware state border, are the exquisite Longwood Gardens.

Morris Arboretum of the University of Pennsylvania
Located in the Chestnut Hill neighborhood, this scenic tract of land includes ponds, greenhouses, meadows, and gardens with thousands of rare plants and "trees-of-record" (see p97).

✓ **Longwood Gardens**
22 miles (35 km)

Longwood Gardens
Industrialist Pierre S. du Pont designed this extravagant horticultural wonderland filled with spectacular choreographed fountains, whimsical topiaries, conservatories with exotic plants, and meadows and gardens replete with more than 11,000 varieties of indoor and outdoor plants (see p128).

Fairmount Park
This extensive greenbelt along the Schuylkill River and Wissahickon Creek is dotted with statues and features miles of running and biking paths (see p97).

0 kilometers   2

0 miles   2

Wissahickon Gorge
The country's only covered bridge within a major city is sited on a hiking trail in this gorge, whose forests and creek are home to over 100 bird species.

Logan Square
This grand square was once used as a burial ground and pastureland. Its center-piece is the majestic, multi-spouted Swann Memorial fountain designed by sculptor Alexander Stirling Calder (see p84).

Washington Square and Tomb of the Unknown Soldier
Named in honor of George Washington, the first president of the US, the centerpiece of this peaceful park is his statue, and the tomb of the unknown soldier of the Revolutionary War (see p60).

Rittenhouse Square
Center City's most popular park often fills with downtown workers who lunch under the trees. Reminiscent of New York's Central Park, it is flanked by upscale restaurants (see p78).

Welcome Park
Named after Penn's ship, this park was completed in 1982, three centuries after the founding of Philadelphia. Marble slabs depicting the city's origi-nal grid crisscross the park (see p55).

PHILADELPHIA THROUGH THE YEAR

Moderating mid-Atlantic coastal waters often temper the effects of extreme heat and harsh cold, making Philadelphia's summers enjoyable and the winters bearable. Spring flowers and warmer temperatures breathe new life into the city, with restaurants and cafés setting up tables outdoors, while city residents head to parks and river-fronts, anticipating summer festivals

Phillies logo

and excursions to beaches and lakes. Activities continue outdoors in fall, which heralds a rush of cool air and colorful foliage to Philadelphia's forested greenbelts. After Thanksgiving, activities tend to move indoors with a rush of Christmas shoppers to quaint boutiques and shopping malls. Sports and cultural activities are in full swing during the winter months, right through to spring.

School and college track teams compete at the Penn Relays

SPRING

Cherry blossoms bloom along the Schuylkill River in early spring, as Philadelphians flock to the Schuylkill river walk to enjoy the warmer weather. April also signals the start of the Philadelphia Phillies' baseball season.

MARCH

Philadelphia Flower Show *(early Mar)*, Pennsylvania Convention Center. Largest indoor flower show in the United States.
St. Patrick's Day Parade *(mid-Mar)*, Center City. A parade celebrating Philadel-phia's strong Irish heritage.

APRIL

Cherry Blossom Festival *(early Apr)*. Features performances of traditional Japanese arts and culture

at various locations through-out the city.
Philadelphia Antiques Show *(early Apr)*, 33rd Street Armory. Dealers from across the United States gather to display their unique finds.
Philadelphia Film Festival *(mid-Apr)*. Showcases the best in independent and foreign cinema.
Philadelphia Furniture and Furnishings Show *(mid-Apr)*, Pennsylvania Convention Center. Exhibition and sale of artisan-designed and manufactured furniture and home furnishings.
Penn Relays *(late Apr)*, Franklin Field. High school and college track stars compete in the longest uninterrupted collegiate

Juggler in action

track meet in the nation.
Equality Forum *(late Apr)*. Begun in the 1960s, this week-long gathering celebrates the cultural and political legacy of the gay, lesbian, bisexual, and transgender communities.
International Children's Festival *(late Apr–early May)*, Annenberg Center for the Performing Arts. Jugglers, folk singers, puppeteers, and dancers delight young audiences.
Philadelphia Phillies Baseball *(Apr–Oct)*, Citizens Bank Park. The season starts with many home games at the 43,500-capacity park.

Blooms at the Philadelphia Flower Show, a spring-time celebration

AVERAGE DAILY HOURS OF SUNSHINE

Hours

Sunshine Chart
This chart shows the average daily number of hours of sunshine in Philadelphia each month. June, July, and August have long days with lots of sunshine. Spring and fall have lesser hours of sunshine, with the shortest days in winter, which can still have ample hours of bright sun on clear, cold days.

MAY

Broad Street Avenue Run *(early May)*, Olney to south Philadelphia. This 10-mile (16-km) run raises funds for the American Cancer Society.
Rittenhouse Row Spring Festival *(early May)*. A spring festival that draws 50,000 visitors to enjoy the best of living, dining, shopping, and entertainment this classy neighborhood has to offer.
Dad Vail Regatta *(second weekend)*, Schuylkill River at Kelly Drive. Largest collegiate regatta in the United States with more than 100 colleges and universities participating.
Devon Horse Show and Country Fair *(late May and early Jun)*, Devon Fair Grounds. Equestrian talents on display at the country's oldest and largest event of its kind.
The Mann Center *(May–Sep)*, Fairmount Park. Performances through the summer by the Philadelphia Orchestra, Philly Pops, and others.
Penn's Landing Festivals *(May–Sep)*. Concerts along with ethnic events for families.
Annual Student Exhibition *(May/Jun)*, Pennsylvania Academy of the Fine Arts. This century-old tradition displays the works of award-winning students.

SUMMER

Summer ushers in a variety of festivals and live music on Penn's Landing. Fairmount Park fills with picnickers and thousands jam roadways to the New Jersey shore. Philadelphians celebrate the nation's birth, which took place in their own city, on the Fourth of July with remembrances, concerts, parades, and a massive display of fireworks above the Philadelphia Museum of Art.

JUNE

TD Bank Philadelphia International Championship *(first week)*. Philadelphia Museum of Art to Manayunk. The country's largest one-day professional cycling race.
Bloomsday *(Jun 16)*, Rosenbach Museum & Library. James Joyce fans celebrate the day on which Leopold Bloom, the protagonist of Joyce's *Ulysses*, made his "odyssey" through Dublin.
Odunde Afrikan American Street Festival *(mid-Jun)*, South Street. Celebrates the Yoruba New Year, beginning with a procession to the Schuylkill River and ending with a lively street fair.
Manayunk Arts Festival *(late Jun)*, Main Street. The region's largest outdoor arts and craft festival.

TD Bank Philadelphia International Championship professional bike race

Fourth of July fireworks over the Philadelphia Museum of Art

JULY

Wawa Welcome America! (week leading up to Jul 4). A week-long celebration with a concert and free events.
Fourth of July Parade *(Jul 4)*, Center City. Parade followed by fireworks.
Let Freedom Ring *(Jul 4)*, Liberty Bell Center. Descendants of those who signed the Declaration of Independence tap the Normandy Bell, an exact cast of the Liberty Bell.
Philadelphia International Gay & Lesbian Film Festival *(mid–late Jul)*. Showcases gay and lesbian films.

AUGUST

Philadelphia Folk Festival *(late Aug)*, Schwenksville. Music, dance, and crafts fair.
Philadelphia Eagles Football *(Aug–Dec)*, Lincoln Financial Field. The season features several home games.
Philadelphia Fringe Festival *(late Aug–early Sep)*. Citywide. Avant-garde theater.

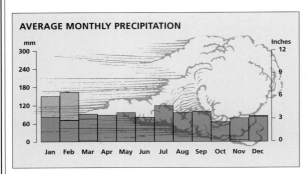

AVERAGE MONTHLY PRECIPITATION

mm | Inches
300 | 12
240 | 9
180 | 6
120 | 3
60 |
0 | 0

Jan Feb Mar Apr May Jun Jul Aug Sep Oct Nov Dec

Rainfall Chart
This chart shows the average monthly rainfall and snowfall. The heaviest rain is in July and August, with a yearly average of 41 inches. Considerable snow falls in January and February. The annual snowfall average is 21 inches.

■ Rainfall (from baseline)
■ Snow (from baseline)

Rowers in Lancaster County in the fall

FALL

Summer gradually gives way to cooler temperatures by mid-September, as thousands of students flock to the city's more than 80 colleges and universities. The bright reds and yellows of fall foliage begin to make an appearance by the end of September, with dramatic colors in October and early November. Football season gets into high gear, as fans head out to watch the Philadelphia Eagles. Autumn also kicks off many cultural activities, signaling a new season for the city's world-class performing arts, opera, and symphony companies.

SEPTEMBER

Von Steuben Day Gala and Parade *(late Sep)*, Center City. Celebrates the city's German heritage and pays tribute to Baron Friedrich von Steuben, a general in the Revolutionary War.

Puerto Rican Day Parade *(last Sun)*, Center City. Celebrating Puerto Rican heritage with a festival and parade.
Philadelphia College Festival *(late Sep or early Oct)*. College Day concert in the Benjamin Franklin Parkway, plus various career fairs and cultural events.

OCTOBER

Pulaski Day Parade *(first Sun)*, Center City. Pays tribute to the Polish Revolutionary War hero, General Casimir Pulaski.
Columbus Day Parade *(second Sun)*, South Broad Street. The parade honors explorer Christopher Columbus and the Italian American community.
Philadelphia Open Studio Tours *(mid-Oct)*. Local artists throughout the city open their workshops for two weekends.
Philadelphia 76ers Basketball *(Oct–Apr)*, Wachovia Center. NBA basketball season begins with a number of home games.

Philadelphia Flyers Hockey *(Oct–May)*, Wachovia Center. The NHL hockey season kicks off with home games.
Terror Behind the Walls *(mid-Oct through Oct 31)*, Eastern State Penitentiary. A "haunted" house in the former prison celebrates Halloween.

NOVEMBER

Philadelphia Museum of Art Craft Show *(early Nov)*, Pennsylvania Convention Center. Features handmade textiles, jewelry, household wares, and more.
Philadelphia Marathon *(third Sun)*. A 26-mile (42-km) run through the city starts and ends at the Philadelphia Museum of Art.
Thanksgiving Day Parade *(fourth Thu)*. Benjamin Franklin Parkway. The oldest such parade in the country.

Colorful floats and giant balloons at the Thanksgiving Day Parade

AVERAGE MONTHLY TEMPERATURE

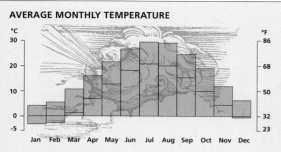

°C: 30, 20, 10, 0, -5
°F: 86, 68, 50, 32, 23

Jan Feb Mar Apr May Jun Jul Aug Sep Oct Nov Dec

Temperature Chart
Spring is usually mild with some brisk days. Summer can be hot and muggy on certain days, although most days are comfortable. Fall brings clear and colder days. In winter, wind chills sometimes drop temperatures to below freezing, but many days are refreshingly chilly and bright.

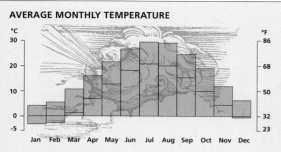

Christmas lights at the Wanamaker Building

WINTER

Strings of sparkling lights illuminate streets, buildings, and trees throughout Center City and beyond, as Christmas shoppers throng the city's main shopping districts. New Year's Day brings the Mummers Day Parade, one of Philadelphia's most honored traditions, in which costumed revelers and string bands march down the street. Sports enthusiasts spend the winter months attending Philadelphia 76ers basketball and Flyers hockey games.

DECEMBER

Christmas Tree Lighting *(Wed after Thanksgiving)*, City Hall. Signals the start of the holiday season.
Philadelphia Holiday Festival *(dates vary)*. Citywide performances by Mummers string bands, festivities, lighting events, and even tax-free shopping for shoes and clothing.

Washington Crossing the Delaware River Reenactment *(Dec 25)*, Washington Crossing. Reenactment of this historic turning point in the American Revolutionary War.
New Year's Eve *(Dec 31)*, Penn's Landing. A night of celebrations with fireworks along the Delaware River.
The Nutcracker *(dates vary)*, Academy of Music. Part of Pennsylvania Ballet's season, productions of this ballet are put on before Christmas.

JANUARY

Mummers Day Parade *(Jan 1)*, Center City. A Philadelphia tradition, where up to 20,000 people in decorative costumes parade to the music of string bands.
Chinese New Year Celebrations *(dates vary)*, Chinatown. Parades and festivities for two weeks.
Welcome Spring *(mid-Jan through Mar)*, Longwood Gardens. Indoor displays of bulbs, trees, and flowers create the illusion of spring during the winter months.

FEBRUARY

Philadelphia International Auto Show *(first week)*, Pennsylvania Convention Center. Highlights the latest in classic and luxury cars.
Mardi Gras *(Fat Tuesday before Ash Wednesday)*, South Street. Day-long revelry and celebration.
African American History Month *(all month)*. Various events throughout the city.

PUBLIC HOLIDAYS
New Year's Day (Jan 1)
Martin Luther King Day (3rd Mon in Jan)
Presidents' Day (3rd Mon in Feb)
Memorial Day (Last Mon in May)
Independence Day (Jul 4)
Labor Day (1st Mon in Sep)
Columbus Day (2nd Mon in Oct)
Veterans Day (Nov 11)
Thanksgiving Day (4th Thu in Nov)
Christmas Day (Dec 25)

Mummers Day Parade, a Philadelphia New Year's Day tradition

PHILADELPHIA AREA BY AREA

OLD CITY

The foundations of Philadelphia, and all of the United States, are rooted in the neighborhood of Old City, which includes the Liberty Bell and Independence Hall, both of which form part of Independence National Historical Park. This area was settled by city founder William Penn and his fellow Quakers in the late 16th century. It later served as the seat of government for rebellious colonial patriots during the American Revolution in the 1770s. Today, well-preserved historical structures, buildings, and homes that date back to the 18th and 19th centuries, some still situated on narrow cobblestoned streets, stand alongside modern buildings and high-rises.

Plaque at Independence Hall

SIGHTS AT A GLANCE

Historical Buildings and Districts

Arch Street Friends Meeting House **8**
Betsy Ross House **21**
Bishop White House **28**
Carpenters' Hall **26**
Christ Church Burial Ground **9**
City Tavern **30**
Curtis Center and Dream Garden Mosaic **14**
Declaration House **16**
Elfreth's Alley **20**
First Bank of the US **25**
Franklin Court and B. Free Franklin Post Office **23**
Free Quaker Meeting House **5**

Independence Hall pp42–3 **1**
Philadelphia Merchants' Exchange **29**
Philosophical Hall and Library **13**
President's House Commemorative Site **3**
Second Bank of the US **12**
Todd House **27**
US Mint **7**

Museums and Galleries

The African American Museum in Philadelphia **17**
Fireman's Hall Museum **19**
Independence Visitor Center **4**
Liberty Bell Center p44 **2**

National Constitution Center pp48–9 **6**
National Liberty Museum **24**
National Museum of American Jewish History **10**
Philadelphia History Museum **15**

Places of Worship

Christ Church **22**
Congregation Mikveh Israel **11**
St. George's United Methodist Church **18**

Parks and Gardens

Welcome Park **31**

KEY

■	Street-by-Street map *see pp40–41*
S	SEPTA subway stop
P	PATCO rail station
i	Visitor information

0 meters — 500
0 yards — 500

GETTING THERE

All sights are within walking distance of each other. Philly Phlash can be accessed along Market Street, and the local rail service makes stops at the Market East Station. The Market-Frankford line has two stops in Old City, at 2nd and Market, and 5th and Market. SEPTA buses 21, 38, and 42 also have stops in Old City.

◁ **The south face of Georgian-style Independence Hall, formerly known as the State House** *(see pp42-3)*

Street-by-Street: Independence National Historical Park

Known locally as Independence Mall, this urban park encompasses several well-preserved 18th-century structures associated with the American Revolution. The Declaration of Independence that heralded the birth of a new nation was written and signed in this historic area. Dominated by the tall brick tower of Independence Hall, the park includes the US Mint and several special-interest museums that explore Philadelphia's colonial and seafaring past, as well as its ethnic heritage. At least 20 of the buildings are open to the public.

Plaque commemorating Independence Hall

US Mint
This mint, the oldest in the country, struck its first coins in 1793. It also mints commemorative coins such as the Eisenhower dollar **7**

Christ Church Burial Ground **9**

★ National Constitution Center
This museum features interactive exhibits explaining the US Constitution. Visitors can walk among life-sized statues of the delegates who were present when this document was adopted in 1787 **6**

Free Quaker Meeting House **5**

KEY

— — — Suggested route

STAR SIGHTS

★ National Constitution Center

★ Liberty Bell Center

★ Independence Hall

Independence Visitor Center
Located in what is called "America's most historic square mile," the Independence Visitor Center provides visitors with practical information and a cultural and historical orientation. Timed tickets for Independence Hall are available here **4**

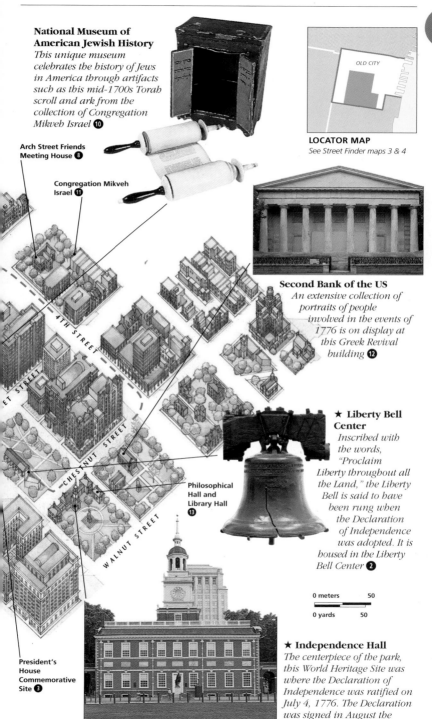

National Museum of American Jewish History

This unique museum celebrates the history of Jews in America through artifacts such as this mid-1700s Torah scroll and ark from the collection of Congregation Mikveh Israel ❿

Arch Street Friends Meeting House ❽

Congregation Mikveh Israel ⓫

LOCATOR MAP
See Street Finder maps 3 & 4

OLD CITY

Second Bank of the US

An extensive collection of portraits of people involved in the events of 1776 is on display at this Greek Revival building ⓬

★ Liberty Bell Center

Inscribed with the words, "Proclaim Liberty throughout all the Land," the Liberty Bell is said to have been rung when the Declaration of Independence was adopted. It is housed in the Liberty Bell Center ❷

Philosophical Hall and Library Hall ⓭

4TH STREET

STREET

STREET

CHESTNUT STREET

WALNUT STREET

0 meters 50
0 yards 50

President's House Commemorative Site ❸

★ Independence Hall

The centerpiece of the park, this World Heritage Site was where the Declaration of Independence was ratified on July 4, 1776. The Declaration was signed in August the same year ❶

Independence Hall ❶

Independence Hall tower clock

This unadorned brick building and clock tower are the most important structures in Independence Hall National Park. Earlier designated the State House of Pennsylvania, it is the site of the drafting and signing of the US Constitution and the Declaration of Independence, the document that declared America's freedom from the British Empire in 1776. Designed by master carpenter Edmund Woolley and lawyer Andrew Hamilton, Independence Hall was completed in 1753, more than two decades after construction began. Today, the meeting rooms are simply furnished, as they were in the late 1700s, and park personnel re-create history by pointing out the Windsor-style chairs from which colonial leaders debated the contents of the Declaration.

Congress Hall
Congress met in this hall from 1790 to 1800. Presidential inaugurations were also held here for George Washington and John Adams.

West Wing

THE DECLARATION OF INDEPENDENCE

Following colonial resistance to British "taxation without representation," the first shots of rebellion rang out in 1775 at the battles of Concord and Lexington outside Boston. Within a year, a strong feeling for independence overwhelmed the colonies. Known for his powerful writing style, Thomas Jefferson, Virginia Delegate and future president, took on the task of drafting a document declaring independence. He eloquently asserted man's right to freedom and rebellion while listing colonial grievances against England's King George III. After making changes, the Continental Congress ratified the Declaration of Independence on July 4, 1776.

An original copy of the 1776 Declaration of Independence

★ **Great Essentials Exhibit**
On display here are original copies of the Declaration of Independence and the US Constitution, as well as this silver Syng inkstand, said to have been used during the signing of the documents.

★ **Assembly Room**
Amidst its simple desks and chairs, delegates of the Continental Congress debated and signed the new nation's Declaration of Independence in 1776. Eleven years later, the Constitution was drafted and signed here as well.

★ **Rising Sun Chair**
The chair used by George Washington during the 1787 Constitutional Convention depicts a symbolic sun rising over the new nation.

Long Gallery
Running the length of the second floor, this light-filled reception room also hosted 18th-century balls and banquets.

East Wing

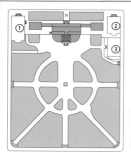

INDEPENDENCE HALL

① Congress Hall
② Old City Hall
③ Philosophical Hall

KEY

Illustrated Area

Lawn

STAR FEATURES

★ Great Essentials Exhibit

★ Assembly Room

★ Rising Sun Chair

Liberty Bell Center ❷

Originally rung to signal Pennsylvania Assembly meetings in the State House (now Independence Hall) in the mid-18th century, the Liberty Bell is one of the world's greatest symbols of freedom, bearing the inscription "Proclaim Liberty throughout all the Land unto all the Inhabitants thereof." Famous for its irreparable crack, the 2,080-lb (940-kg) bell was moved to its current home in the Liberty Bell Center in 2003. The center details the bell's history and significance, and how it became an icon for other freedom struggles. Clearly visible on the bell is the unsuccessful "stop drilling" repair, where, in 1846, the edges of the fracture were filed down to reduce friction and stress in an effort to slow the growth of the crack.

VISITORS' CHECKLIST

Market St between 5th & 6th Sts.
Map 4 D3. **Tel** *(215) 965-2305.*
🚊 *Market East Station.* 🚌 *5th St.*
🚌 *Philly Phlash.* 🕐 *9am–5pm.*
♿ **www**.nps.gov/inde

The Liberty Bell
The bell cracked the first time it was rung in 1753. Recast twice by Philadelphia's Pass and Stow Foundry, it was placed in the steeple of the State House (now called Independence Hall). It is said to have been first referenced as "Bell of Liberty" by 19th-century abolitionists.

Multimedia Display Gallery
This gallery displays old newspaper reports, videos, and photographs of people who have fought for liberty, such as the Dalai Lama and Nelson Mandela.

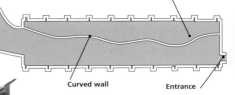

Curved wall   Entrance

Liberty Bell Center
The center is an elongated building where visitors first walk through a multimedia display gallery. This leads to the bell itself, set next to a large window with an excellent view of Independence Hall. A commemorative installation, "The President's House", sits adjacent to the Liberty Bell. This was the official residence of the US President before the White House.

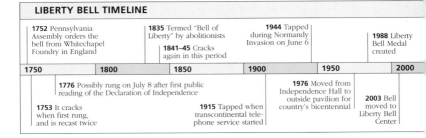

LIBERTY BELL TIMELINE

1752 Pennsylvania Assembly orders the bell from Whitechapel Foundry in England

1835 Termed "Bell of Liberty" by abolitionists

1841–45 Cracks again in this period

1944 Tapped during Normandy Invasion on June 6

1988 Liberty Bell Medal created

1750	1800	1850	1900	1950	2000

1776 Possibly rung on July 8 after first public reading of the Declaration of Independence

1753 It cracks when first rung, and is recast twice

1915 Tapped when transcontinental telephone service started

1976 Moved from Independence Hall to outside pavilion for country's bicentennial

2003 Bell moved to Liberty Bell Center

President's House Commemorative Site ❸

6th & Market Sts. **Map** 4 D3.
🚇 *Market East Station.* 🚆 *5th St.*
🚌 *Philly Phlash.* ⏰ *24 hrs a day.* ♿

Focusing on the untold stories of slavery in Philadelphia, the President's House brings to light the people and events that shaped the history of the slave trade in America. The outdoor installation sits on the site where America's first president, George Washington, resided. At the time he owned nine slaves, whose stories are told here. America's second president, abolitionist John Adams, also resided here.

This outdoor installation allows guests to walk through the house's footprint and examine important artifacts, including letters from George and Martha Washington urging the return of one escaped slave, Oney Judge. Visitors can learn about the political climate of the time by looking at exhibits that show the dynamics of the abolitionist movement in Philadelphia and the relationship between free blacks and slaves, as well as the laws signed by Washington and Adams and how they defined the American Presidency.

The site's location is one of the most significant features of the attraction. The Liberty Bell, a nation's symbol of freedom, sits atop the land where the slave quarters were located. Though Philadelphia was the epicenter of the fight for freedom in the 18th century, it was still a place where not all men were free.

The Independence Visitor Center in "America's most historic square mile"

Independence Visitor Center ❹

6th & Market Sts. **Map** 4 D2.
Tel *(215) 965-7676.* 🚇 *Market East Station.* 🚆 *5th St.* 🚌 *Philly Phlash.* ⏰ *Oct– Jun: 8:30am–5pm Mon–Sun; Jul–Sep: open later.*
🚫 *Jan 1, Thanksgiving, Dec 25.*
♿ 🛍 🚻 **www.**
independencevisitorcenter.com

One of the first stops for any visitor to Philadelphia should be the Independence Visitor Center, part of the Independence National Historical Park redevelopment project, along with the Liberty Bell and National Constitution Centers.

This expansive center offers information on more than 4,000 attractions in the city and the region. Apart from screening historical and orientation films, such as the short film *Independence* directed by John Huston, it has maps and brochures, touch-screen information kiosks, daily listings of events, and trip-planning services. Both National Park Service rangers and City of Philadelphia tourism specialists provide assistance and advice about historical sights, attractions, shopping, and dining. A gift shop has all manner of souvenirs themed around Philadelphia.

Of particular interest is a rotating exhibition of original engravings of colonial Philadelphia by William Russell Birch, which were first published in 1800. Prints of these line the Market Street entrance corridor.

The Visitor Center is also the place to obtain timed-entry tickets for Independence Hall. These are available on a first-come-first-served basis.

Plain brick façade of the 18th-century Free Quaker Meeting House

Free Quaker Meeting House ❺

Arch & 5th Sts. **Map** 4 D2.
🚇 *Market East Station.*
🚆 *5th St.* 🚌 *Philly Phlash.*
⏰ *1–5pm Wed– Sun.* 📷 ♿

This simple Georgian brick building was built in 1783 for Quakers who were compelled to bear arms in the American Revolution. Bearing arms meant defying the pacifist beliefs of the order, which led to expulsion from the main Quaker community. About 200 such people called themselves the "Free Quakers" and founded their own meetinghouse. However, in the years that followed, attendance dropped to just a few dozen, and by 1834, only two Free Quakers, Betsy Ross and John Price Wetherill, still attended meetings. Shortly thereafter, the meetinghouse was permanently closed. Since then, the building has served as a school, a library, and a warehouse.

Today, the building contains two benches and a window from colonial times. Also on display is Betsy Ross's five-pointed star tissue pattern, which she is said to have used to shape stars to make the colonial-era American flag. Today, the descendants of the original Free Quakers hold annual meetings here to decide how to distribute funds generated by rental of the hall and how best to invest income for charitable purposes. Actors dressed in colonial garb give lectures on the building's history, and guides demonstrate how to cut a five-pointed star in one snip.

National Constitution Center ❻

See pp48–9.

US Mint ❼

5th & Arch Sts. **Map** 4 D2.
Tel *(215) 408-0112.* 🚇 *Market East Station.* 🚌 *5th St.* 🚋 *Philly Phlash.*
🕐 *9am–3pm Mon–Fri.* 🎫 *group tours by prior arrangement.*
www.usmint.gov
Federal Reserve Bank of Philadelphia 6th & Arch Sts.
Tel *(215) 574-6000.* 🕐 *photo ID required to enter.*

The Philadelphia mint, the oldest in the US, produces gold bullion coins and medals, and also makes most of the coins that Americans use everyday. The first US coins, minted in 1793, were copper pennies intended solely for commerce in the colonies. Today, 24 hours a day, five days a week, hundreds of machines and operators, in a room the size of a football field, blank, anneal, count, and bag millions of dollars worth of pennies, dimes, and quarters. The gift shop, open on a limited basis, sells commemorative coins and numismatic collectables.

A related exhibit, Money in Motion, is on display at the **Federal Reserve Bank of Philadelphia**, which is located one block west of the US Mint. It explains US monetary policy and history with the help of interactive computer screens and impressive exhibits.

Philadelphia's oldest Quaker meetinghouse, on Arch Street

Arch Street Friends Meeting House ❽

4th & Arch Sts. **Map** 4 E2. ***Tel*** *(215) 627-2667.* 🚇 *Market East Station.*
🚌 *2nd St.* 🚋 *Philly Phlash.*
🕐 *10am–4pm Mon–Sat.*
✝ *10:30am Sun; 7pm Wed.*
www.archstreetfriends.org

This brick structure is the oldest Quaker meeting house still in use in Philadelphia. Built in 1804, the site first served as a Quaker burial ground, but later accommodated victims of the yellow fever epidemic in the 1790s. Today, the house has a central hall and two adjacent meeting rooms. The East Room features Quaker artifacts and six dioramas depicting William Penn's life as a Quaker. The West Room contains worn wooden benches and now serves as the main meeting and worship hall.

Christ Church Burial Ground ❾

5th & Arch Sts. **Map** 4 D2.
Tel *(215) 922-1695.* 🚇 *Market East Station.* 🚌 *5th St.* 🚋 *Philly Phlash.*
🕐 *10am–4pm Mon–Sat, noon–4pm Sun (burial ground); 9am–5pm Mon–Sat, noon–5pm Sun (church).*
🎫 🛇 **www**.oldchristchurch.org

This crammed cemetery dates back to 1719, and is an expansion of the church's original graveyard. More than 5,000 people are buried here, most from colonial times. The burial ground is the final resting place of Benjamin Franklin, his wife Deborah, and their daughter and son-in-law Sarah Franklin and Richard Bache. Four other signers of the Declaration of Independence – Dr. Benjamin Rush, Francis Hopkinson, George Ross, and Joseph Hewes – are also buried here. Franklin's grave is on the perimeter of the grounds, and is visible through an iron grating. Passers-by toss pennies on the grave, both to show respect and to bring good luck. With headstones already deteriorating by the mid-19th century, all gravestone inscriptions were copied and published in 1864 in order to preserve records of people interred in this graveyard.

Headstone, Christ Church Burial Ground

National Museum of American Jewish History ❿

Independence Mall East, 55 N 5th St.
Map 4 D2. ***Tel*** *(215) 923-3811.*
🚇 *Market East Station.* 🚌 *5th St.*
🚋 *Philly Phlash.* 🕐 *10am–5pm Mon–Thur, 10am–3pm Fri, noon–5pm Sun.* 🎫 *Sat, Jewish holidays.* ♿
www.nmajh.org

This is the only institution in the nation dedicated solely to the story of the American Jewish experience. The core exhibition traces the lives of American Jews from 1654 to the present, exploring how they created a new home in

Inspecting coins at the US Mint

a free land and examining how this country shaped their lives, communities, and livelihoods.

The museum includes nearly 1,100 artifacts, films, and state-of-the-art technology that provide a powerful testament to what free people can accomplish for themselves and for society at large.

Exhibits devoted to everyday relationships and popular culture make the collection accessible to both Jewish and non-Jewish audiences. The *Only in America Gallery/ Hall of Fame* illustrates the accomplishments of prominent American Jews.

Federal-style façade of Library Hall, a reproduction of the 1789 original

Congregation Mikveh Israel ⓫

44 N 4th St. **Map** 4 E2. **Tel** *(215) 922-5446.* 🚇 *Market East Station.* 🚋 *5th St.* 🚌 *Philly Phlash.* ⏱ *10am–5pm daily.* ⭐ *7:15am daily; Fri evening; 9am Sat.* ♿ **www**.mikvehisrael.org

Philadelphia's oldest Jewish congregation, Mikveh Israel, dates to before the 1740s. The congregation built its first synagogue in 1782, and moved into its current building in 1976.

Mikveh Israel's archival collection includes two pairs of Torah finials crafted by silversmith Myer Myers in 1772 and letters written by US Presidents George Washington and Abraham Lincoln. Past congregation members included colonial patriot and financier Haym Salomon; Nathan Levy, whose ship brought the Liberty Bell to America; and Rebecca Gratz, who founded educational and social institutions. The synagogue still holds a traditional service, which has remained virtually unchanged since the colonial era.

Second Bank of the United States ⓬

420 Chestnut St. **Map** 4 D3. **Tel** *(215) 965-7676, (800) 537-7676.* 🚇 *Market East Station.* 🚋 *5th St.* 🚌 *Philly Phlash.* ⏱ *11am–4pm Wed–Sun.* ♿ **www**.nps.gov/inde

Built between 1819 and 1824, this is one of America's finest examples of Greek Revival architecture. Once a repository that provided credit for federal government agencies and private businesses, it now houses a collection of 185 paintings from the late 18th and early 19th centuries. On view are portraits of colonial and federal leaders, military officers, explorers, scientists, and founding fathers.

Many of the portraits are by Charles Willson Peale (1741–1827), his brother James, and their respective children, who together form America's most distinguished family of artists. Peale began collecting portraits after the Revolutionary War. Today, 94 of his paintings, including likenesses of George Washington, Thomas Jefferson, and the Marquis de LaFayette, the Continental Army's French ally, are on display, along with portraits by other artists.

Philosophical Hall and Library Hall ⓭

5th St between Chestnut & Walnut Sts. **Map** 4 D3. **Tel** *(215) 440-3400.* 🚇 *Market East Station.* 🚋 *5th St.* 🚌 *Philly Phlash.* ⏱ *Philosophical Hall: 10am–4pm Thu–Sun, varies with exhibits; Library Hall: 9am–4:45pm Mon–Fri (lobby exhibit).* **www**.amphilsoc.org

A Colonial-era "think tank," the American Philosophical Society was founded in 1743 by Benjamin Franklin to promote the study of government, nature, science, and industry. Built in 1789, the Federal-style Philosophical Hall was a meeting place for doctors, clergymen, and the founding fathers of the nation. Reopened in 2001 for the first time since the early 19th century, the hall today hosts art, history, and science exhibitions.

The society also owns Library Hall, once the home of the Library Company founded by Franklin in 1731. The company's vast collections served as the Library of Congress until 1800. The current building, a reconstruction of the 1789 original, stores some of the society's most precious works, including the title page of an 1859 manuscript of Darwin's *Origin of Species,* the journals of explorers Lewis and Clark, and Jefferson's handwritten Declaration of Independence.

Redbrick exterior of Congregation Mikveh Israel

National Constitution Center ⑥

The inscription "We the People" is boldly engraved on the massive Indiana limestone façade of this sprawling center, which was opened on July 4, 2003. It explains the US Constitution through more than 100 interactive and multimedia exhibits, including artifacts, sculptures, photographs, video, and film. Visitors can listen to President Franklin Delano Roosevelt's speeches or to actual arguments from Supreme Court cases at a replica of the Supreme Court Bench, or walk through a re-creation of the 19th-century Senate floor. The circular main hall also contains displays that illuminate the text of the Constitution and highlight the themes of liberty and freedom.

Washington's statue in Signers' Hall

Engraved Façade
"We the People," part of the opening words of the US Constitution, engraved on the façade of the center.

THE US CONSTITUTION

After the Revolutionary War, delegates from the original 13 states, except Rhode Island, gathered in Philadelphia for the Constitutional Convention in 1787. It took them nearly four months to draft a document creating a strong centralized government for the new nation. Adopted on September 17, the Constitution ensures individual liberties and defines distinct powers for Congress, the president, and the federal courts, while also establishing a system of "Checks and Balances" so that no branch of government can dominate the others.

A copy of the Constitution of the United States

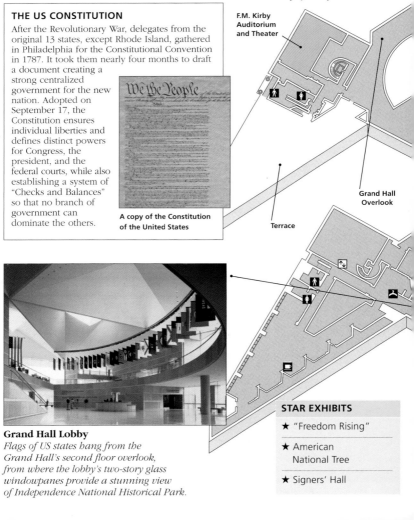

F.M. Kirby Auditorium and Theater

Grand Hall Overlook

Terrace

Grand Hall Lobby
Flags of US states hang from the Grand Hall's second floor overlook, from where the lobby's two-story glass windowpanes provide a stunning view of Independence National Historical Park.

STAR EXHIBITS

★ "Freedom Rising"

★ American National Tree

★ Signers' Hall

VISITORS' CHECKLIST

525 Arch St. **Map** 4 D2.
Tel (215) 409-6600. 🚇 Market
East Station. 🚏 5th St. 🚌 Philly
Phlash. ⏰ 9:30am–5pm Mon–
Fri, 9:30am–6pm Sat, noon–5pm
Sun. ⚫ Thanksgiving, Dec 25.
📷 ♿ 🍴 🏛
www.constitutioncenter.org

Second Floor

★ "Freedom Rising"
*The circular, 350-seat
Kimmel Theater features
"Freedom Rising," a multimedia production that
narrates the story of the US Constitution. This
17-minute show is projected on a 360-degree screen.*

★ American National Tree
*With the "We the People" wall in the foreground,
the circular American National Tree features
stories of more than 100 Americans who have
influenced the Constitution. Each story exemplifies
tolerance, diversity, and opportunity.*

Box Office

First Floor

Main Entrance

KEY
- ☐ Richard and Helen DeVos Exhibit Hall
- ☐ Kimmel Theater
- ☐ Posterity Hall
- ☐ Signers' Hall
- ☐ F.M. Kirby Auditorium and Theater
- ☐ First Public Printing of the Constitution
- ☐ Non-exhibition space

CENTER GUIDE
*The Grand Hall Lobby
and Kimmel Theater are
on the ground floor.
Permanent displays and
interactive exhibits are
situated on the second
floor in the circular
DeVos Hall.*

★ Signers' Hall
*Walk among life-sized bronze
statues of the 39 men who
signed the Constitution
(including that of Benjamin
Franklin, seated in the front),
and the three who dissented.*

Curtis Center and Dream Garden Mosaic ⑭

6th & Walnut Sts. **Map** 4 D3.
Tel (215) 238-6450. 🚇 *Market
East Station.* 🚋 *5th St.* 🚌 *Philly
Phlash.* ⬤ *8am–6pm Mon–Fri,
10am–1pm Sat.* ♿

This Beaux-Arts building is
where Cyrus Curtis kicked off
his publishing empire in 1883
with the founding of the
Ladies Home Journal. His
publishing company also
breathed new life into the
Saturday Evening Post,
and created popular
magazines such as
*American Home, Jack
and Jill, Holiday*, and
Country Gentleman.

Inside the building is the
enormous *Dream Garden
Mosaic*, a 49ft x 15ft (15m x
4.5m) glasswork that domi-
nates the lobby. Designed
by Maxfield Parrish, the
mosaic was completed in
1916 by Louis Comfort
Tiffany and Tiffany Studios.
The artwork, depicting a
garden with trees and
streams, has more than
100,000 pieces of hand-
fired favrile glass. In
1998, it was sold to a
Las Vegas casino
owner, but the people
of Philadelphia resisted the
move. Local artists and histo-
rians helped in raising $3.5
million for the Pennsylvania
Academy of the Fine Arts
(see pp74–5) to buy back the
mosaic. It later underwent
painstaking restoration.

**Atwater Kent
exterior detail**

Philadelphia History Museum at Atwater Kent ⑮

15 S 7th St. **Map** 4 D3. *Tel* (215)
685-4830. 🚇 *Market East Station.*
🚋 *8th St.* 🚌 *Philly Phlash.*
⬤ *1–5pm Wed–Sun.* ⬤ *Jan 1,
Thanksgiving, Dec 25.* 🎟️ 📷
www.philadelphiahistory.org

Philadelphia's official history
museum since 1938, the former
Atwater Kent Museum was
refurbished and rebranded (to
its current name) in 2010. Its
collection of 100,000 objects
and images spanning over
300 years remains the
museum's foundation.
Designed by John Haviland
in Greek Revival style and
completed in 1826, this
was the original home of
The Franklin Institute. The
nation's first architecture
classes were taught here.
The building was saved from
demolition in 1935 when A.
Atwater Kent purchased it
for a museum.

A colorful walk-on map of
the city covers the first floor
gallery. Past exhibitions
have included furniture
used by President George
Washington while living
in Philadelphia and
Benjamin Franklin's
wine glass. The museum
has an expansive collection of
Saturday Evening Post covers
showing "vignettes of daily
life" in America by Norman
Rockwell, who created 322
images for the Philadelphia-
based magazine between
1916 and 1963.

**Declaration House, reconstructed
in 1975 by National Park Service**

Declaration House ⑯

7th & Market Sts. **Map** 4 D2.
Tel (215) 965-7676, (800) 537-7676.
🚇 *Market East Station.* 🚋 *8th St.*
🚌 *Philly Phlash.* ⬤ *hours vary, call
to confirm.*

The current brick structure of
Declaration House is a 1975
reconstruction of the
Georgian-style home where
Thomas Jefferson drafted the
Declaration of Independence
(see p42) from June 11 to 28,
1776. He had rented two
upstairs rooms from bricklayer
Jacob Graff, who had built
the house in 1775. Although
only a few blocks from
Independence Hall, the house
faced a field and stable, and
offered Jefferson a quieter
setting to write the Declaration.

Today, along with a bust of
the famous American statesman and third president, the
house includes copies of
Jefferson's rough drafts of
the Declaration. The two

***Dream Garden Mosaic**, an enormous glass artwork gracing the Curtis Center lobby*

rooms upstairs contain period furnishings, and include recreations of Jefferson's bedroom and parlor, where he wrote the document.

The African American Museum in Philadelphia ⓱

701 Arch St. **Map** 4 D2. **Tel** (215) 574-0380. 🚇 Market East Station. 💲 5th St. 🚌 Philly Phlash. 🕙 10am–5pm Tue–Sat; noon–5pm Sun; Martin Luther King Day. 🔴 Mon, public hols. 🎫 🎥 🚹 🔵 www.aampmuseum.org

A Smithsonian affiliate, this museum is one of several founded in Philadelphia during the nation's bicentennial year. The museum is dedicated to "collecting, preserving, and interpreting the material and intellectual culture of African Americans" in the local area and the Americas. Since opening in 1976, the collection has swelled to more than 500,000 artifacts, including photographs, documents, fine and folk art, costumes, books, periodicals, and a number of other memorabilia.

Permanent and changing exhibitions celebrate important aspects of African-American life and history, including the Civil Rights movement, and contributions in the arts, entertainment, sports, medicine, politics, religion, law, and technology. The permanent exhibit, "Audacious Freedom: African Americans in Philadelphia in 1776–1876", uses interactive displays to recount the stories and contributions made by people of African descent in Philadelphia. Previous exhibitions have showcased African woodcarvings and textile designs while interpreting the traditions and ceremonies of several African countries. Others have focused on struggles against slavery and oppression, including the Haitian Revolution, which resulted in Haiti establishing

L'Ouverture by Ulrick Jean-Pierre, **African American Museum**

the world's first Black republic in 1804. The museum also organizes regular workshops and demonstrations.

St. George's United Methodist Church ⓲

235 N 4th St. **Map** 4 E2. **Tel** (215) 925-7788. 🚇 Market East Station. 💲 5th St. 🚌 Philly Phlash. 🕙 10am–3pm Mon–Fri; Sun morning after worship; Sat by appt. 🎫

The American Methodist movement began in St. George's United Methodist Church in 1769, making it the country's oldest Methodist church in continuous use. This simple brick structure, its inside walls adorned with a muted blue tint, has not changed much since it was remodeled in 1792. Colonial-era wooden pews and floorboards remain, as do the wrought iron candle chandeliers and candelabra, although now wired with electric lights. A two-room museum has 18th- and 19th-century artifacts, hymnals, bibles, and other important church keepsakes. They include a 1785 silver chalice from John Wesley, the founder of the movement, the original handwritten journals of Joseph Pilmoor, the first pastor of the church, and a bible from Francis Asbury, considered

Exhibit at the African American Museum

the father of the American United Methodist Church.

St. Augustine's Church across the street dates back to 1796. Burned down in 1844 by anti-Catholic rioters, the current building was designed by architect Napoleon LeBrun and rebuilt in 1847.

Fireman's Hall Museum ⓳

147 N 2nd St. **Map** 4 E2. **Tel** (215) 923-1438. 🚇 Market East Station. 💲 2nd St. 🚌 Philly Phlash. 🕙 10am–4:30pm Tue–Sat (until 9pm 1st Fri of month). 🔵 www.firemanshall.org

Housed in an old firehouse that was operational between 1902 and 1952, this unique museum narrates the history of firefighting in Philadelphia, back to colonial times. The building still contains the original brass sliding pole used for quick access to fire trucks. Several pieces of old equipment are on display, including an 1896 hook-and-ladder, a 1903 high-pressure Cannon Wagon, and a 1907 steam-powered pumper. Of special note are two well-preserved hand-pumpers, one from 1815, and the other from 1730, six years before Benjamin Franklin founded the nation's first fire department. Also on display are axes, saws, nozzles, old fire plaques indicating insured buildings, and leather fire hats from the early 19th century. A large stained-glass window memorializes fallen firefighters.

Façade of the Fireman's Hall Museum

Elfreth's Alley ⑳

N 2nd St between Arch & Race Sts.
Map 4 E2. ⚑ *Elfreth's Alley Museum,
126 Elfreth's Alley, (215) 574-0560.*
🚇 *Market East Station.* 🚌 *2nd St.*
🚌 *Philly Phlash.* 🏛 ⌚ *10am–5pm
Tue–Sat, noon–5pm Sun.* 🖼 ✂ ⬜
www.elfrethsalley.org

The oldest continuously
occupied residential street in
the country, this narrow
cobblestoned lane is lined
with 33 historic homes, most
in simple Georgian style.
Named after Jeremiah Elfreth,
a blacksmith who built and
rented out some of the first
homes, the alley dates back
to 1702, when it was a path
used by carts hauling goods
from the Delaware River
docks. Its early occupants
were tradespeople, artisans,
and sea captains, while the
industrial boom later brought
in laborers and tailors.

The oldest homes are at 120
and 122, built between 1724
and 1728. The street's Mantua
Maker's Museum House, at 126,
has been restored to resemble
the period between 1762 and
1794, when it was owned by
sisters-in-law Mary Smith and
Sarah Milton, makers of
mantuas and dresses. The
home at 124 is now a gift shop.

Halfway down the street is
another smaller alley, Bladen
Court, which includes three
houses and a courtyard.
Visitors can take a guided or
self-guided audio tour. Twice
a year, in June and December,
many Elfreth Alley residents
open their homes for tours
during Fete Days celebrations.

**Betsy Ross House, where the first
American flag was sewn**

Betsy Ross House ㉑

239 Arch St. **Map** 4 E2. **Tel** *(215)
686-1252.* 🚇 *Market East Station.*
🚌 *2nd St.* 🚌 *Philly Phlash.*
⌚ *Apr–Sep: 10am–5pm; Oct–Mar:
10am–5pm Tue–Sun.* ● *Jan 1,
Thanksgiving, Dec 25.* ♿ *limited
access.* **www**.betsyrosshouse.org

One of Philadelphia's most
visited historic sites, this
simple colonial home was
where Quaker seamstress and
upholsterer Betsy Ross is said
to have sewn the first
American flag – although no
official documentation exists
to prove it. Instead, the story
was handed down through
generations of her family.
Nonetheless, the 1740 row
house has been restored to
around 1777, when Ross was
supposedly commissioned
by George Washington to
create the "Stars and Stripes"
for the struggling new nation.
The home, with narrow
stairwells and low ceilings,
is decorated with period
antiques and reproduction
pieces, but also has a few
original items that once
belonged to Ross, including
her eyeglasses, a family bible,
and an American Chippendale
walnut chest-on-chest.

Christ Church ㉒

2nd St above Market St. **Map** 4 E2.
Tel *(215) 922-1695.* 🚇 *Market East
Station.* 🚌 *2nd St.* 🚌 *Philly Phlash.*
⌚ *9am–5pm Mon–Sat; 12:30pm–
5pm Sun.* ● *Jan & Feb: Mon & Tue.*
✝ *9am & 11am Sun, noon Wed.*
www.oldchristchurch.org

Founded in 1695, Christ
Church was Philadelphia's
only Church of England parish
for 66 years. The existing
structure, built in 1754 in
Georgian style, after Wren's
London churches, was the
town's tallest building at the
time. Often called the "Nation's
Church," it was where revolu-
tionary leaders, including
Benjamin Franklin, Betsy
Ross, and George and Martha
Washington, once worshiped.
Plaques mark some pews
used by the colonial elite.

Inside is the baptismal font
in which William Penn was
baptized, dating from the
14th century and donated by
London's All Hallows Church
in 1697. Bishop William White
(see p54), parish rector for
57 years, is buried in the
chancel of the church.

Franklin Court and B. Free Franklin Post Office ㉓

Between 3rd & 4th Sts and Chestnut
& Market Sts. **Map** 4 E3. **Tel** *(215)
965-7676, (800) 537-7676.*
🚇 *Market East Station.* 🚌 *2nd St.*
🚌 *Philly Phlash.* ⌚ *court: hours vary;
post office: 9am–5pm Mon–Sat.* ♿

This expansive court, which
cuts through an entire city
block, is where Benjamin
Franklin's home once stood.
Although razed in 1812, a
"Ghost House" frame depicts
the exact positions of the
house and adjacent print
shop, while excavations

Elfreth's Alley, dating to the early 18th century

underneath reveal the original foundations. An impressive, underground museum has exhibits explaining Franklin's life. On the court grounds are several former residences once owned by Franklin, which now house artifacts, replicas and demonstrations of colonial printing and book-binding operations, and the B. Free Franklin Post Office and Museum, which has an active post office. Another building houses the restored offices of *The Aurora*, the newspaper published by Franklin's grandson, Benjamin Franklin Bache.

Tribute to valor – the National Liberty Museum

National Liberty Museum ㉔

321 Chestnut St. **Map** 4 E3. **Tel** (215) 925-2800. 🚇 Market East Station. 🚋 2nd St. 🚌 Philly Phlash. 🕐 10am–5pm. 🌑 Mon (first Mon in Sep–last Mon in May), Jan 1, Thanksgiving, Dec 25. 🎟 for adults. 🚻 www.libertymuseum.org

Through exhibits heralding freedom and diversity, the National Liberty Museum takes an unconventional approach to its mission of defusing violence and bigotry. The museum honors 1,000 people worldwide who have stood up against repression. On display are life-sized dioramas of South Africa's Nelson Mandela in his jail cell, and concentration camp victim Anne Frank's Amsterdam bedroom, in which she hid

Classical façade of the First Bank, designed by Samuel Blodgett

from the Nazis. Another display has photographs of every rescue worker who died in the September 11, 2001 attacks. With more than 100 glass artworks, the museum is the only one in the world to use glass as a symbol for freedom, and has a two-story structure, the *Flame of Liberty*, by Dale Chihuly, as its centerpiece.

First Bank of the United States ㉕

116 S 3rd St between Chestnut & Walnut Sts. **Map** 4 E3. **Tel** (215) 965-7676. 🚇 Market East Station. 🚋 2nd St. 🚌 Philly Phlash. 🌑 closed to the public.

The dispute over building the First Bank instigated the new nation's first debate on the interpretation of the US Constitution *(see pp48–9)*, which neither allowed nor prohibited the building of a federal bank. Alexander Hamilton, treasury secretary from 1789 to 1795, led the charge to provide the nation with a firm financial footing and a means to pay off the Revolutionary War debt. Chartered by President Washington and Congress in 1791, the bank building was completed six years later, with its classical design signifying culture and political maturity.

In 1811, Congress voted to withdraw the charter. The building was then occupied by Girard Bank through the 1920s, and finally taken over by the National Park Service in 1955. Original brick rooms and sheet iron vault doors still remain in the building, which now houses the Civil War and Underground Museum of Philadelphia.

BENJAMIN FRANKLIN

One of America's finest statesmen, Benjamin Franklin wore many hats as a printer, inventor, author, philosopher, postmaster, and diplomat. Born in Boston in 1706, Franklin moved to Philadelphia in 1723. He established the first library and fire department in the city, and upgraded its postal services. Franklin also founded the University of Pennsylvania and the Pennsylvania Hospital. In the Revolutionary War, he presided over the 1776 Constitutional Convention and helped draft the Declaration of Independence *(see p42)*. He won favor with the French who would come to America's aid against the British. In 1787, he signed the US Constitution, and died in Philadelphia three years later. In 2006, the city honored Franklin with a year-long celebration of his 300th birthday.

Benjamin Franklin (1706–90)

Carpenters' Hall 26

320 Chestnut St. **Map** 4 E3.
Tel (215) 925-0167. 🚇 *Market East
Station.* 🚌 *5th St.* 🚋 *Philly Phlash.*
🔴 *Jan–Feb: 10am–4pm Wed–Sun;
Mar–Dec: 10am–4pm Tue–Sun.*
⚫ *Jan 1, Thanksgiving, Dec 25.*
www.carpentershall.org

This two-story structure was
built for the Carpenters'
Company, the country's oldest
trade guild, established in
1724. It played an important
role in the Revolutionary War,
secretly hosting the First
Continental Congress in 1774.
  Today, the Carpenters' Hall
houses displays of original
Windsor chairs, used during
the Congress, and colonial-era
carpenters' tools. Two rebuilt
structures share the grounds –
Pemberton House, named
after a Quaker merchant, is
now a gift shop, while the
New Hall Military Museum
displays weapons of the
colonial army and navy. The
original 1791 building housed
War Department offices.

Reconstructed dining room of Bishop White House

Georgian-style Carpenters' Hall,
designed by Robert Smith in 1770

Todd House 27

4th & Walnut Sts. **Map** 4 D3.
Tel (215) 965-7676. 🚇 *Market East
Station.* 🚌 *5th St.* 🚋 *Philly Phlash.*
📷 *compulsory; free tickets available
at Independence Visitor Center on
first-come, first-served basis.* ♿

This Georgian-style home
reflects the way the middle
class lived in late 18th-century
Philadelphia. What makes
Todd House particularly
interesting is its famous

resident, Dolley Payne, who
later married James Madison,
the fourth president of the
US. Built in 1775, the home
was occupied by Dolley and
her first husband, lawyer John
Todd, both Quakers, from
1791 to 1793. Dolley lost
Todd and their infant son in
1793 during the city's yellow
fever epidemic. The following
year, she met Madison during
an arranged meeting.
  Today, the three-story home
has been restored to when John
and Dolley Todd lived here,
with furnishings that reflect
subtle Quaker conservatism.
Period items include replicas
of Dolley's dressing table,
and John Todd's first-floor
law library, which contained
more than 300 volumes.

Bishop White House 28

309 Walnut St. **Map** 4 E3. **Tel** (215)
965-7676. 🚇 *Market East Station.*
🚌 *5th St.* 🚋 *Philly Phlash.*
📷 *compulsory; free tickets available
at Independence Visitor Center on
first-come, first-served basis.* ♿

The residence of Bishop
William White for nearly 50
years, this three-story Federal
structure, built in 1786, is an
excellent example of a late
18th-century upper-class
Philadelphia home. Dr. White,
the first Episcopal Bishop of
Pennsylvania and rector of
Christ Church (see p52) and
St. Peter's Episcopal Church
(see p61), often entertained
the colonial elite here, including George Washington and

Benjamin Franklin. The house
has been restored, and period
and original family pieces
decorate the rooms, including
whale oil lamps on the
fireplace mantel and an
assortment of silver pieces
in the dining room. Chair
placement and bookcases in
Dr. White's upstairs study
have been accurately reconstructed, thanks to a painting
of the room commissioned
after his death. An inside
privy, which remains today,
is indicative of the home's
upper-class status.

Philadelphia Merchants' Exchange,
designed in Greek Revival style

Philadelphia Merchants' Exchange 29

143 S 3rd St at Walnut St.
Map 4 E3. **Tel** (215) 965-2305.
🚇 *Market East Station.* 🚌 *2nd St.*
🚋 *Philly Phlash.* 🔴 *8:30am–4:30pm
(lobby exhibit).*

The oldest stock exchange
building in the country, this

imposing edifice is one of Old City's finest architectural gems. Completed in 1834, it was designed in Greek Revival style by the up-and-coming architect William Strickland, already noted for designing the new steeple atop Independence Hall (see pp42–3) and for his work on the Second Bank of the US (see p47). Strickland's admiration of classical Greek design is reflected by the columned Corinthian portico at one end and the unusual, semi-circular portico at the other.

With the financial district shifting to Center City in the late 19th century, the building soon became neglected. The National Park Service took it over in 1952, making it a part of Independence National Historical Park. Today, the Park Service maintains offices in the building. Although the exchange is closed to the public, visitors are permitted to enter the lobby and view a small exhibit that details the history and architecture of the exchange.

City Tavern ③⓪

138 S 2nd St between Walnut & Chestnut Sts. **Map** 4 E3. **Tel** (215) 413-1443. 🚇 Market East Station. 🚊 2nd St. 🚌 Philly Phlash. ⏱ from 11:30am; reservations taken until 8:30pm. ♿ **www**.citytavern.com

Recalling the atmosphere of an authentic London tavern, the City Tavern also boasted the second largest ballroom in the colonies when it first opened in 1773.

City Tavern, still a popular dining spot in Philadelphia

Welcome Park, dedicated to city founder William Penn

However, just a year later, with the Revolutionary War in the offing, the three-story building was used by members of the First Continental Congress as an unofficial gathering place. Later, in 1777, when he became the leader of the Continental Army, Washington used the tavern as his headquarters.

After the Revolutionary War, the Constitutional Convention held its closing banquet here in 1787. Frequented by the likes of George Washington, Thomas Jefferson, and other colonial notables, it was once called "the most genteel tavern in America," by John Adams, the second president of the United States.

However, by the 1790s, the City Tavern had lost its prominence and served as a merchants' exchange until 1834, when it was partially destroyed by fire. The original structure was finally demolished in 1854 to make way for new brownstone buildings.

After careful research, the National Park Service reconstructed the tavern in 1975. Today, the inn is almost identical to the original, with serving staff in period dress and colonial-style dishes on the menu. These include such delicacies as sweet potato biscuits, said to be a favorite of Jefferson, turkey pot pie based on Martha Washington's recipe, West Indies pepperpot soup, and ales brewed according to Washington's and Jefferson's original recipes.

Statue of William Penn

Welcome Park ③①

S 2nd St at Walnut St (2nd St & Sansom St Alley). **Map** 4 E3. 🚇 Market East Station. 🚊 2nd St. 🚌 Philly Phlash.

Named after the ship that ferried Penn and the first Quakers from England to the New World, the Welcome, this open city square is dedicated to the city's founder, William Penn. It was constructed in 1982 to commemorate the 300th anniversary of the founding of the colony of Pennsylvania. The centerpiece of the park is a smaller version of Penn's statue from City Hall (see p72). Emblazoned along the south wall of the park is a timeline of Penn's life and the events leading to the creation of the new colony. The park is located where the Slate Roof House – Penn's home and the Pennsylvania Seat of Government from 1700 to 1701 – once stood. This postmodernist square is made of concrete crisscrossed by marble slabs, depicting the main streets of the original city grid planned by William Penn and his surveyor Thomas Holmes.

At the park's north end sits the Thomas Bond House, named after the surgeon who, in 1751, along with Benjamin Franklin and others, founded Pennsylvania Hospital, the nation's first public hospital (see p67). The restored 1769 Georgian-style home is now a bed-and-breakfast (see p134).

SOCIETY HILL AND PENN'S LANDING

William Penn first stepped ashore on the banks of the Delaware River at what is today known as Penn's Landing, the eastern edge of this neighborhood. An elongated and tree-lined promenade, Penn's Landing includes a plaza for concerts, historic ships and dinner boats along the piers, and the Independence Seaport Museum.

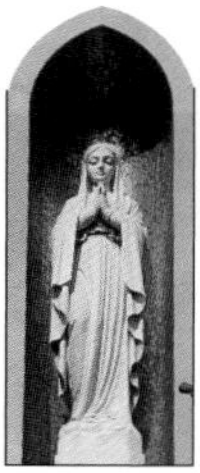

Detail, Old St. Mary's Church

Heading west, several walkways lead to Society Hill, a well-preserved area with churches, synagogues, and 18th-century homes. The area's southern border, South Street, contrasts with the more serene Society Hill, indulging in the excitement derived from a trendy and eclectic mix of cafés, restaurants, shops, nightclubs, and bars.

SIGHTS AT A GLANCE

Historical Buildings and Districts
New Market and Head House Square 15
Penn's Landing 14
Pennsylvania Hospital 17
Physick House 6
Powel House 12
South Street and Walkway 16

Parks and Gardens
Rose Garden and Magnolia Garden 9
Washington Square 1

Places of Worship
Mikveh Israel Cemetery 18
Mother Bethel AME Church 2
Old Pine Street Church 3
Old St. Joseph's Church 10
Old St. Mary's Church 8
Society Hill Synagogue 7
St. Peter's Episcopal Church 4

Museums and Galleries
Independence Seaport Museum pp64–5 13
Polish American Cultural Center Museum 11
Thaddeus Kosciuszko National Memorial 5

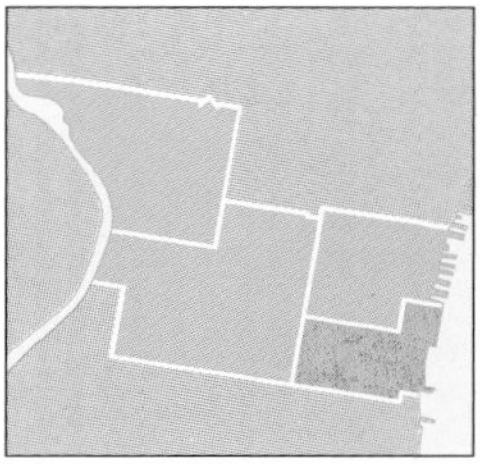

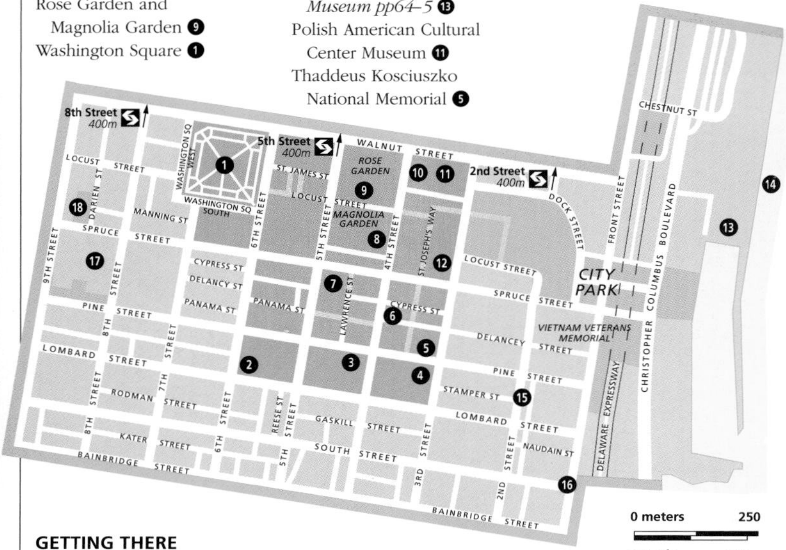

0 meters 250
0 yards 250

GETTING THERE

Most sights here are a 5- to 15-minute walk from Independence Mall. Philly Phlash buses run May–Oct and are accessible on Market Street, while the Market-Frankford line has stops at 2nd and Market, 5th and Market, and 8th and Market. SEPTA bus 42 runs along Spruce and Walnut Streets.

KEY

Street-by-Street map *see pp58–9*

SEPTA subway stop

◁ **Penn's statue outside Pennsylvania Hospital, founded in 1751** ***(see p67)***

Street-by-Street: Society Hill and Penn's Landing

Flowers laid at the Tomb of the Unknown Soldier

This historic neighborhood dates back to 1682 when William Penn chartered the "Free Society of Traders" to help develop a fledgling Philadelphia. The area was home to many notable colonial figures and members of the new Federal government, which was formed after the Revolutionary War. In the late 1950s, the Philadelphia Redevelopment Authority saved hundreds of 18th- and early 19th-century homes from likely demolition, selling them to private citizens who agreed to restore them. Today, a walk through the neighborhood reveals surviving narrow streets and courtyards, and houses in a mix of architectural styles, including Georgian, Federal, Greek Revival, and Beaux-Arts.

Mother Bethel AME Church
Founded in 1791, this site is the oldest piece of land continuously owned by African Americans. A lower level museum includes the tomb of founder Richard Allen ❷

Old Pine Street Church
The cemetery of "the Church of the Patriots" also contains the grave of Eugene Ormandy, director of the Philadelphia Orchestra from 1938 to 1980 ❸

KEY

--- — Suggested route

0 meters	100
0 yards	100

STAR SIGHTS

★ Powel House

★ Washington Square and Tomb of the Unknown Soldier

St. Peter's Episcopal Church
Completed in 1761, this Anglican church has an unusual double-ended interior, with the altar at one end, and the pulpit at the other ❹

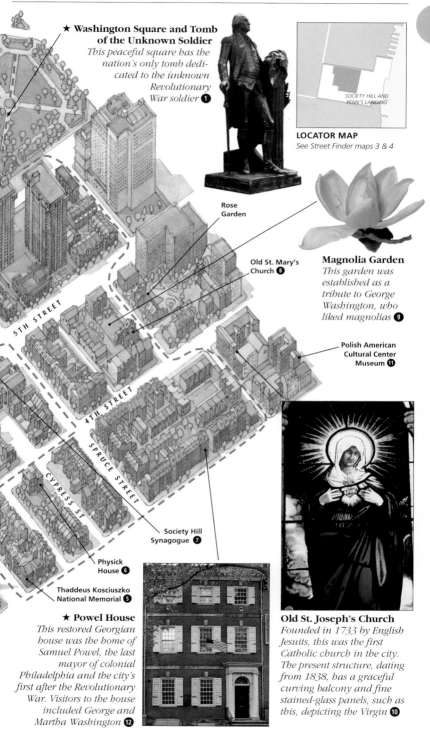

★ Washington Square and Tomb of the Unknown Soldier
This peaceful square has the nation's only tomb dedicated to the unknown Revolutionary War soldier ❶

LOCATOR MAP
See Street Finder maps 3 & 4

Rose Garden

Old St. Mary's Church ❽

Magnolia Garden
This garden was established as a tribute to George Washington, who liked magnolias ❾

Polish American Cultural Center Museum ⓫

5TH STREET

4TH STREET

SPRUCE STREET

CYPRESS ST

Society Hill Synagogue ❼

Physick House ❻

Thaddeus Kosciuszko National Memorial ❺

★ Powel House
This restored Georgian house was the home of Samuel Powel, the last mayor of colonial Philadelphia and the city's first after the Revolutionary War. Visitors to the house included George and Martha Washington ⓬

Old St. Joseph's Church
Founded in 1733 by English Jesuits, this was the first Catholic church in the city. The present structure, dating from 1838, has a graceful curving balcony and fine stained-glass panels, such as this, depicting the Virgin ❿

Washington Square, one of the five original squares in Penn's grid

Washington Square and Tomb of the Unknown Soldier [1]

Walnut St between 6th & 7th Sts. **Map** 4 D3. 🚆 *Market East Station.* 🚇 *5th, 8th, 9th-10th Sts.* 🚌 *42, Philly Phlash.*

One of the five original squares in Penn's city grid, Washington Square, named after the nation's first president, is a pleasant park with benches and towering trees. This quiet space is also hallowed ground, having served as a cemetery for 90 years until the late 18th century. More than 2,000 Revolutionary War soldiers and prisoners of war were buried in massive pits here. Congressman John Adams described the pathos in a letter to his wife Abigail in 1777, writing that he spent an hour "in the Congregation of the dead" and that "I never in my whole life was affected with so much melancholy." In 1793, mass graves were again dug for victims of the city's yellow fever epidemic. Today, the park's centerpiece is the Tomb of the Unknown Soldier, with a statue of Washington, which was erected in the 1950s as a tribute to those who fought in the Revolutionary War. The tomb includes the remains of a revolutionary soldier who was buried on the site.

Washington's statue at Washington Square

Mother Bethel AME Church [2]

419 S 6th St. **Map** 4 D4. ***Tel*** *(215) 925-0616.* 🚆 *Market East Station.* 🚇 *5th St.* 🚌 *42, Philly Phlash.* 🕐 *10am–3pm Mon only by appt.* **www**.motherbethel.org

Standing on the oldest piece of land to be continuously owned by African Americans in the US, Mother Bethel traces its roots to former slave Richard Allen (1760–1831), the first Bishop of the African Methodist Episcopal Church. Allen began preaching in 1786 at St. George's United Methodist Church *(see p51)*, where he successfully built up a black parish. He founded his own church in 1794, by buying and moving a blacksmith's shop to the current site, and using the anvil as his pulpit. The current structure was built in 1889 and still contains the original curved pews and stained-glass windows.

In 1830, the church hosted the first national convention for African Americans, and for years was a stop along the Underground Railroad, the system set up by abolitionists to transport fugitive slaves to Canada and the free states. Today, a museum in the lower level houses the tomb of Allen and his wife Sarah, along with historic church artifacts, including the original pews from the blacksmith shop.

Old Pine Street Church [3]

412 Pine St. **Map** 4 D4. ***Tel*** *(215) 925-8051.* 🚆 *Market East Station.* 🚇 *2nd, 5th Sts.* 🚌 *42, Philly Phlash.* 🕐 *10am–3pm Mon–Sat, call in advance.* ✝ *9:30am Sun.* ♿ *limited access.* **www**.oldpine.org

The only remaining colonial Presbyterian place of worship in Philadelphia today, Old Pine Street Church was founded in 1768. Designed in Georgian style by Robert Smith, it was later remodeled into an imposing columned Greek Revival building. George Duffield, the church's first pastor, served as chaplain to the Continental Congress of 1774 and second US President John Adams and Dr. Benjamin Rush, the "Father of American Psychiatry," were parishioners here, earning it the moniker "Church of the Patriots."

In 1777, occupying British forces used the church as a hospital and stable, also burying 100 Hessian soldiers in a mass grave outside the church wall. Today, there are more than 3,000 tombs in the surrounding cemetery, including that of Eugene Ormandy, conductor of the Philadelphia Orchestra from 1938 to 1985.

Detail of a gravestone from the Old Pine Street Church graveyard

Interior and altar of St. Peter's Episcopal Church

St. Peter's Episcopal Church ❹

313 Pine St. **Map** 4 D4. ***Tel*** *(215) 925-5968.* 🚆 *Market East Station.* 🚇 *2nd, 5th Sts.* 🚌 *42, Philly Phlash.* 🕒 *8am–4pm Mon–Fri; 11am–5pm Sat; 1–3pm Sun.* ✝ *9am, 10am & 11am Sun.* ♿ **www**.stpetersphila.org

Opened for worship in 1761, St. Peter's was founded by Society Hill Anglicans who were members of a then overcrowded Christ Church *(see p52)*, and who wanted a church closer to their homes. Christ Church and St. Peter's functioned as one parish until 1832, with Bishop White *(see p54)* serving as rector of both churches.

St. Peter's, built in Georgian style by Robert Smith, has a unique design. The placement of the wine-glass pulpit and altar at opposite ends of the building, and the seats in boxed pews facing either way, give the church no definitive front or back. In 1842, well-known architect William Strickland designed the landmark tower and spire that still house bells from London's Whitechapel Foundry, which had forged the first Liberty Bell in 1753 *(see p44)*.

Buried in the graveyard are several important colonial Americans, including portrait painter Charles Willson Peale, naval hero Stephen Decatur, and George M. Dallas, vice president of the US from 1845 to 1849, after whom counties were named in Texas, Iowa, Arkansas, and Missouri.

Thaddeus Kosciuszko National Memorial ❺

301 Pine St. **Map** 4 D4. ***Tel*** *(215) 597-9618.* 🚆 *Market East Station.* 🚇 *2nd St.* 🚌 *42, Philly Phlash.* ♿ *limited access.* 🕒 *noon–4pm Wed–Sun.* **www**.nps.gov/thko

Remembered as the "Hero of Two Continents," General Thaddeus Kosciuszko fought for freedom in both his native Poland and colonial America. During the Revolutionary War, he designed and built fortifications at Saratoga and West Point that proved critical to American victories over the British troops.

After the war, Kosciuszko returned to Poland in 1784 and took part in its fight for independence from Russia, but he was wounded and imprisoned by the Russians. He was released only upon the condition that he leave Poland. He then returned to Philadelphia to recuperate from his war wounds for nine months in this Society Hill house. His upstairs room has been restored and furnished with period pieces similar to those he owned. It also contains his medals, walking crutch, and a sable fur given to him on his release by Russia's Tsar Paul I. While nursing his injuries, Kosciuszko spent most of his time reading, sketching, and receiving guests, including his close friend and then US Vice President, Thomas Jefferson.

Physick House ❻

321 S 4th St. **Map** 4 D4. ***Tel*** *(215) 925-7866.* 🚆 *Market East Station.* 🚇 *2nd, 5th Sts.* 🚌 *42, Philly Phlash.* 🕒 *noon–4pm Thu–Sat; 1–4pm Sun.* 🌐 **www**.philalandmarks.org

Named after Dr. Philip Syng Physick, the "Father of American Surgery" and grandson of silversmith Philip Syng, who designed the inkwell used during the signing of the Declaration of Independence *(see p42)*, this is one of the few free-standing colonial homes that remain today. Built in 1786 by wine importer Henry Hill, this Federal-style house has what was believed to be the largest fanlight in colonial Philadelphia over its door. After acquiring the home in 1815, Physick set up his medical practice, treating such prominent patients as Dolley Madison *(see p54)* and President Andrew Jackson.

Physick lived there until his death in 1837, and the house has been restored to that period. Original, locally quarried Pennsylvania Blue Marble can be seen in the hall and on fireplace mantels. Family pieces, such as an unusual mid-18th-century oval wooden case that belonged to William Penn's grandson, a British Wagstaff grandfather clock belonging to Physick's father, and original silver items are also displayed. Physick's medical instruments can be seen in an upstairs room, and include surgical tools and medicine chests with bottles.

Physick House entrance fanlight

Interior of Physick House, containing original colonial-era furnishings

Society Hill Synagogue ❼

418 Spruce St. **Map** 4 D4. **Tel** (215) 922-6590. 🚇 *Market East Station.* 🚊 *5th St.* 🚌 *42, Philly Phlash.* ⏱ *9am–4pm Mon–Thu; call in advance.* ⭐ *Fri night & Sat morning.* ♿ *www.*societyhillsynagogue.org

Originally built as a Baptist church, this impressive structure was designed by 19th-century architect Thomas Ustick Walter, who was most noted for his design of the dome and House and Senate wings of the US Capitol in Washington DC. The original struc-ture was built in Greek Revival style in 1830, but two decades later, Walter was again commis-sioned to design a new Italianate façade, much of which remains today. The building was home to Baptist worshippers for more than 80 years, until a group of Romanian Jews acquired it in 1912.
By 1916, the build-ing was known as the Great Romanian Synagogue. The name, written in Yiddish, is still visible over the entrance. In the mid-1960s, it became the

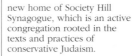

Detail from Old St. Mary's Church

new home of Society Hill Synagogue, which is an active congregation rooted in the texts and practices of conservative Judaism.

Old St. Mary's Church ❽

252 S 4th St. **Map** 4 D4. **Tel** (215) 923-7930. 🚇 *Market East Station.* 🚊 *5th St.* 🚌 *42, Philly Phlash.* ⏱ *9am–5pm Mon–Fri.* ⛪ *Sun.* ♿ *www.* ushistory.org/tour/tour_stmary.htm

Founded to take on parishioners from an over-crowded Old St. Joseph's Church, this redbrick church was built in 1763. Together, the two houses of wor-ship served the city's Catholic population as one parish until the 1820s. Old St. Mary's witnessed several significant events in the years leading up to the birth of the nation. During the American Revolutionary War, members of the Continental Congress attended services here. The first pub-lic religious com-memoration of the Declaration of Independence took place here in 1779, on the third anniversary of its adoption. Following the British surrender at Yorktown in 1781, the church held a Thanksgiv-ing service, with the flags of the conquered army laid on the altar steps. In 1810, Old St. Mary's was enlarged to its present size and became the first Catholic cathedral of the new diocese of Philadelphia. Its graveyard, dating to 1759, contains the tombs of Commodore John Barry, "Father of the American Navy," and the first to capture a British ship during the

Revolutionary War, Thomas Fitzsimons, one of the signers of the Constitution, Mathew Carey, 18th-century American publisher and bookseller, and Michael Bouvier, the great-great-grandfather of first lady Jacqueline Kennedy Onassis.

Roses in full bloom in Society Hill's Rose Garden

Rose Garden and Magnolia Garden ❾

Locust St between 4th & 5th Sts. **Map** 4 D3. 🚇 *Market East Station.* 🚊 *5th St.* 🚌 *42, Philly Phlash.*

These two public gardens, directly across each other on Locust Street, are nestled within shaded and quiet court-yards, characteristic of Society Hill's charm. The Rose Garden stretches through the center of the entire block, all the way up to Walnut Street. It commemorates the signers of both the Declaration of Independence and the US Constitution. The funding to plant roses, which flower during spring and summer, is povided by The Daughters of the American Revolution, an organization whose members are drawn from the direct descendants of those who fought in the Revolutionary War. Inside the garden is a section of a cobblestoned street dating back to 1800.
The Magnolia Garden was established as a tribute to George Washington, who had often expressed an interest in horticulture and, in particu-lar, magnolia trees. Different varieties of magnolias are planted around the restful garden, whose centerpiece is a small fountain.

Italianate façade of Society Hill Synagogue

Interior of Old St. Joseph's Church with its unusual curving balcony

Old St. Joseph's Church ❿

321 Willings Alley. **Map** 4 D3.
Tel (215) 923-1733. 🚇 Market East
Station. 🚌 5th St. 🚌 42, Philly
Phlash. ⬜ 9:30am–4pm Mon–Fri
(to 6:30pm Sat), 7:30am–2pm Sun.
✝ noon–Sat, 7:30am & 9:30am
Sun. ♿ www.oldstjoseph.org

Located in a narrow alleyway,
Old St. Joseph's was Philadelphia's first Catholic church.
Reverend Joseph Greaton, an
English Jesuit,
founded it in
1733. In 1734,
efforts were made
to thwart Roman
Catholic church
services, but these
were unsuccessful,
with religious
freedom for all
assured by Penn's
1701 Charter of
Privileges.
The old chapel
was replaced by a
larger building in
1757, and six years later, Old
St. Mary's was built a block
away to handle the growing
number of members. St.
Joseph's current structure dates
from 1838 and features a grand
columned altar and a curved
balcony at the sanctuary's
front end. On the ceiling is the
fresco, *The Exaltation of Saint
Joseph into Heaven*, painted
by 19th-century Italian artist
Filippo Costaggini, whose
work can also be seen in the
US Capitol in Washington DC.

Polish American Cultural Center Museum ⓫

308 Walnut St. **Map** 4 E3. **Tel** (215)
922-1700. 🚇 Market East Station.
🚌 2nd, 5th Sts. 🚌 42, Philly Phlash.
⬜ May–Dec: 10am–4pm Mon–Sat;
Jan–Apr: 10am–4pm Mon–Fri.
⬤ public hols. 🖥 www.
polishamericancenter.org

Through portraits and
memorabilia from Poland,
this small museum's mission
is to promote
awareness and
appreciation of
Polish culture and
history. It honors
Poles who have
made significant
contributions to
history, ranging
from figures such
as Nicholas
Copernicus, the
astronomer, and
composer Frédéric
Chopin, to such
modern-day lumi-
naries as the late Pope John
Paul II and politician and
Nobel Peace Prize winner Lech
Walesa. Of particular note are
displays on the heroes of the
American Revolutionary War,
Thaddeus Kosciuszko and
General Casimir Pulaski, the
namesake of an annual city
parade that celebrates Polish
heritage (see p34). Also on
display is traditional Polish
folk art – festive garb, Easter
eggs, decorative paper
cutouts, and wooden plates.

Portrait of General
Pulaski, Polish American
Cultural Center Museum

Powel House ⓬

244 S 3rd St. **Map** 4 E4. **Tel** (215)
627-0364. 🚇 Market East Station. 🚌
2nd St. 🚌 42, Philly Phlash. ⬜ noon–
5pm Thu–Sat, 1–5pm Sun. 🎫 🖥
compulsory. www.philalandmarks.org

This grand Georgian home
built in 1765 is an exquisite
example of how the colonial
elite lived. Samuel Powel, one
of the wealthiest men in colonial America, was its second
owner, purchasing it in 1769
when he was about to marry
Elizabeth Willing. Powel was
Philadelphia's last mayor
before the Revolutionary War
and the first after the nation's
birth. He died in 1793, a
victim of the city's yellow
fever epidemic.
The Powels used their
lavish home to entertain the
country's most important
citizens, including Benjamin
Franklin, George Washington,
and John Adams, the second
president of the US. Original
features that remain today
include a Pennsylvania Blue
Marble fireplace on the first
floor, the stairwell of Santo
Domingo mahogany, and the
cypress front door. Noteworthy
furnishings include a small
scale from Benjamin Franklin,
original china and a sewing
cabinet gifted to Mrs. Powel
by the Washingtons, Gilbert
Stuart portraits, and original
silhouettes of Washington cut
on cobalt blue paper by
Samuel Powel at a social
event. Outside the house is a
peaceful garden dating back
to the late 1700s.

Powel House, an elegant upper-
class colonial-era residence

Independence Seaport Museum ⑬

Olympia exhibit

Located on Penn's Landing waterfront, the mandate of this museum is to preserve US maritime history and traditions with a special focus on Delaware Bay and the Delaware River and its tributaries. Displays combine artifacts and paintings of naval encounters, along with computer games, large-scale ship models, and audiovisuals that include sounds of ship horns and accounts by sailors and shipbuilders. The museum re-creates the Benjamin Franklin Bridge as a three-story replica that spans a carpeted Delaware River. Exhibits include a replica of the bridge of the destroyer USS *Lawrence*, and of steerage compartments in which many immigrants traveled to America. There is an active boatbuilding workshop, and berthed nearby are the World War II submarine *Becuna*, commissioned in 1944, and the *Olympia*, Admiral George Dewey's flagship in the 1898 Spanish-American War.

Waterfront Museum
This expansive facility is the centerpiece of Penn's Landing.

Museum Library

Submarine Becuna
This World War II vessel with torpedo launching tubes was the submarine flagship of the Southwest Pacific Fleet, which was under the command of General Douglas MacArthur.

First Floor

What Floats Your Boat? is an interactive exhibit exploring the science, art, and history of boats.

★ **Workshop on the Water**
Craftspeople build and restore traditional boats of the 19th century at this workshop dedicated to the skills and traditions of wooden boatbuilding and sailing in the Delaware River Valley and the New Jersey shore.

MUSEUM GUIDE

The first floor houses most of the exhibits, the museum shop, and visitor information. The second floor includes On the Rivers, On the Shores and the Quarterdeck Gallery with the Olympia exhibit. The Olympia and the Becuna are berthed outside the museum.

KEY

- Workshop on the Water
- What Floats Your Boat?
- Home Port Philadelphia
- Divers of the Deep
- River Gallery
- Quarterdeck Gallery
- On the Rivers, On the Shores
- Non-exhibition space

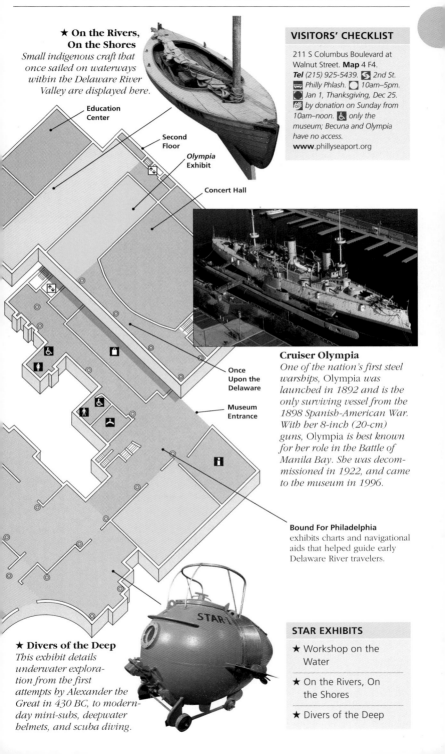

★ **On the Rivers, On the Shores**
Small indigenous craft that once sailed on waterways within the Delaware River Valley are displayed here.

Education Center

Second Floor

Olympia Exhibit

Concert Hall

Once Upon the Delaware

Museum Entrance

VISITORS' CHECKLIST

211 S Columbus Boulevard at Walnut Street. **Map** 4 F4.
Tel *(215) 925-5439.* 🚇 *2nd St.*
🚌 *Philly Phlash.* 🕐 *10am–5pm.*
⬤ *Jan 1, Thanksgiving, Dec 25.*
💲 *by donation on Sunday from 10am–noon.* ♿ *only the museum; Becuna and Olympia have no access.*
www.phillyseaport.org

Cruiser Olympia
One of the nation's first steel warships, Olympia was launched in 1892 and is the only surviving vessel from the 1898 Spanish-American War. With her 8-inch (20-cm) guns, Olympia is best known for her role in the Battle of Manila Bay. She was decommissioned in 1922, and came to the museum in 1996.

Bound For Philadelphia
exhibits charts and navigational aids that helped guide early Delaware River travelers.

★ **Divers of the Deep**
This exhibit details underwater exploration from the first attempts by Alexander the Great in 430 BC, to modern-day mini-subs, deepwater helmets, and scuba diving.

STAR EXHIBITS

★ Workshop on the Water

★ On the Rivers, On the Shores

★ Divers of the Deep

Small boats at Penn's Landing marina with the Benjamin Franklin Bridge in the background

Penn's Landing ⑭

Western shore of the Delaware River between Market & South Sts. **Map** 4 F3. 🚇 *Market East Station.* 🚊 *2nd St.* 🚌 *21, Philly Phlash.* **www**. delawareriverwaterfrontcorp.com

A popular waterfront on the Delaware River, Penn's Landing is where city founder William Penn first stepped onto his new colony in 1682 *(see p18)*. Development of the docks seen today began in 1967, before which it was an unappealing stretch of land. Among its attractions are grassy areas with trees, walkways, and an amphitheater where summer festivals and concerts are held. Several vessels are anchored here, including the century-old sailing ship *Moshulu* *(see p148)*, the dinner cruise boat *Spirit of Philadelphia*, the 1883 three-masted barkentine *Gazela*, once a Portuguese fishing boat, and the paddle-boat charter *Liberty Belle*.

Nearby is the Independence Seaport Museum *(see pp64–5)* with its two historic vessels – the cruiser *Olympia* and the submarine *Becuna* – docked in a small harbor.

Penn's Landing offers outstanding waterfront views of the Benjamin Franklin and Walt Whitman Bridges, and the Camden Waterfront, where *Battleship New Jersey* is moored. Along the Chestnut Street overpass is the impressive Irish Memorial, a bronze sculpture with 35 life-sized figures, which honors the

more than one million people who died and the others who fled Ireland during the Great Hunger of the 1840s.

New Market and Head House Square ⑮

2nd St between Pine & Lombard Sts. **Map** 4 E4. 🚇 *Market East Station.* 🚊 *2nd St.* 🚌 *42, Philly Phlash.*

One of the oldest in America, this covered marketplace was established in 1745. Called the "Shambles," meaning butcher shop, it was the second public marketplace in colonial Philadelphia – the first was located at the eastern end of High Street, now called Market Street. It was where vendors sold fresh produce, meat, poultry, and fish two days a week. The original New Market stretched two blocks from Pine Street to South Street and was flanked

by two firehouses, known as head houses. The two firehouses once contained fire gear and apparatus for three volunteer fire companies.

Today, only the firehouse at 2nd and Pine Streets remains. Built in 1805, it is thought to be the country's oldest existing firehouse. New Market was restored in the 1960s, and has since housed the Crafts and Fine Arts Fair on summer weekends.

South Street and Walkway ⑯

South St. **Map** 4 E5. 🚇 *Market East Station.* 🚊 *2nd St.* 🚌 *42, Philly Phlash.*

Known as Cedar Street in colonial times, and bordering on what was then New Market and Head House Square, South Street remains a marketplace of sorts today, but with an emphasis on pop culture and counterculture.

South Street, promising revelry and an exciting atmosphere

The South Street Head House District, which stretches from Front to 11th Streets and includes some surrounding streets, is an eclectic melting pot of more than 300 shops, galleries, cafés, restaurants, bars, and more. Eateries range from pizzerias and sushi bars to vegetarian cafés and fine-dining restaurants, while shops sell everything from jewelry and fine art to funk culture items and grunge-style clothing. There are also body piercing and tattoo parlors, jazz clubs, and rocking nightclubs. The strip often overflows with younger revelers on weekend nights that usually extend into the early hours of the morning. A walkway over I-95 (also called the Delaware Expressway) links Columbus Boulevard to South Street, offering fine views of Penn's Landing, and *Battleship New Jersey* across the Delaware River.

Pennsylvania Hospital's surgical amphitheater

Exterior of Pennsylvania Hospital with a statue of William Penn

Pennsylvania Hospital ⓱

800 Spruce St. **Map** 3 C4. *Tel* (215) 829-6799. 🚇 Market East Station. 🚏 8th St. 🚌 42, Philly Phlash. 🕐 8:30am– 4:30pm Mon–Fri. 📷 book in advance. ♿ **www**.pahosp.com

Founded by surgeon Thomas Bond and Benjamin Franklin in 1751 to care for the "sick-poor and insane," Pennsylvania Hospital was the nation's first public hospital. The old section, the Pine Building, was built in stages. The wings are Georgian, the east wing being completed in 1755, and the west in 1796. The Federal center section was built in 1804 and includes the Great Court, the area open for self-guided tours.

Inside the center section is artist Benjamin West's masterpiece, *Christ Healing the Sick in the Temple*, which was delivered to the hospital in 1817, along with portraits of colonial physicians, including Dr. Philip Syng Physick *(see p61)* and Benjamin Rush, well-known for his contributions to the field of psychiatry. In the Great Court are the hospital's early fire pumper, purchased in 1803, and the musical planetarium clock constructed by colonial clockmaker and astronomer, David Rittenhouse, in 1780.

On the second floor is a medical library founded in 1762 with a collection of more than 13,000 volumes, some dating back to the 15th century. The library, located in this room since 1807, houses the country's most complete collection of medical books published between 1750 and 1850. Under a skylight on the top floor is the nation's first surgical amphitheater, called the "dreaded circular room," which was used for operations from 1804 to 1868. Outside, an 18th-century statue of William Penn stands over a peaceful courtyard overflowing with wisteria shrubbery.

Marker at Mikveh Israel cemetery

Mikveh Israel Cemetery ⓲

44 N 4th St. **Map** 3 C3. *Tel* (215) 922-5446. 🚇 Market East Station. 🚏 8th St. 🚌 42, Philly Phlash. 🕐 10am–5pm Tue–Sat, and by appt. **www**.mikvehisrael.org

This burial ground, the oldest Jewish cemetery in the city and one of the oldest in America, was founded in 1740 after shipper and merchant Nathan Levy sought a place to bury one of his children according to Jewish law. Governor Thomas Penn, son of William Penn, granted land here and deemed it a Jewish graveyard. Levy, whose ship brought the Liberty Bell to Philadelphia, is also buried here. Other notables include members of the prominent Gratz family, including philanthropist Rebecca Gratz, the inspiration for the eponymous character in Sir Walter Scott's novel *Ivanhoe*, fur trader Aaron Levy, founder of Aaronsburg, Pennsylvania, rabbis of the congregation, and financier Haym Salomon. His grave is unmarked, only noted by a memorial at the entrance. Jewish soldiers of the Revolutionary War, the War of 1812, and the Civil War are also buried here. The cemetery was walled in the late 18th century to protect it from people "setting marks and firing shots."

CENTER CITY

This sprawling, modern downtown district is Philadelphia's financial and business center. The city's tallest skyscraper, Comcast Center, is situated west of City Hall, on 17th Street and JFK Boulevard. At the neighborhood's eastern end is Chinatown, flanking the newly expanded Pennsylvania Convention Center and adjacent Reading Terminal Market, with Center City's

Classical urn at
Rittenhouse Square

major department store, Macy's, nearby. Along Broad Street, the central north-south artery, are 19th-century buildings that house the Masonic Temple and the Pennsylvania Academy of the Fine Arts in the north, while the theater district is located in the south. In Rittenhouse Square, some of the city's most lavish apartment buildings and hotels tower over town homes that line quiet streets.

SIGHTS AT A GLANCE

Historical Buildings and Districts
Chinatown ❼
City Hall ❹
Liberty Place ❶❺
Library Company of Philadelphia ❽
Masonic Temple ❸
Reading Terminal Market ❺
Rittenhouse Square ❶❸

Places of Worship
Arch Street United Methodist Church ❷
St. Mark's Episcopal Church ❶❹

Museums and Galleries
College of Physicians of Philadelphia/Mütter Museum ❶❻
Rosenbach Museum and Library ❶❷

Cultural Venues
Academy of Music ❾
Kimmel Center for the Performing Arts ❶❿
Pennsylvania Academy of the Fine Arts pp74–5 ❶
Pennsylvania Convention Center ❻
Suzanne Roberts Theatre ❶❶

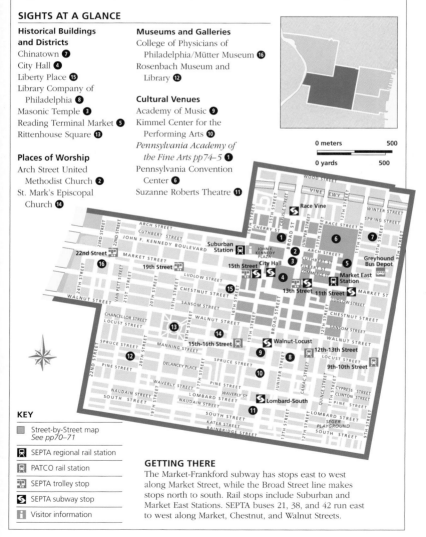

0 meters   500
0 yards   500

KEY

▢   Street-by-Street map
See pp70–71

🚇   SEPTA regional rail station

🚇   PATCO rail station

🚃   SEPTA trolley stop

🅂   SEPTA subway stop

ℹ️   Visitor information

GETTING THERE

The Market-Frankford subway has stops east to west along Market Street, while the Broad Street line makes stops north to south. Rail stops include Suburban and Market East Stations. SEPTA buses 21, 38, and 42 run east to west along Market, Chestnut, and Walnut Streets.

◁ **High-rise office buildings dominating the skyline in Center City, Philadelphia's business district**

Street-by-Street: Center City

City Hall sits in the heart of Center City, where
Market Street and Broad Street – the city's main
east-west and north-south arteries – converge. Most
of this area, dominated by 19th- and 20th-century
architecture, was developed well after the American
Revolutionary War. Diagonally across from City Hall
is JFK Plaza, where Philadelphia's famous LOVE statue
stands next to a pool and fountain, providing respite
from the area's heavy commercial activity. Just a block
north of City Hall are the landmark Masonic Temple
and the Pennsylvania Academy of the Fine Arts.

The Union League of Philadelphia
on Broad Street, is a classic French
Renaissance-styled building.

JFK Plaza features Robert
Indiana's iconic 1960s
LOVE artwork.

JOHN F.

MARKET ST

CHESTNUT STREET

SANSOM STREET

JUNIPER STREET

13TH STREET

WALNUT STREET

★ City Hall
*A 37-ft (11-m) high statue
of William Penn stands atop
this Beaux-Arts building,
one of the largest and most
elaborate city halls in the
country* ❹

| 0 meters | 250 |
| 0 yards | 250 |

KEY

− − − Suggested route

STAR SIGHTS

★ City Hall

★ Pennsylvania
   Academy of
   the Fine Arts

★ Reading Terminal
   Market

The Wanamaker Building is designed
in Beaux-Arts style with a restrained
Renaissance exterior. It is built around a
soaring central atrium, which houses an
enormous pipe organ. The building hosts
an annual holiday light-and-sound show
and is home to Macy's department store.

★ Pennsylvania Academy of the Fine Arts
America's oldest fine art museum was founded in 1805 by portrait artist Charles Willson Peale. Its collection spans three centuries ❶

LOCATOR MAP
See Street Finder maps 1, 2, & 3

Pennsylvania Convention Center
Opened in 1993, the center has since undergone extensive expansion to increase the amount of space to a massive 1 million square feet (92,900 square meters) for exhibitions, trade shows, and conventions ❻

Arch Street United Methodist Church
This Gothic Revival church is the square's oldest structure ❷

Masonic Temple
Home to the Grand Lodge of Freemasons, the impressive interiors and architecture of this temple feature Spanish, Italian, and Egyptian influences. It is also revered for its ornate Romanesque Revival façade ❸

★ Reading Terminal Market
Once the largest arched-roof train shed in the world, this is now one of the best farmers' markets in the country ❺

Pennsylvania Academy of the Fine Arts ❶

See pp74–5.

Arch Street United Methodist Church ❷

55 N Broad St. **Map** 2 F4.
Tel (215) 568-6250. 🚉 Suburban
Station. 🚇 15th St, City Hall.
🚌 Philly Phlash. ○ 10am–3pm
Mon–Fri. ✝ 8:30am & 11am Sun.
♿ www.archstreetumc.org

This Gothic Revival marble
building, constructed in two
sections between 1864 and
1870, is the oldest structure
on William Penn's original
Center Square. The church
was founded in 1862 during
the American Civil War and
was still being built when the
funeral procession of President
Abraham Lincoln passed by it
in 1865. It was designed by
Quaker Addison Hutton,
whose architectural plan
called for a radical change
from the unadorned and plain
Quaker meetinghouses of
the 18th and 19th centuries.

The original construction
included the installation of a
2,322-pipe organ by J.C.B.
Standbridge, Philadelphia's
leading builder of organs.
The organ has been restored
twice, once in 1916 and again
in 1959. The sanctu-
ary's spacious

**Philadelphia's Masonic Temple, an
architectural masterpiece**

atrium is detailed with a
Victorian stenciling pattern
and stained glass. Today, a
diverse congregation from the
Center City neighborhood
worships at the church.

Masonic Temple ❸

1 N Broad St. **Map** 2 F4. *Tel* (215)
988-1900. 🚉 Suburban Station.
🚇 15th St, City Hall. 🚌 Philly Phlash.
○ Jul–Aug: Sat; Mon, public hols. 🎟
by donation. 🎫 11am, 2pm, & 3pm
Tue–Fri, 10am & 11am Sat (call to verify
times). ♿ www.pagrandlodge.org

An architectural jewel, dedicated as the Grand Lodge of
Free and Accepted Masons
of Pennsylvania in 1873, this
remarkable building contains a
number of ornate meeting
halls in various styles. Among
them, the Oriental Hall's
(1896) ornamentation and

coloring have been
copied from the Alhambra
in Granada, Spain; the
Renaissance Hall (1908)
follows an Italian Renaissance motif; while the
Egyptian Hall (1889) takes
its inspiration from the
temples of Luxor, Karnak,
and Philae. High arches,
pinnacles, and spires
form the Gothic Hall, and
the cross-and-crown
emblem of Sir Knights –
"Under this sign you will
conquer" – hangs over a
replica of the Archbishop's
throne in Canterbury
Cathedral, England.

The halls were created to
honor the building trades,
and much of the stone and
tilework are imperceptibly
faux finished – an attestation
to the skill of the men who
made them. President George
Washington, a Freemason,
wore his Masonic apron when
he laid the cornerstone of the
US Capitol in Washington DC.
The apron is on display, along
with other Masonic rarities, in
a museum on the first floor.

City Hall ❹

Broad & Market Sts. **Map** 2 F4.
Tel (215) 686-2840. 🚉 Suburban
Station. 🚇 15th St, City Hall. 🚌 38,
Philly Phlash. 🎫 building and
tower:12:30pm Mon–Fri; tower:
every 15 mins from 9:30am–4:30pm
Mon–Fri. ♿ www.phila.gov

Built on Penn's original Center
Square, this imposing marble,
granite, and limestone landmark is the largest and perhaps
the nation's most ornate city
hall. The building, which took
30 years to build and was
completed only in 1901, is
designed in French Second
Empire style with a mansard
roof and prominent 548-ft
(167-m) high tower. City Hall
was the nation's tallest occupied building until 1909. The
tower, with four clocks and a
37-ft (11-m) tall statue of
Penn, was the city's highest
structure until 1987 *(see box)*.

Philadelphia artist Alexander
Milne Calder designed the
60,000-lb (27-ton) statue, the
largest atop any building in the
world. Calder also designed

NO BUILDING HIGHER THAN
WILLIAM PENN'S STATUE

**City Hall with
Penn's statue**

While skyscrapers sprang up across America
in the 20th century, Philadelphia maintained
a "gentlemen's agreement" not to build higher
than 491 ft (150 m) – lower than the statue
of William Penn on top of City Hall. Honoring
Penn and the city's colonial heritage, the rule
remained unchallenged for almost a century.
But lured by new revenues and jobs, the
agreement was broken in 1987 when the
61-story One Liberty Place *(see p79)* was
built. It towers over City Hall by more than
400 ft (122 m). Within just five years, several
other skyscrapers followed, including Two
Liberty Place, the Mellon Bank Center, the
Bell Atlantic Tower, and, in 2008, the city's
tallest skyscraper, the Comcast Center.

Ornamental, French-influenced City Hall in the midst of Center City

more than 250 other sculptures in the building, including the tower's bronze eagles, and the bronze figures of Native American and Swedish settlers.

Inside, rooms not to be missed include the Mayor's Reception Room, and Conversation Hall, which has statues of George Washington and other colonial notables. The Council Caucus Room, with its grand domed ceiling, features carvings representing the four seasons as stages in life. An elevator takes visitors to a deck on the tower that offers spectacular city views while on the ground level the visitor center stocks maps and brochures of the city's sights.

Reading Terminal Market ❺

12th & Arch Sts. **Map** 3 B2. **Tel** (215) 922-2317. 🚇 Market East Station. 🚏 11th St. 🚌 Philly Phlash. 🕐 8am–6pm Mon–Sat. 🔴 Jan 1, Easter, Jul 4, Memorial Day, Thanksgiving, Dec 25. ♿
www.readingterminalmarket.org

Once a Center City railroad terminal and marketplace, Reading Terminal Market is now considered by many to

be one of the finest farmers' markets in the United States. It was created in 1892, after two farmers' markets on this site were leveled to make space for a new train terminal. These markets were relocated beneath the new train shed. So modern was the market for its time that people came from as far off as the New Jersey shore to buy fresh Lancaster County produce. Over the years, the market gradually declined and was nearly destroyed in the 1970s. New construction routed the city's trains around the old terminal in the 1980s, and the market was refurbished in the early 1990s.

Today, the revitalized Reading Terminal Market houses more than 80 vendors, 6 days a week, selling an extensive variety of free-range meats and poultry, seafood, country vegetables, pastas, Amish specialties, and baked goods, as well as other items such as books, clothing, flowers, jewelry, crafts, unique spices, and hard-to-find specialties and ethnic foods. Several stands also offer freshly-made and prepared foods, ranging from Pennsylvania Dutch country breakfasts to soul food.

Jars of preserves at Reading Terminal Market

Pennsylvania Convention Center ❻

Between Market & Race Sts and 11th & 13th Sts. **Map** 2 F3. **Tel** (215) 418-4700, (800) 428-9000. 🚇 Market East Station. 🚏 11th St, 13th Sts. 🚌 38, Philly Phlash. 🕐 for conventions; Head House entrance open 24 hrs. **www**.paconvention.com

A sprawling 1 million sq ft (92,900 sq m) of meeting and exhibition space make up one of the country's most unique convention centers. The building's Grand Hall, above Reading Terminal Market, was once a bustling train terminal for the Reading Railroad. Reopened in 1994, the hall retains its Victorian features, including the majestic ceiling that had once made it the largest single-arch train shed in the world. Much of the original wooden roof and milk-glass windows remain, now casting natural light onto the terrazzo marble floor with simulated tracks where commuter trains once awaited passengers. Visitors can enter through the old railroad headhouse (now part of the Philadelphia Downtown Marriott) on the Market Street side for a peek at the Grand Hall, where a storyboard outlines its history. A second entrance on North Broad Street is part of a striking floor-to-ceiling glass façade.

Scattered throughout the multiblock complex is a collection of contemporary works of art by nearly 60 artists.

Colorful wares for sale at Reading Terminal Market

Pennsylvania Academy of the Fine Arts ❶

Founded by Colonial painter and scientist Charles Willson Peale and sculptor William Rush in 1805, the Pennsylvania Academy of the Fine Arts is America's oldest art museum and fine arts school. Its galleries display works by some of the world's best-known artists. One of them, the classical stylist Benjamin West (1738–1820), a Quaker from Pennsylvania, helped organize the British Royal Academy in 1768. Former student, the Impressionist Mary Cassatt (1844–1926), and modern abstractionist Richard Diebenkorn (1922–93), among others, share its wall space. The academy's main building, the distinctive National Historic Landmark Building, with its ornate arched foyer, is considered one of the finest examples of Victorian architecture in America. The contemporary Samuel M.V. Hamilton Building, with new galleries, opened in 2005 as part of the museum's 200th anniversary celebrations.

National Historic Landmark Building
Designed by Furness and Hewitt, the academy's main building opened during the nation's centennial in 1876.

Sculpture Exhibit
The 1873 marble sculpture Semiramis, *by William Wetmore Story (1819–95).*

National Historic Landmark Building Second Floor

★ **The Cello Player**
One of America's greatest painters, Thomas Eakins (1844–1916) taught at the academy from 1876 to 1886. This penetrating study of a cello player, capturing a moment of intense concentration, was painted in 1896. Rudolph Hennig, a leading musician, posed for it.

STAR EXHIBITS

★ The Cello Player

★ The Fox Hunt

★ Pantocrator

★ **The Fox Hunt**
This 1893 masterpiece by naturalist painter Winslow Homer (1836–1910), considered one of the greatest American artists of the 19th century, is among the academy's vast collections.

Lenfest Plaza

★ **Pantocrator**
Vincent Desiderio's monumental 2002 oil-on-linen triptych, 8 ft (2.5 m) tall and 17 ft (5 m) wide, is part of the Academy's collection of contemporary American art.

VISITORS' CHECKLIST

118 N Broad St at Cherry St.
Map 2 F3. *Tel* (215) 972-7600.
🚆 Suburban Station. 🅂 City Hall. 🚌 Philly Phlash. ◯ 10am–5pm Tue–Sat, 11am–5pm Sun. ● Mon, public hols. 🎨 Morris Gallery free. 🎟 11:30pm & 12:30pm Tue–Sat, noon & 1pm Sat–Sun. ♿ www.pafa.org

Samuel M.V. Hamilton Building Second Floor

Upper Foyer Gallery

Samuel M.V. Hamilton Building First Floor

Entrance

Lower Foyer Gallery

Samuel M.V. Hamilton Building
Adjacent to the National Historic Landmark Building, this contemporary structure doubles the academy's available display space, and includes a sculpture study center and a painting deck.

Fisher Brooks Gallery
This expansive new space on the first floor of the Samuel M.V. Hamilton Building houses the academy's post-World War II collection and also holds special exhibitions.

KEY

- ☐ Fisher Brooks Gallery
- ☐ Foyer Galleries
- ☐ 18th–20th century art
- ☐ Exhibit gallery
- ☐ Tuttleman Sculpture Gallery
- ☐ Non-exhibition space

GALLERY GUIDE

The grand staircase of the National Historic Landmark Building leads up to the gallery level on the second floor, which displays sculpture and 18th- to early 20th-century works, including portraiture, Impressionist, American genre, and landscape paintings. The Samuel M.V. Hamilton building houses contemporary artworks after 1945.

Ornamental gate at the entrance of Chinatown

Chinatown ❼

North of Arch St at 10th St.
Map 3 C1. 🚇 *Market East Station.*
🚊 *11th St.* 🚌 *Philly Phlash.*

This thriving neighborhood
spans an area nearly four
blocks wide and includes
more than 50 restaurants, a
score of grocery stores, and
other shops and boutiques.
Chinatown's origin dates to
the 1860s when the first
Chinese laundry was
established in the area.
It witnessed rapid
growth after World
War II owing to
a huge influx
of immigrants.
  In the US's fourth
largest Chinatown,
behind those in
New York, San
Francisco, and
Washington, D.C.,

**Dragon figurine in a
Chinatown shop**

visitors can still find a variety of
Asian fare including traditional
eel, squid, and duck dishes,
and Chinese cultural gifts such
as porcelain, wooden Buddhas,
and dragons. The colorful
Friendship Gate, with its ornate
dragons and Chinese art, is
at 10th and Arch Streets and
should not be missed.

Library Company
of Philadelphia ❽

1314 Locust St. **Map** 2 F5. **Tel** (215)
546-3181. 🚇 *Suburban Station.*
🚊 *Walnut-Locust.* 🚌 *21, 42.*
🕐 *9am–4:45pm Mon–Fri.*
www.librarycompany.org

Founded as the country's
first lending library by
Benjamin Franklin in 1731,
the Library Company has the

distinction of being America's
oldest cultural institution.
Its extraordinary collection
of historic books, papers
and images – numbering
more than 500,000 books,
75,000 graphics, and 160,000
manuscripts – documents
American culture from the
colonial era through the
19th century.
  The **Historical Society of
Pennsylvania**, housed on
the same block as Library
Company, was founded
in 1824 and is one of
the oldest historical
societies in the US.
Its stockpile has
600,000 printed
items, and more
than 19 million
manuscripts and
graphic materials
from the 17th
century onwards.

🏛 **Historical Society
of Pennsylvania**
1300 Locust St. **Tel** (215) 732-6200.
🕐 *12:30–5:30pm Tue & Thu,
12:30–8:30pm Wed; 10am–5:30pm
Fri (last admittance at 4:45pm).*
● *public hols.* ♿ **www**.hsp.org

Academy of
Music ❾

S Broad & Locust Sts (1420 Locust
St). **Map** 2 E5. **Tel** (215) 893-1935.
🚇 *Suburban Station.* 🚊 *Walnut-
Locust.* 🚌 *21, 42, Philly Phlash.*
🔵 *for performances.* 🎫 *tickets sold
one hour before a performance &
until half-an-hour after the last performance begins; tickets also sold at
the Kimmel Center 10am–6pm.*
🎫 *by appt; call (215) 893-1935.*
www.academyofmusic.org

Often referred to as the
"Grand Old Lady of Locust
Street," the Academy of Music
was the city's foremost
performing arts venue before
the construction of the
Kimmel Center in 2001. It
remains the country's oldest
grand opera house still in use.
  Designed by Philadelphia
architects Napoleon LeBrun
and Gustavus Runge, the
Victorian Italianate style structure took two years to build
and was completed in 1857.
The interior's horseshoe design
offers greater visibility to the
audience seated on both sides
of the balconies, which are
supported by Corinthian-style
columns. While the façade has
ornate gas lamps, the main hall
still has a glittering, 5,000-lb
(2,300-kg) crystal chandelier,
originally with 240 gas burners,
and later wired for electricity.
Statues representing Poetry
and Music crown the prosceni-
um arch. The former home
of the Philadelphia Orchestra
– which now performs in the
Kimmel Center – the academy
today hosts the Pennsylvania
Ballet and the Opera Company
of Philadelphia *(see p164).*

The Academy of Music, home to Philadelphia's opera and ballet

The Kimmel Center's glittering, modern façade

Kimmel Center for the Performing Arts ❿

260 S Broad St. **Map** 2 E5. **Tel** (215) 790-5800, (215) 893-1999 (tickets). 🚇 Suburban Station. 🚃 Walnut-Locust. 🚌 21, 42, Philly Phlash. 🕐 10am–6pm; later for performances. **www**.kimmelcenter.org

The centerpiece of the city's performing arts district, this modern complex includes two venues in a spacious atrium under a 150-ft (46-m) high barrel-vaulted glass roof. The center is named after philanthropist and businessman Sidney Kimmel, who made the single-largest private donation towards the complex.

The cello-shaped Verizon Hall, whose acoustics have been designed specifically for the Philadelphia Orchestra, seats more than 2,500 people. The Perelman Theater seats 650 people and has a rotating stage for chamber music, dance, and theatrical shows.

Other highlights include an expansive lobby with a stage for separate functions, an education center for performing arts classes, and a smaller studio and theater. The center's glass-enclosed roof garden offers great city views.

The center was the inspiration for the Philadelphia International Festival of the Arts, a city-wide event in spring 2011 featuring more than 100 performances across the city.

Suzanne Roberts Theatre ⓫

480 S Broad St. **Map** 3 A4. **Tel** (215) 982-0420. 🚇 Suburban Station. 🚃 Lombard-South. 🚌 21, 42. 📷 ♿ **www**.philadelphiatheatre company.org

The Suzanne Roberts Theatre, is home to the Philadelphia Theatre Company. The theater is named after former actress, playwright, director, and philanthropist Suzanne Roberts, who, for more than 40 years, has devoted her energy and talent to the city's theater community. It is housed in a modern facility that boasts a dramatic glass façade, two-story lobby, mezzanine level reception areas, and a 365-seat auditorium with state-of-the-art lighting and sound facilities. A second, 100-seat flexible stage is used for more intimate performances.

Rosenbach Museum and Library ⓬

2008-2010 DeLancy Pl at 20th St. **Map** 2 D5. **Tel** (215) 732-1600. 🚇 Suburban Station. 🚃 Lombard-South. 🚌 21, 42. 🕐 noon–5pm Tue & Fri, noon–8pm Wed & Thu, noon–6pm Sat & Sun. 🔴 Mon, public hols. 📷 🎥 **www**.rosenbach.org

Home to Dr. Rosenbach, one of America's most prominent rare book and manuscript dealers, this 1865 townhouse with a museum and research library sits on a quiet and shaded Rittenhouse street. Dr. Abraham Simon Wolf Rosenbach (1876–1952) and his brother Philip ran their company during the first half of the 20th century, combining great scholarship and business acumen. Apart from books, they also bought and sold 18th- and 19th-century artifacts such as silver, furniture, sculptures, drawings, and paintings.

So precious were many of their acquisitions that the brothers kept them for their own collection, which includes 30,000 books and 300,000 manuscripts and letters. Some of these are displayed today, including manuscript pages of James Joyce's *Ulysses*, over 100 personal letters of George Washington, and three of President Lincoln's speeches in manuscript form. In the house are the brothers' original possessions, including Chippendale furniture, gold-plated silver, and portraits by American artist Thomas Sully.

The museum's Maurice Sendak Gallery showcases the works and personal collections of the celebrated children's author, Maurice Sendak, best known for his 1963 classic *Where the Wild Things Are*.

Suzanne Roberts Theatre, Avenue of the Arts

Shaded walkway and benches at Rittenhouse Square, a favored outdoor park

Rittenhouse Square ⑬

Walnut St between 18th & 19th Sts. **Map** 2 D5. 🚇 *Suburban Station.* 🚆 *Walnut-Locust.* 🚌 *21, 38, 42, Philly Phlash.*

One of Center City's most popular outdoor parks, on any sunny day shaded Rittenhouse Square teems with local residents and downtown workers relaxing under the trees. One of the five public areas planned by Penn in his 1682 city grid, it was originally known as Southwest Square. It was renamed in 1825 in honor of David Rittenhouse (1732–96), first director of the US Mint, astronomer, clockmaker, and a descendant of Wilhelm Rittenhouse, who established the nation's first papermill near Wissahickon Creek in 1690.

In the mid-19th century, the first house was built opposite the square, which soon became a prominent public garden. The park was given its present-day appearance in 1913 by French American Beaux-Arts architect Paul Cret, who also designed the Barnes Foundation's gallery building and the Valley Forge memorial arch. Benches line the many walkways that crisscross the park and lead to the small fountain and reflecting pool at its center. Flowers add color in spring and summer.

Since its development, the square has been a desirable address in town. Extravagant high-rise apartments and hotels, and upscale restaurants and cafés surround the square, reminiscent of a New York City park scene.

St. Mark's Episcopal Church ⑭

1625 Locust St. **Map** 2 E5. **Tel** (215) 735-1416. 🚇 *Suburban Station.* 🚆 *Walnut-Locust.* 🚌 *21, 38, 42, Philly Phlash.* ⛪ *daily.* 📷 *only by appointment.* **www.** saintmarksphiladelphia.org

Founded by a local group of Anglican worshippers in 1847, St. Mark's Episcopal Church is one of the nation's

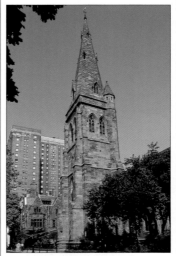

Downtown Philadelphia's Gothic-style St. Mark's Episcopal Church

best examples of Gothic Revival architecture. The parishioners raised $30,000 and hired John Notman, a prominent Philadelphia architect, to design and build a new church in the medieval designs of the 14th- and 15th-century high Gothic period. The church was opened in 1849 during the early development of the Rittenhouse Square neighborhood.

Inside is a baptistry made of inlaid Italian marble and colorful panels in a spacious sanctuary that is reminiscent of an old English church.

Not to be missed is the adjoining structure, the spectacular Lady Chapel. It was donated by Rodman Wanamaker as a memorial to his wife, who died in 1900 and is buried in the chapel's crypt. The 12 panels in this chapel have ornate carvings depicting scenes from the life of St. Mary the Virgin. Its ornate and beautiful marble altar, encased in silver, was made by Carl Krall and is one of only three such in the world. Still used for mass, it is the most well-known of St. Mark's ecclesiastical treasures. In 1937, the organ, considered to be one of the best examples of tonal construction in the nation, was dedicated to the church.

Liberty Place 🅯

16th & Chestnut Sts. **Map** 2 E4.
Tel (215) 851-9055. 🚉 *Suburban
Station.* 🚇 *Broad St.* 🚌 *Philly
Phlash.* 🕐 *9:30am–7pm Mon–Sat;
noon–6pm Sun.* ♿ **www**.
shopsatliberty.com

This gleaming, modern office
complex, which sprawls over
a vast area, is built on two
city blocks and anchors what
were once Philadelphia's
tallest skyscrapers. Designed
by Murphy and Jahn
Associates and built by
Rouse & Associates, the two
steel towers with sapphire
blue glass sheathing have a
postmodern architectural
aesthetic. Built in 1987 with
pyramidal tops and spires
reminiscent of New
York's Chrysler
Building, the 945-ft
(288-m) One Liberty
Place tower was
the first structure

to break the 86-year gentlemen's agreement not to build
higher than the height of the
hat on Penn's statue on top of
City Hall *(see p72)*. The 61-story
One Liberty Place stretches
almost 100 ft (30 m) higher
than its 58-story companion
tower Two Liberty Place,
which houses the national
headquarters of the CIGNA
Insurance Corporation and
new luxury condominiums.
   The mall complex that
connects the two towers
houses 60 stores that cover
the needs and fashion
desires of Center City office
workers, running the gamut
from specialty food shops,
chic boutiques, and trendy
shoe shops to more practical outlets such as book-
stores and newsstands.
A food court has sev-
eral vendors dishing
up everything from
spicy Cajun dishes
to smoothies.

**Joseph Hyrtl's collection of 139
skulls, Mütter Museum**

College of Physicians of Philadelphia/Mütter Museum 🅰

19 S 22nd St. **Map** 1 C4. *Tel* (215)
563-3737. 🚉 *Suburban Station.*
🚇 *15th St.* 🚌 *21, 38, 42.* 🕐
10am– 5pm. ● *Jan 1, Thanksgiving,
Dec 25.* 📷 **www**.collphyphil.org

A non-profit society founded
in 1787 "to advance the
Science of Medicine," the
College of Physicians provides
health education to medical
professionals and the public
through the C. Everett Koop
Community Health Information
Center, the Historical Medical
Library, the Free Library, and
computerized databases.
   For a visitor, the college's
most fascinating resource is
the Mütter Museum. Named
after professor of surgery
Thomas Mütter, who in 1858
donated 2,000 specimens he
had used for teaching, the
museum displays some curious
and unusual items, including
preserved specimens and wax
anatomical and pathological
models. These were used for
educational purposes in the
mid-1800s, when diseases and
genetic defects were identifi-
able only by their physical
manifestations.
   Key exhibits include the
skull collection of Joseph
Hyrtl, a 19th-century Viennese
anatomist, a plaster cast of the
original Siamese twins, Chang
and Eng, who died in 1874,
and *When the President is the
Patient*, one of the only major
exhibitions in the US to focus
on the long, hidden history
of illness in the White House.
Memorabilia from famous
scientists and physicians is
also on display.

One Liberty Place, with Two Liberty Place behind it

LOGAN SQUARE AND THE MUSEUM DISTRICT

Logan Square, with its multispouted Swann Memorial Fountain, is the centerpiece of the Museum District, bordered by the Schuylkill River on the west and the Cathedral of Saints Peter and Paul on the east. Benjamin Franklin Parkway, often referred to as the Champs Elysées of Philadelphia, is the route

Detail, Philadelphia Museum of Art façade

for most parades held in the city. It runs through the heart of this area and is flanked by buildings with imposing architectural styles, reminiscent of the ancient temples of Greece and Rome. To the north is the Eastern State Penitentiary, a fortress-turned-museum that once housed some of the country's most notorious criminals.

SIGHTS AT A GLANCE

Historical Buildings and Districts
Eakins Oval **9**
Fairmount Water Works Interpretive Center **11**
Free Library of Philadelphia **2**
Logan Square **3**
Thomas Eakins House **13**
Boathouse Row *(see p98)*

Museums and Galleries
Academy of Natural Sciences **5**
Barnes Foundation pp86–7 **1**
Eastern State Penitentiary **12**
The Franklin Institute **7**
Moore College of Art and Design **6**
Philadelphia Museum of Art pp90–93 **10**
Rodin Museum **8**

Places of Worship
Cathedral of Saints Peter and Paul **4**

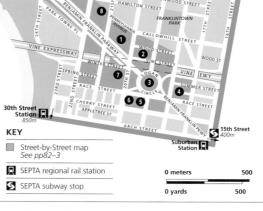

GETTING THERE
The easiest way to get around the Museum District is by Philly Phlash buses, which run along Benjamin Franklin Parkway to the Philadelphia Museum of Art (Mar–Nov only). SEPTA bus 38 runs from Center City along Market Street, and then up 22nd Street to Logan Square before turning onto the Parkway toward the Museum of Art. Regional trains stop at either Suburban or 30th Street Stations, while the subway stops are at 15th and 30th Streets. Once at Logan Square, most of the sights are within walking distance.

KEY

☐ Street-by-Street map See pp82–3

🚊 SEPTA regional rail station

🚇 SEPTA subway stop

0 meters		500
0 yards		500

◁ **The Swann Memorial Fountain located in the center of Logan Square**

Street-by-Street: Logan Square and the Museum District

Central to this neighborhood is the Benjamin Franklin Parkway – a grand boulevard lined with trees and grassy areas stretching from Center City to the Philadelphia Museum of Art. Statues and sculptures around the museum add to the area's European flair. Imposing structures housing many of the city's other key museums were built along the Parkway and around Logan Square in the 19th and early 20th centuries. Today, they hold some of the world's most prized antiquities, artworks, and natural history collections. Among them are the Rodin Museum, and The Franklin Institute. From 2012 the Barnes Foundation will relocate here.

Fairmount Water Works Interpretive Center

Stately temple-like façades that once housed the nation's first municipal water-pumping station now serve as home to a diving, entertainment, and education center, as well as an excellent restaurant **⓫**

Statue of George Washington

Eakins Oval

Ornate fountains and statues are the centerpieces of this traffic circle named after the 19th-century Philadelphia artist Thomas Eakins **➒**

★ The Franklin Institute

A massive statue of Benjamin Franklin sits in the atrium of this popular interactive science museum. The museum highlights Franklin's discoveries in technology and also houses a planetarium and IMAX theater **➐**

WINTER

RAC

STAR SIGHTS
★ Barnes Foundation
★ The Franklin Institute
★ Philadelphia Museum of Art
★ Rodin Museum

Academy of Natural Sciences

The oldest continuously operating natural history museum in the Western hemisphere has dinosaur fossils among its more than 17 million specimens **➎**

**Moore Colleg[e]
Art and Desig[n]**

★ **Philadelphia Museum of Art**
*The country's third largest fine art museum, sited in a
landmark building, has vast collections of paintings,
sculptures, and decorative arts showcasing more
than 2,000 years of human creativity* ⑩

★ **Rodin Museum**
*This small museum has more
than 130 sculptures by Auguste
Rodin, including* The Thinker.
*This is the largest collection
of his works outside France* ⑧

★ **Barnes Foundation**
*From 2012, the Barnes
Foundation will be re-
located here. Famed for
Impressionist and Mod-
ernist works (like Roger
de La Fresnaye's), the
collection is revered for
its depth and quality.* ①

Logan Square
*Originally called Northwest Square, Logan Square
is now centered by the Swann Memorial Fountain
and flanked by the Free Library of Philadelphia* ③

Cathedral of
Saints Peter
and Paul ④

KEY

– – – Suggested route

0 meters	200
0 yards	200

Barnes Foundation ❶

See pp86–7.

The Beaux-Arts façade of the Free Library of Philadelphia

Free Library of Philadelphia ❷

1901 Vine St. **Map** 2 E2. *Tel (215)*
686-5322. Suburban Station.
Race-Vine. 38, Philly Phlash.
9am–9pm Mon–Wed, 9am–5pm
Thu–Sat, 1–5pm Sun. Sun in
summer, public hols. tour starts
at Rare Book Dept at 11am.
www.library.phila.gov

Opened in 1894, this library
first occupied rooms in City
Hall. It relocated a few times
before moving into its current
Beaux-Arts building in 1927.

Today, the library has up to
1.75 million volumes, and its
key collections include maps,
children's books, social sciences and history books, and

the largest public library
chamber music collection in
the eastern US. The Rare Book
Department is also one of the
nation's largest, with holdings
that span 4,000 years and
include Sumerian cuneiform
tablets, medieval manuscripts,
incunabula, early American
children's books, and letters
and manuscripts from authors
such as Charles Dickens and
Edgar Allen Poe *(see p96)*.

Logan Square ❸

19th St at Benjamin Franklin Parkway.
Map 2 D3. Suburban Station.
Race-Vine. 38, Philly Phlash.

Part of William Penn's
original grid plan, Logan
Square (then known as
Northwest Square) was initially used as a burial ground,
then for pastureland, and
later for public executions.
It was renamed Logan
Square in 1825 in
honor of Penn's
secretary James Logan.
The square changed
dramatically during
the 1920s, when the
construction of the
Benjamin Franklin
Parkway turned it
into a traffic circle,
which is why it is
today also referred to
as Logan Circle.

At its center is the Swann
Memorial Fountain, designed
by Alexander Stirling Calder
in 1924. It features three
statues, meant to represent
the city's three main

waterways – the Delaware
and Schuylkill Rivers, and
Wissahickon Creek. Today,
the shaded area is a popular
spot along the Parkway, with
children often dipping in the
fountain on hot summer days.

Cathedral of Saints Peter and Paul ❹

18th St at Benjamin Franklin Parkway.
Map 2 E3. *Tel (215)* 561-1313.
Suburban Station. Race-Vine.
38, Philly Phlash. 7am–4:30pm
Mon–Sat. daily.

This grand cathedral, with a
copper dome more than 60 ft
(18 m) high, is a prominent
city landmark. Designed by
architects John Notman and
Napoleon LeBrun, the
Victorian Italianate basilica
with Renaissance features was
modeled after the Lombard
Church of St. Charles in
Rome and completed in
1864. The sanctuary is
shaped in the form of
a cross with a white
marble floor, a marble
altar, and six marble
columns rising more
than 40 ft (12 m) along
the curved walls of
the apse. Stained-glass
windows add a touch
of beauty to the main
altar area, side altars,
and the eight side

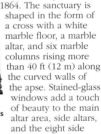

Window of the Cathedral of Saints Peter and Paul

chapels. Of particular note is
the organ, one of the largest
in the city, with 75 pipes and
four manuals. The cathedral is
now the seat of Philadelphia's
Roman Catholic Archdiocese.

Logan Square's Swann Memorial Fountain, named after the founder of the Philadelphia Fountain Society

Exhibit at Dinosaur Hall, Academy of Natural Sciences

Academy of Natural Sciences ❺

1900 Benjamin Franklin Parkway.
Map 2 D3. **Tel** (215) 299-1000.
🚆 Suburban Station. 🚇 Race-Vine.
🚌 38, Philly Phlash. ⏱ 10am–4:30pm
Mon–Fri, 10am–5pm Sat & Sun.
🚫 Jan 1, Thanksgiving, Dec 25. 📷
♿ www.acnatsci.org

A natural history museum and research library, the Academy of Natural Sciences was founded in 1812 by seven naturalists, who pooled their fossils and specimens to foster education and research about the earth's diverse species. Its collection has since swelled to 17 million specimens. Exhibits are housed on four levels, and include mounted animals, ranging from birds native to Pennsylvania to bison from North America and cape buffalo from Africa. Dinosaur Hall is a favorite with children, while the live butterfly exhibit is a reproduction of a tropical rainforest. The animals in the Live Animal Center cannot survive in the wild and are thus used for teaching purposes.

Moore College of Art and Design ❻

20th St & Benjamin Franklin Parkway.
Map 2 D3. **Tel** (215) 965-4000.
🚆 Suburban Station. 🚇 Race-Vine.
🚌 38, Philly Phlash. ⏱ galleries:
10am–5pm Tue–Fri, noon–4pm Sat &
Sun. 🚫 Mon, public hols. ♿
www.moore.edu

This school is the first and only women's art and design college in the United States, and one of only two in the world. It was founded as the Philadelphia School of Design for Women in 1848 by Sarah Worthington Peter (1800–77). Her aim was to educate women for careers that would lead to financial independence, and in accordance with that, the original curriculum provided training in the new fields spawned by the Industrial Revolution, such as textile design. Today, the college offers nine undergraduate degree programs in fine arts and design.

Two galleries of the college are open to the public. Rotating exhibitions highlight the works of alumnae and women artists. The Paley Gallery exhibits national and international artists, while the Levy Gallery showcases local artists and provides a center for exploration and experimentation for emerging and established talent. Past shows have featured work by Mary Cassatt, Karen Kilimnik, and Jacqueline Matisse.

The Franklin Institute ❼

222 N 20th St at Benjamin Franklin
Pkwy. **Map** 2 D3. **Tel** (215) 448-1200.
🚆 Suburban Station. 🚇 Race-Vine.
🚌 38, Philly Phlash. ⏱ museum:
9:30am–5pm daily; IMAX theater:
10am–6pm daily (to 9pm Fri & Sat).
📷 📱 ♿ www.fi.edu

The oldest science and technology institution in continuous use in North America, this museum was founded in 1824. Named after Benjamin Franklin (see p53), the institute's first location was in the building that now houses the Philadelphia History Museum at Atwater Kent (see p50). The current building opened in the 1930s and contains a spacious rotunda with a 21-ft (6-m) tall marble statue of Franklin. Exhibits highlight Franklin's accomplishments in medicine, astronomy, meteorology, and optics. Among the museum's attractions are Electricity Hall, which showcases his discovery of electricity, the Giant Walk-Through Heart with interactive devices (see p26), and the Train Factory, which has an original Baldwin steam locomotive.

Franklin's statue in the museum atrium

The KidScience exhibit, for five to eight year olds, is designed to teach basic principles of science. Children are taken on a fictional journey across *The Island of the Elements* where they learn about Light, Water, Earth, and Air.

Moore College of Art and Design, housed in a modern building

Barnes Foundation ❶

Floral motif, chest detail

Established in 1922 by pharmaceutical magnate Albert C. Barnes on his estate in the Philadelphia suburb of Merion, the Barnes Foundation has one of the world's best displays of Impressionist, French Modern, and Postimpressionist paintings. There are more than 800 works on view, including pieces by Renoir, Cezanne, and Matisse. It also contains exhibits on ancient Egyptian and Greek art, American furniture, and African sculpture. Grouped into 96 ensembles, the collection is displayed without labels and with little regard for chronology, so as to highlight artistic affinities between diverse works. The collection is in keeping with the foundation's aim of promoting "the advancement of education and the appreciation of the fine arts." In 2011, it will close at its location in Merion and will reopen at a larger site on Franklin Parkway in 2012.

★ **The Postman**
Painted by Vincent van Gogh in 1889 in Arles, France, this is a portrait of postman Joseph Roulin. The foundation is home to seven van Gogh paintings.

Gardanne
Paul Cezanne, the renowned French artist, painted this scenic landscape of the town of Gardanne in the mid-1880s. 69 of Cezanne's works are at the Barnes, helping to make it one of the finest Impressionist collections in the world.

Library

Auditorium

★ **Group of Dancers**
Over half of the Impressionist Edgar Degas's pieces depict dancers; this painting, completed c1900, is just one of the many fine examples of his work on view at the Barnes Foundation.

STAR EXHIBITS

★ The Postman

★ After the Concert

★ Card Players and Girl

GALLERY GUIDE
Artworks can be viewed on both the first and second floors. Galleries in the foundation display various paintings and sculptures that highlight different themes. An artist's oeuvre is not necessarily displayed together.

Models
*(1886-1888)
Georges Seurat
was a pioneer
of Pointilism,
an Impression-
ist technique
in which paint-
ings are made
from colored
dots, as this
piece shows.*

VISITORS' CHECKLIST

Benjamin Franklin Parkway.
Tel (610) 667-0290.
Suburban Station. Spring
Garden. 38, Philly Phlash.
opening in 2012. Call or
check website for details.
public hols.
www.barnesfoundation.org

★ **After the Concert**
*The Barnes has over
180 works by Pierre-
Auguste Renoir, including
this one, which was completed by the famous French
Impressionist in 1877.
Renoir painted several
thousand works over
60 years, even
while suffering
from severe
arthritis
toward the end
of his life.*

★ **Card Players and Girl**
*Often referred to as the father of
modern art, Paul Cezanne completed this painting in 1892. Cezanne's
compositions and use of color
greatly influenced 20th-century art.*

Dogone Couple
*While many of his contem-
poraries viewed African art
as "primitive" artifacts,
Albert C. Barnes was an
early and active collector of
it. As a result, in addition to
modern American and
European art, the founda-
tion holds a distinguished
collection of African art.*

KEY

☐	Joy of Life gallery
☐	Permanent exhibition
☐	Temporary exhibition
☐	Non-exhibition space

Rodin's sculpture, *The Thinker*, outside the Rodin Museum

Rodin Museum ❽

22nd St at Benjamin Franklin Parkway. **Map** 2 D2. *Tel* (215) 568–6026. 🚉 Suburban Station. 🚌 Spring Garden. 🚌 38, Philly Phlash. ⭕ 10am–5pm Tue–Sun. ⬤ Mon, public hols. 📷 ♿ 🎬 www.rodinmuseum.org

French sculptor Auguste Rodin's (1840–1917) most famous artwork, *The Thinker*, sits outside the columned façade that leads into the courtyard of this small, temple-like museum. With nearly 130 sculptures, it contains the largest collection of Rodin's work outside of Paris.

Opened in 1929, the Rodin Museum's entrance showcases the impressive, 20-ft (6-m) high *The Gates of Hell*, which Rodin worked on for 37 years until his death. Inside is the life-sized sculpture of six heroes of the Middle Ages, known as *The Burghers of Calais*. Other notable works include *Apotheosis of Victor Hugo*, a sculpture of the French writer, and different sculptures of kissing lovers, known as *Eternal Springtime*.

Eakins Oval ❾

Benjamin Franklin Parkway. **Map** 1 C1. 🚉 30th St Station. 🚌 Spring Garden. 🚌 38, Philly Phlash.

Named after prominent Philadelphia artist Thomas Eakins, this oval was part of the Benjamin Franklin Parkway project in the 1920s. Located opposite the entrance to the Philadelphia Museum of Art, Eakins Oval has a prominent equestrian statue of President George Washington at its center. The center also features a fountain, which has figurines of wild animals surrounding four statues that symbolize four of the country's major rivers – the Delaware, Mississippi, Hudson, and Potomac. Two smaller fountains flank the large central one – the Ericsson fountain, named for the engineer who designed the USS *Monitor*, a Union naval vessel of the Civil War, and another named after Fairmount Park Commission chairman Eli Kirk Price (1797–1884) who led efforts to build the parkway. Today, the oval is at the center of a traffic circle and includes a shaded green area with park benches and a parking lot.

Washington's statue at Eakins Oval

Philadelphia Museum of Art ❿

See pp90–93.

Fairmount Water Works Interpretive Center ⓫

640 Waterworks Dr. **Map** 1 B1. *Tel* (215) 685-0723. 🚉 30th St Station. 🚌 Spring Garden. 🚌 38, Philly Phlash. ⭕ 10am–5pm Tue–Sat, 1–5pm Sun. ⬤ Mon, public hols. 📷 ♿ www.fairmountwaterworks.org

Situated on the elevated banks of the Schuylkill River, these impressive Greek Revival buildings were constructed between 1812 and 1871 to supply drinking water to Philadelphia – the first American city to take on providing water as a municipal responsibility. When it opened in 1822, its huge water wheels, turbines, and pumps and the beauty of the site made it a destination for engineers and visitors from the US and Europe. Water pumping ended in 1909, and today the restored buildings house old pumping apparatuses and an interpretive center with a number of fascinating interactive exhibits. All the exhibits here are based on the theme "Water Is Our World" and challenge children and adults alike to learn about water resources. Other exhibits include a real-time fish migration up the river, a virtual helicopter tour of the watershed, and a computer simulation of historic technology. The on-site restaurant offers beautiful city views.

Fairmount Water Works Interpretive Center, now a National Historic Landmark

Reconstruction of Al Capone's cell at the Eastern State Penitentiary

Eastern State Penitentiary ⑫

22nd St at Fairmount Ave.
Map 2 D1. **Tel** (215) 236-3300.
🚇 Spring Garden. 🚌 38, Philly Phlash. ◯ 10am–5pm daily. ● Jan 1, Easter, Thanksgiving, Dec 24, 25, & 31. 🚫 children under 7 not allowed. 🅿️ 👤 **www**.easternstate.org

Named the "House" by inmates and guards, the Eastern State Penitentiary was a revolutionary concept in criminal justice. Prior to its opening, convicts lived in despicable conditions and suffered brutal physical punishments. The Philadelphia Quakers proposed an alternative in the form of a facility where a lawbreaker could be alone to ponder and seek penitence for his misdeeds. This led to the opening of the penitentiary in 1829. During incarceration, with sentences seldom less than five years, prisoners were hooded when outside their cells to prevent interaction with others.

The prison, with its fortress-like Gothic Revival façade, had a single entrance and 30-ft (9-m) high boundary walls. Inside, seven cellblocks extended from a central rotunda, and each solitary cell had a skylight and private outdoor exercise yard. In the early 20th century, the isolation form of imprisonment was abandoned, and more cellblocks were added. Over the years, the prison has housed several infamous personalities including the gangster Al Capone.

Officially closed in 1971, it is now a National Historic Landmark and museum.

Today, the structure's chipped walls and aging cellblocks host changing exhibitions from its collections of old artifacts and photographs. The prison also conducts tours, with audio excerpts from former guards and inmates, and each Halloween it hosts *Terror Behind the Walls*, a "haunted" house experience *(see p34)*.

Thomas Eakins House ⑬

1729 Mt Vernon St. **Map** 2 E1.
Tel (215) 685-0750. 🚇 Spring Garden. 🚌 38, Philly Phlash. ◯ hours vary.

This brick row house was home to the artist Thomas Eakins for most of his life, with the exception of the time he spent abroad: first in Paris studying art at the École des Beaux-Arts from 1866 to 1868, and then traveling to Spain in 1869 before returning home in 1870. One of the country's most renowned Realist painters of the late 19th and early 20th centuries, Eakins' works often reflected life in Philadelphia through portraits and family paintings, as well as through his popular city and nature paintings, which included sculling and sailing scenes on the Schuylkill and Delaware Rivers.

Today, the Thomas Eakins House is home to the city's Mural Arts Program. Changing exhibitions in the building's galleries highlight artwork created by Philadelphia's youth participating in the Mural Arts and other outreach programs.

Façade of Thomas Eakins House, home to the Mural Arts Program

MURAL ARTS PROGRAM

Philadelphia has America's largest collection of colorful, outdoor and indoor murals, which are emblazoned on walls all across the city. Through artists' visions and the sheer manpower of inspired local youth, more than 3,000 variegated and vibrant murals have been painted since the Mural Art Program's inception in 1984 as an anti-graffiti initiative. With extensive preparation including scaffolding and undercoating, a typical mural is completed within two months and can cost as much as $20,000. The murals often highlight famous community leaders, role models, artistic cityscapes, and themes of culture, history, diversity, and anti-drug messages.

Murals on city walls, a tradition in the city of Philadelphia

Philadelphia Museum of Art ❿

Beaux-Arts roof detail

Founded in the country's centennial year of 1876, Philadelphia's most prominent museum attracts major exhibitions to supplement its superlative permanent collections. More than 200 galleries showcase works of art spanning more than 2,000 years, with some Asian exhibits dating from the third millennium BC. The medieval cloister courtyard and fountain on the second floor is very popular, as are the French Gothic chapel and the pillared temple from Madurai, India. In addition to outstanding collections of Old Master, Impressionist, and Postimpressionist paintings, Pennsylvania Dutch and American decorative arts are also featured with American art. Scattered throughout the museum are computerized stations with information on the exhibits.

Mask of Shiva
A 9th-century copper alloy artifact from India.

★ Sunflowers
Impressionist painter Vincent van Gogh (1853–90) is perhaps best known for his series of sunflower paintings. This version was painted just 18 months before his death.

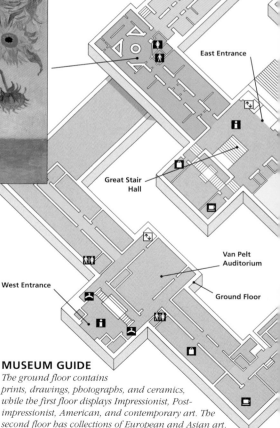

East Entrance

Great Stair Hall

West Entrance

Van Pelt Auditorium

Ground Floor

KEY

☐	Julien Levy Gallery
☐	Modern and Contemporary Art
☐	European Paintings, Sculpture, Decorative Arts, and Architecture
☐	Special Exhibition Galleries
☐	American Art
☐	Arms and Armor
☐	Dutch Ceramics
☐	Middle East and Asian Art
☐	Non-exhibition space

MUSEUM GUIDE

The ground floor contains prints, drawings, photographs, and ceramics, while the first floor displays Impressionist, Postimpressionist, American, and contemporary art. The second floor has collections of European and Asian art. First Floor refers to the floor above ground level.

The West Entrance of the Philadelphia Museum of Art

★ **Ming Dynasty Ceramics**
Delicate ceramics, fine hardwood furniture, and other objects of the Ming Dynasty are on display in the Chinese gallery, including this 15th-century bowl, the Three Friends.

Second Floor

Cloister with Elements from the Abbey of Saint-Genis-des-Fontaines
Surrounded by marble arcaded walkways and centered by a rare fountain, this cloister is based on medieval French design.

First Floor

American Art
The museum has an impressive collection of American art that includes Noah's Ark, *painted in 1946 by Edward Hicks (1780–1849).*

★ **Thomas Eakins Collection**
Portrait of Dr. Samuel D. Gross (The Gross Clinic) *(1875) by Thomas Eakins, acclaimed Philadelphian artist, forms a part of the museum's collection of works by local artists.*

STAR EXHIBITS

★ Sunflowers

★ Ming Dynasty Ceramics

★ Thomas Eakins Collection

Exploring the Philadelphia Museum of Art

Stained glass roundel, France (1246–48)

The Museum of Art is home to over 300,000 objects from Europe, Asia, and the Americas, spanning more than 4,000 years. Its key exhibits include European paintings, from medieval and Renaissance to Impressionist and Postimpressionist pieces. Modern art collections feature works by Pablo Picasso and Henri Matisse, while Asian art includes furniture and ceramics. American art sections contain extensive works by Philadelphia artists Thomas Eakins and Charles Willson Peale, and the museum's collections of prints, drawings, and photographs feature works by 19th- and 20th-century US and European artists. It also has one of the oldest and largest collections of costumes and textiles in America.

Fra Angelico's *Dormition of the Virgin* (c. 1427)

EUROPEAN PAINTINGS, SCULPTURE, DECORATIVE ARTS, AND ARCHITECTURE

Most of the museum's second floor is devoted to European art from 1500 to 1850. In addition, it has rooms with sculpture, furniture, descriptive interiors, and original façades that highlight periods of European history from 1100 to 1800. The Portal from the Abbey Church of Saint-Laurent dates to 1125. Its imposing stone arched walls were once the main entrance to the Augustinian abbey church of Saint-Laurent in France.

The Cloister with Elements from the Abbey of Saint-Genis-des-Fontaines is based on one in a late 13th-century abbey in Roussillon in

Jester Vase (1894) by Marc-Louis-Emmanuel Solon

southwestern France. Other decorative arts include ceramic vases, stained and painted glass, stone sculptures, and metal and wooden objects ranging from candelabra to mahogany furniture and glass goblets. Key European paintings include masterpieces by Fra Angelico, Sandro Botticelli, Rogier van der Weyden, Peter Paul Rubens, and Nicolas Poussin, as well as classic European views and land- and cityscapes from 18th-century verdute artists Canaletto, his nephew and pupil Bernardo Bellotto, and Francesco Guardi. Renaissance portraits and religious paintings include Jan van Eyck's *Saint Francis of Assisi Receiving the Stigmata* (1428–30), Botticelli's *Stories of Saint Mary Magdalene* (1484–91) and Joos van Cleve's *King Francis I* (1525).

Ruben's *Prometheus Bound* (1618) is a centerpiece painting combining historical and mythological subjects.

The first floor has some excellent Impressionist and Postimpressionist paintings by artists such as Renoir, Monet, Cezanne, Pissarro, and van Gogh. Works include Renoir's *Great Bathers* (1884–87), van Gogh's *Sunflowers* (1889), Cezanne's *Large Bathers* (1906), and Monet's *Poplars* (1891), to name just a few.

AMERICAN ART

One of the finest public holdings of American art, this collection is sourced from the Philadelphia area. Decorative arts, paintings, and sculptures include 18th- and 19th-century silver, ceramics, and porcelain, as well as Pennsylvania German items including toys, textiles, furniture, and illuminated folk art called fraktur. Impressive bookcases, desks, chairs, and chests made in colonial Philadelphia, along with other decorative arts, demonstrate the cultural links

The Staircase Group (1795) by Charles Willson Peale

Japanese ceremonial teahouse, surrounded by a bamboo garden

between European and early American lifestyles and designs. Key paintings include Charles Willson Peale's *Rachel Weeping* (1772) and *The Staircase Group* (1795), in which he painted his sons ascending a staircase. Thomas Eakins' works, including *The Gross Clinic* (1875), are the most significant part of the museum's collection of 19th-century paintings. Sculptures and sketches by the renowned artist are also housed here. Other paintings include Sanford Gifford's *A Coming Storm* (1863) and Edward Hick's *Noah's Ark* (1846).

Bird Tree, Pennsylvania (1800–1830)

MIDDLE EAST AND ASIAN ART

Within the second-floor galleries of Asian Art are exquisite carpets, delicate jade carvings, porcelains, ink paintings, and sculptures forming part of the museum's collections of Southeast Asian, Korean, Chinese, Japanese, Persian, and Turkish art.

The Chinese Ming Dynasty (1368–1644) is represented by a room brought from China, the imposing Reception Hall from a Nobleman's Palace, and ceramics and hardwood furniture. Works by Japanese artists from the 12th to 20th centuries include exquisitely painted scrolls and screens, decorative arts, and fine modern designs. A centerpiece exhibit is *Evanescent Joys*, a ceremonial teahouse acquired from Japan in 1928. Korean art includes ceramics, lacquer, and sculpture, of which an example is a rare 15th-century cast-iron tiger. Also on display are outstanding Persian and Turkish carpets, including the showpiece 16th- to 17th-century *Tree Carpet*. The carpets were gifted by collectors Joseph L. Williams and John D. McIlhenny in the 1940s and 50s. The museum's Indian art collection includes *Nandi, the Sacred Bull of Shiva*, a 13th-century schist carving from Mysore, and the impressive Pillared Hall from Madurai. Reconstructed from the ruins of three temples, its granite pillars are the only examples of stone architecture from India in an American museum.

MODERN AND CONTEMPORARY ART

The museum's modern art collection began with acquisitions of works by Pablo Picasso and Constantin Brancusi in the 1930s. Today key holdings include Picasso's *Self-Portrait* (1906) and *Three Musicians* (1921), encompassing his decade-long study of Synthetic Cubism. Works by Marcel Duchamp include the *The Large Glass* (1915–23), applied on two planes of glass with lead foil, fuse wire and dust, and the 1912 *Nude Descending a Staircase (No. 2)*, a mechanical portrayal of a subject with Cubist qualities. Salvador Dali's surrealistic 1936 painting *Soft Construction of Boiled Beans (Premonition of Civil War)* and Henri Matisse's *Breakfast* (1920) also form part of the collection.

COSTUMES AND TEXTILES

Acquisitions from the 1876 Centennial Exposition initiated the museum's costume and textile collections. The first textiles showcased designs and techniques used in India, Europe, and the Middle East. The collections grew in the early 20th century with the addition of 18th- and 19th-century French textiles, and today number over 20,000 objects, including fashionable Philadelphia apparel, Pennsylvania Dutch quilts, weaving pattern books, and colonial-era clothing. One of the most famous costumes is the wedding dress worn by Princess Grace of Monaco, a Philadelphian. Other items include African-American quilts, 20th-century hats, 19th-century needlework, church embroideries and vestments, and three-century old Japanese Noh robes, dating from between 1615 and 1867.

Gala Ensemble, Italy (late 19th to early 20th century)

FARTHER AFIELD

The growth of neighborhoods away from the historic center of Philadelphia only began in the 19th century, with the exception of areas such as Germantown and Fairmount Park, which were distinct areas even as far back as colonial times. These are home to some of the city's most renowned sights, including the University of Pennsylvania just

Statue at Fairmount Park

beyond the Schuylkill River. Fairmount Park runs along the river, leading to the chic neighborhoods of Manayunk and Chestnut Hill. Sights to the south include the Italian Market and the Mummers Museum, while to the east, just across the Delaware River in the bordering state of New Jersey, are the varied attractions of the Camden Waterfront.

SIGHTS AT A GLANCE

Historical Buildings and Districts
Boathouse Row and Kelly Drive **6**
Camden Waterfront **14**
Chestnut Hill **3**
Edgar Allen Poe National Historic Site **1**
Fort Mifflin **13**
Germantown **2**
Italian Market **10**
Main Street Manayunk **4**
University of Pennsylvania and University City **8**
Walt Whitman House **15**

Parks, Gardens, and Zoos
Fairmount Park **5**
Philadelphia Zoo **7**

Museums and Galleries
Mario Lanza Institute and Museum **11**
Mummers Museum **12**
University of Pennsylvania Museum of Archaeology and Anthropology **9**

KEY

	Main sightseeing area
	Urban area
✈	Airport
═	Highway
═	Major road
═	Minor road
—	Railway
- -	State border

0 kilometers 4

0 miles 4

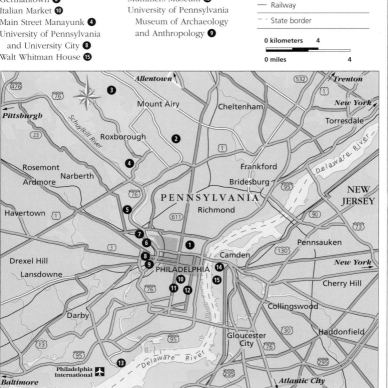

◁ **Turrets punctuate the roofline of Rosemont College, near Philadelphia**

Three-story brick house rented by Edgar Allan Poe in the mid-1840s

Edgar Allan Poe National Historic Site ❶

532 N 7th St. *Tel (215) 597-8780.*
🚇 *Spring Garden.* 🚌 *47.* 🕐 *9am–5pm Wed–Sun.* ⬤ *Mon, Tue; Jan 1, Veterans Day, Thanksgiving, Dec 25.* ♿ *limited.* **www**.nps.gov/edal

The great American writer Edgar Allan Poe (1809–49) lived in Philadelphia for six years from 1838 to 1844 in several residences. This three-story brick house was his rented residence for about a year between 1843 and 1844, and his only home that remains today in the city.

The inside, with original walls and creaking wooden floors, is empty as there are no accurate descriptions of what the house looked like during Poe's time, and none of his personal belongings have survived. The visitor area, though, has exhibits and a video highlighting his life and a room decorated as depicted in his essay "The Philosophy of Furniture."

In fact, Poe's years in the city were some of his most productive with the publishing of "The Murders in the Rue Morgue," "The Gold Bug," and "The Tell-Tale Heart." Poe fans seem to think that the house's basement may have inspired him to write "The Black Cat." One wall has brick columns similar to where, in the story, the murderer had entombed his victim. The raven statue outside is a tribute to one of his poems, "The Raven."

Germantown ❷

Centered by Germantown Avenue at Chelten Ave.
🚉 *Chestnut Hill West SEPTA regional rail to Chelten Ave station.* 🚌 *23.*

A few miles northwest of Philadelphia, this neighborhood was first inhabited in 1683 by German settlers wooed by Penn's promise of religious freedom. Its most prominent historical period was during and after the American Revolutionary War. It was the site of the Battle of Germantown in 1777, when British troops withstood an attack by the Continental Army, forcing the Americans to retreat to Valley Forge for the winter *(see pp20–21)*. In 1793, President Washington and his family moved here to escape the yellow fever epidemic in the city. Several historic homes in this now urban neighborhood have been preserved and are open to visitors *(see pp106–107)*.

At its center is Market Square, a busy marketplace in colonial times and now a small park dominated by a Civil War memorial. Flanking the square are the Deshler-Morris House, and the

Germantown Historical Society Museum and Library. The center's museum features rotating exhibitions chosen from among its 20,000 historical artifacts and documents, some of which date back to the 1600s. To its north is the **Awbury Arboretum**, a landscaped area with gardens, ponds, and a Victorian estate originally owned by a Quaker family. This neighborhood is safer to visit during the day.

🏛 **Germantown Historical Society Museum and Library**
5501 Germantown Ave. *Tel (215) 844–1683.* 🕐 *9am–5pm Tue, 1–5pm Thu; call for Sun hours.* 📷 ♿

🌿 **Awbury Arboretum**
1, Awbury Rd. *Tel (215) 849-2855.* 🕐 *dawn–dusk.* ♿ *limited access.*

Chestnut Hill ❸

Centered by Germantown Ave at Chestnut Hill Ave. 🚉 *Chestnut Hill East or Chestnut Hill West SEPTA regional rail to Chestnut Hill stations.*

What began as a settlement of farmhouses and taverns in the mid-1700s is now one of Philadelphia's most upscale neighborhoods. Located on the city's northern border, Chestnut Hill is an urban village bisected by Germantown Avenue. Its shaded, cobblestoned streets

Boutiques and cafés line the sidewalks of Chestnut Hill

are lined with boutiques, fine-food restaurants, cafés, and galleries. Within its hilly terrain are the Wissahickon Gorge greenbelt and the **Morris Arboretum of the University of Pennsylvania**, an immense area that includes thousands of rare plants and "trees-of-record," greenhouses, ponds, and meadows. Some of the other attractions in this area include the **Woodmere Art Museum**, which is housed in a Victorian mansion and features a collection of more than 300 paintings and sculptures. The **Chestnut Hill Historical Society** has a collection of more than 15,000 items that date from the 1680s to the present, including artifacts, documents, and photographs.

Rose at Morris Arboretum

🌺 **Morris Arboretum of the University of Pennsylvania**
100 E Northwestern Ave. *Tel (215)* 247-5777. ☐ *10am–4pm daily (Jun–Aug: to 8:30pm Thu; Apr–Oct: to 5pm Sat & Sun).* ▨ 🅱
www.morrisarboretum.org

🏛 **Woodmere Art Museum**
9201 Germantown Ave. *Tel (215)* 247-0476. ☐ *10am–5pm Tue–Sat, 1–5pm Sun.* ▨ 🅱
www.woodmereartmuseum.org

🏛 **Chestnut Hill Historical Society**
8708 Germantown Ave. *Tel (215)* 247-0417. ☐ *9:30am–2:30pm Tue & Fri; appointments preferred.*
www.chhist.org

Main Street Manayunk ❹

Main St, Manayunk. *Tel (215) 482-9565.* 🚉 *Manayunk/Norristown SEPTA regional rail Manayunk Station.* 🚌 *61.* **www**.manayunk.com

Once an industrial urban village, this neighborhood has been revitalized in recent years with trendy stores, galleries, restaurants, and cafés lining the fashionable Main Street. In 1824, it changed its name to Manayunk, from the Lenape word *manaiung*, which means, "Where we go to drink." With the completion

of the Manayunk Canal, the early 19th-century town grew into a thriving mill and industrial town. Today, the old mills are home to upscale apartments and an eclectic mix of storefronted shops. Main Street comes to life especially on weekends when sidewalk café tables fill up. The pedestrian walk along the canal is also popular with walkers and bikers.

Fairmount Park ❺

On both sides of the Schuylkill River & along Wissahickon Creek. *Tel (215) 683-0200.* 🚉 *30th St Station.* 🚊 *Spring Garden.* **www**.phila.gov/fairpark

Stretching along the shores of the Schuylkill River and Wissahickon Creek, Fairmount Park forms part of an extensive greenbelt. Its grassy fields and dense wooded areas are dotted with statues and crisscrossed by miles of hiking paths. The most popular path runs parallel to Kelly and Martin Luther King Jr. drives and stretches 8 miles (13 km) along both sides of the river.

West of the Schuylkill River is The Mann Center, an outdoor amphitheater and summer home of the Philadelphia Orchestra *(see p164)*. The nearby **Horticulture Center** has elongated ponds with fountains, while the **Shofuso Japanese House and Garden** is a 17th-century-

Outdoor seating at a café along Manayunk's Main Street

style Shoin mansion that has a koi pond. The grand Memorial Hall, a centerpiece during the country's centennial celebration, was formerly the city's art museum. It was dedicated by President Ulysses S. Grant, but is now home to the **Please Touch Museum** for children *(see p170)*.

Other key attractions include 18th- and early 19th-century mansions that were once the rural homes of prominent colonial families *(see pp108–109)*.

🌺 **Horticulture Center**
Tel (215) 685-0096. ☐ *Apr–Oct: 8am–6pm; Nov–Mar: 8am–5pm.* ▨ 🅱

🌺 **Shofuso Japanese House and Garden**
Tel (215) 878-5097. ☐ *May–Oct: 10am–4pm Tue–Fri, 11am–5pm Sat & Sun.* ⚫ *Nov–Apr.* ▨

🏛 **Please Touch Museum**
Tel (215) 963-0667. ☐ *9am–5pm Mon–Sat, 11am–5pm Sun.*

Geese at Fairmount Park, part of Philadelphia's greenbelt

Boathouse Row and Kelly Drive ⑥

West of Philadelphia Museum of Art along Kelly Drive. 🚇 *30th St Station.* 🚌 *38, Philly Phlash.*

This row of quaint stone and brick boathouses is home to what's affectionately known as the "Schuylkill Navy," namely rowing and sculling clubs patronized by area universities and high schools. Situated on the river's eastern shore, some feature Victorian Gothic architecture and date back to the 19th century. These boathouses, and others farther upstream, host the country's largest intercollegiate sculling contest in May, the annual Dad Vail Regatta *(see p33).*

At one end of Boathouse Row is the Azalea Garden, where people picnic under the magnolias and large oaks. At the other end is the small 1887 lighthouse that once flashed beacons to warn barges and steamboats of the nearby Fairmount dam. Also close to Boathouse Row is Icelandic sculptor Einar Jonsson's 1918 statue of Thorfinn Karlsefni, the Viking explorer who is said to have landed in America a millennium ago. At night, strings of lights illuminating the boathouses reflect

off the river, creating an idyllic scene often highlighted on calendars and postcards. A popular path along Kelly Drive offers miles of walking and biking on both sides of the Schuylkill River.

Philadelphia Zoo ⑦

3400 Girard Ave. ***Tel*** *(215) 243-1100.* 🚇 *30th St Station.* 🚇 *34th St.* 🚌 *38.* ⭘ *Mar–Oct: 9:30am–5pm daily (to 4pm Dec–Feb).* ⬤ *Jan 1, Jun 9, Thanksgiving, Dec 24, 25, & 31.* 🗓 **www**.philadelphiazoo.org

Boasting Victorian gardens and historic architecture, including the country home of William Penn's grandson John, the Philadelphia Zoo was opened in 1874. The zoo is the country's oldest and is home to more than 1,600 exotic animals from around the world. The zoo houses several rare species such as naked mole rats and blue-eyed lemurs. A walk-through giant otter habitat shows these animals at their playful best. The magnificent big cats – clouded leopards, lions, tigers (including rare white tigers), and jaguars – are kept in near-natural habitats or inside the Bank of America Big Cat Falls exhibit, in weather-protected cages that provide a close-up view. Other features are an

Hummingbird at Philadelphia Zoo

open birdhouse with uncaged finches and hummingbirds; the Reptile and Amphibian House with venomous king cobras, giant tortoises, and alligators basking in a tropical paradise; and a large reserve area for ten primate species. The Zooballoon takes passengers aloft for panoramic views of the city.

University of Pennsylvania and University City ⑧

Main Campus between Chestnut St & University Ave and between 32nd & 40th Sts. ***Tel*** *(215) 898-5000.* 🚇 *SEPTA Airport, Warminster, or Media/Elwyn line regional rail to University City Station.* 🚇 *34th St.* 🚌 *42.* **www**.upenn.edu

This highly regarded Ivy League school has the honor of being America's first university. Founded by Benjamin Franklin in 1749, the University of Pennsylvania started classes two years later, beginning what would become the nation's first liberal arts curriculum. The university is also home to the country's first medical school, student union, and the oldest collegiate football field still in use.

Today, with more than 20,000 students enrolled in undergraduate, graduate, and professional school programs, it is often listed among America's top ten universities.

Scenic Boathouse Row along Schuylkill River, to the west of the city

Shaded walkway at the University of Pennsylvania campus

Its vast urban campus features 19th-century buildings along grassy areas and shaded walkways, including Locust Walk, its main pedestrian street. Among the notable sculptures on the campus are two of Franklin along Locust Walk, one with the statesman and inventor seated on a bench.

The Penn campus is located within University City, a revitalized neighborhood with one of the Philadelphia area's most ethnically diverse and educated populations. It has Victorian-era homes, as well as its own brand of galleries, cafés, and restaurants. Within University City are also several medical centers and other institutions of higher learning, including Drexel University.

University of Pennsylvania Museum of Archaeology and Anthropology 9

3260 South St. ***Tel*** *(215) 898-4000.* 🚆 *Airport, Warminster, or Media/Elwyn lines to University City Station.* [S] *34th St.* 🚌 *42.* 🕘 *10am–4:30pm Tue–Sat, 1pm–5pm Sun.* ● *Mon, public hols; Sun in summer.* 📷 🛍 ☕ 🍴 📖 ♿ **www**.museum.upenn.edu

A world-class museum with nearly one million artifacts, this institute is one of Philadelphia's best. The museum's expansive 90 ft (27 m) rotunda is the largest unsupported masonry dome in the country, and features Chinese art and early Buddhist sculpture. The museum's collections have been gathered since its founding in 1887 through more than 400 archaeological digs and research expeditions around the world. More than 30 galleries spread over three floors house impressive remnants of civilizations past and present spanning the earth, including a 13-ton (28,650-lb) granite Sphinx of Rameses II from 1200 BC, well-preserved mummies, an Etruscan warrior helmet from the 7th century BC, Zapotec figures from Mexico, African stringed musical instruments, and an Alaskan Umiak, a whaling boat with a skin hull.

A flower stall at the Italian Market

Italian Market 10

Along 9th St between Christian & Wharton Sts. [S] *Ellsworth-Federal.* 🚌 *47.* 🕘 *9am–5pm Tue–Sat, 9am–2pm Sun.* ● *Mon.* **www**.phillyitalianmarket.com

Under numerous awnings and corrugated tin roofs, this open-air market is the largest and oldest of its kind in the country. The market dates to the late 1800s, when Italian immigrants sold meats and produce, and Jewish merchants sold clothing. Although still predominantly Italian, today it comprises a mix of nationalities. The sights and sounds of the market, however, have not changed much from a century ago. Several stalls offer fresh fruit and vegetables, butcher shops sell prime cuts, poultry and game meats, while seafood vendors stack fish and shellfish on ice. Other specialties include pastas, cheeses from all over the world, spices, coffees, and teas. Bakeries have pastries ranging from ricotta-filled Italian cannolies to Amish baked goods. Food stands and cafés dish up Philly cheesesteaks, pizzas, and traditional Italian dishes.

Mural depicting the Italian Market and Frank Rizzo, 1970s city mayor

Art Deco façade of the three-story Mummers Museum

Mario Lanza Institute and Museum ⓫

Columbus House, 712 Montrose St. *Tel* (215) 238-9691. 🚇 Ellsworth-Federal. 🚌 47. 🕙 11am–3pm Mon–Sat. 🔴 Sun, public hols. 🏠 **www**.mario-lanza-institute.org

Housed in a former church rectory, the museum honors the world-famous Philadelphia tenor and movie star, Mario Lanza (1921–59). Lanza developed an interest in opera as he grew up, and his talents were soon recognized. His career flourished with best-selling recordings and starring roles in several major films of the 1940s and 50s, such as *The Great Caruso* and *For The First Time*.

Through posters, newspaper clippings, photographs, and other memorabilia, the museum charts his life from his childhood to his death in Rome from a heart attack. The museum shop sells many of the 460 songs Lanza recorded during his career.

Mummers Museum ⓬

1100 S 2nd St. *Tel* (215) 336-3050. 🚌 57. 🕙 May–Sep: 9:30am–4:30pm Wed, Fri & Sat (to 9:30pm Thu); Oct–Apr: 9:30am–4:30pm Wed–Sat. 🔴 Mon, public hols. 🎦 🏠 ♿ **www**.mummersmuseum.com

Opened during the nation's bicentennial year in 1976, this museum celebrates the city's Mummers tradition and annual New Year's day Mummers Parade where thousands of

people strut to the rhythm of marching string bands *(see p35)*. Permanent and rotating exhibits showcase the museum's extensive collections. Artifacts from past parades are displayed to re-create the excitement of the event. They include floats, musical instruments used in the parades, and plumed and sequinned costumes. The museum's library has newspaper clippings dating back to the late 19th century, and more than 6,000 manuscripts, photographs, works of art, and films that highlight the parade's history and tradition. Every Thursday, May through September, string bands perform a free concert at 8pm so that visitors can sample the sounds of the Mummers celebrations.

Mario Lanza bust

Fort Mifflin ⓭

Fort Mifflin Rd near Island Ave. *Tel* (215) 685-4167. 🕙 Apr–Nov: 10am–4pm Wed–Sun. 🔴 public hols; Dec–Mar, except for groups. 🎦 🎦 **www**.fortmifflin.us

Historic Fort Mifflin, with its well-preserved ramparts and soldiers' barracks, is the only fort in Philadelphia. Surrounded by a moat, it overlooks the Delaware River and offers views of the city skyline, and the nearby and often noisy Philadelphia airport.

Construction of the fort began with the installation of sturdy granite walls in 1771 – the only remnants of the original fortification that remain today – and the fort stayed in continuous use through the Korean War in the 1950s.

Its most prominent moment, however, was during the Revolutionary War, when the Continental troops in the fort managed to keep the British at bay for seven weeks. This allowed Washington to retreat to Valley Forge and thwarted British efforts to open a supply route along the Delaware River for their troops who had occupied Philadelphia.

Today, Fort Mifflin is a popular tourist attraction. The former soldiers' barracks

MUMMERS TRADITION AND PARADE

The Mummers tradition dates to the late 1600s when Swedish and Finnish settlers ushered in the new year with parades and masquerades. Others soon joined in with the use of costumes based on Greek celebrations of King Momus, the Italian feast of Saturnalia, and the British Mummery Play. Today, the parade features the Comics, who dress as hobos and clowns and poke fun at the crowds; the Fancies, who dazzle in sequined outfits; the Fancy Brigades, who perform themed shows; and the String Bands, where marchers play banjos, drums, and glockenspiels. The parade is followed by the Fancy Brigade Finale, held at the Pennsylvania Convention Center.

Costumed revelers at a Mummers Day parade

Moat around 18th-century Fort Mifflin, Philadelphia's lone fort

now house a small museum and a diorama depicting the siege of 1777. On display are tools, cannonballs, and grapeshot from the Revolutionary War, as well as items from the American Civil War, when Confederate soldiers, Union deserters, and civilian lawbreakers were imprisoned at the fort.

Camden Waterfront ⓮

Delaware River, NJ. **Tel** (856) 757-9154. 🚉 PATCO Speedline from Center City, New Jersey Transit. 🚌 New Jersey Transit. ⛴ RiverLink Ferry. **www**.camdenwaterfront.com

This spacious riverfront area in New Jersey, opposite Penn's Landing, has gardens, a music venue, a minor league baseball stadium, art galleries, a theater, and other attractions.

One of the biggest draws is the **Adventure Aquarium**. It boasts one of the largest tanks

in North America and contains over 5,000 aquatic creatures, such as sharks, seals, and stingrays. Nearby is the floating museum, the **Battleship New Jersey**, with nine 16-inch (40-cm) guns in three triple turrets. One of the nation's most decorated battleships, she served in World War II and the Vietnam War. The waterfront is also home to the 6,500-seat Campbell's Field, which hosts the Camden Riversharks baseball team. For concerts, head to the 7,000-seat Susquehanna Bank Center, an indoor and outdoor amphitheater. The **RiverLink Ferry** (see p186) offers a scenic ride across the Delaware River to and from Penn's Landing.

Adventure Aquarium, exterior detail

🐟 **Adventure Aquarium**
1 Aquarium Dr. **Tel** (856) 365-3300. ⏱ 9:30am–5pm daily. 🏷 📷 🛗 **www**.adventureaquarium.com

🏛 **Battleship New Jersey**
Clinton Street at the waterfront. **Tel** (856) 966-1652. ⏱ Feb 6–mid-Mar: 9:30am–3pm Sat–Sun; mid-Mar–end Mar & Oct–Dec: 9:30am–3pm daily; Apr–Sep: 9:30am–5pm daily. 🏷 **www**.battleshipnewjersey.org

⛴ **RiverLink Ferry**
Tel (215) 925-5465. ⏱ Memorial Day–Labor Day: 9am–6pm daily; May & Sep: Sat & Sun. 🏷 ♿ **www**.riverlinkferry.org

Walt Whitman House ⓯

330 Mickle Boulevard, NJ. **Tel** (856) 964-5383. 🚉 PATCO Speedline, New Jersey Transit. 🚌 New Jersey Transit. ⛴ RiverLink Ferry. ⏱ only by appointment: 10am–noon, 1–4pm Wed–Sat.

This modest, two-story house two blocks east of the Camden Waterfront is the only home that renowned American poet Walt Whitman (1819–92) ever owned. He lived here from 1884 until his death in 1892.

Whitman left Washington DC after suffering a stroke in 1873, coming to live with his brother George in Camden. When his brother decided to move to a nearby rural area, Whitman opted to stay on here. With the surprising success of the 1882 edition of his most famous volume of poetry, *Leaves of Grass*, he was able to purchase this home. Already a prominent poet, Whitman was visited in Camden by famous writers, such as Charles Dickens and Oscar Wilde, and Philadelphia artist and friend Thomas Eakins (see p87), who photographed and painted the aging poet.

Today, the house, a National Historic Landmark, contains some of Whitman's personal belongings, letters, and old photographs, including the earliest known image of the poet from 1848.

USS New Jersey, berthed at the dock adjacent to the Susquehanna Bank Center at Camden Waterfront

TWO GUIDED WALKS
AND A DRIVE

Philadelphia's colonial history around Society Hill and Independence National Historical Park, also called "America's most historic square mile," is best explored on foot. However, for those who wish to explore other historical areas, this section introduces some neighborhoods that can be explored through a guided walk or drives.

Maritime painting in the Seaport Museum

The first is a walking tour around the Penn's Landing area along the scenic Delaware River. This tour includes stops at Gloria Dei (Old Swedes') Church, the oldest church in Pennsylvania, and the Irish, Korean, and Vietnam memorials. The second walk explores colonial-era homes along Germantown, which was settled in 1683. This 90-minute walk includes the "White House," where the first president of the US, George Washington, and his family stayed to escape the city's 1793 yellow fever epidemic. The third is a drive through Fairmount Park, close to the Philadelphia Museum of Art on the banks of the Schyulkill River. This tour also highlights historic homes, many of which were once the summer retreats of the colonial elite. This drive includes splendid panoramic views of the city skyline at Belmont Plateau.

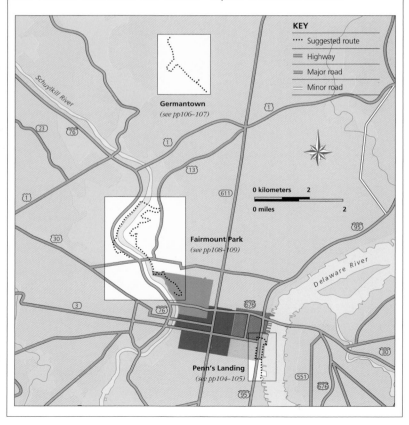

KEY

····· Suggested route
═══ Highway
══ Major road
── Minor road

Schuylkill River

Germantown
(see pp106–107)

Fairmount Park
(see pp108–109)

Delaware River

0 kilometers 2
0 miles 2

Penn's Landing
(see pp104–105)

◁ One of the rowing teams of the "Schuylkill Navy" brings its boat ashore at Boathouse Row *(see p96)*

A Two-Hour Walk Along Penn's Landing

Penn's statue at Welcome Park ①

Penn's Landing's plaza, walkways, marina, and Christopher Columbus Park provide the setting for a scenic walk along the Delaware River, the natural boundary between the states of Pennsylvania and New Jersey. Docked along the riverside are some of Philadelphia's historic ships and popular dinner cruise boats, as this area is now a commercial and entertainment zone. The walk, which starts in the neighborhood of Old City and includes historic sights, stretches south along the river to the Gloria Dei Church and then doubles back to include the city's monuments to the Vietnam War and Korean War.

Independence Seaport Museum ⑥, showcasing US maritime heritage

Corn Exchange National Bank, with a unique domed clock tower ②

Welcome Park to Irish Memorial

The walk begins in Welcome Park ① *(see p55)* at 2nd Street and the Sansom Street alley. Dedicated to William Penn, the park is located where his home, the Slate Roof House, once stood. Pass by the historic Thomas Bond House Bed and Breakfast *(see p134)* along 2nd Street to Chestnut Street, where the Corn Exchange National Bank building ② sits across the street. Designed in Colonial Revival style, the structure dates back to the mid-19th century and now contains a bank, restaurants, and a newspaper office.

Turn right onto Chestnut Street and stop in front of 126 Chestnut ③. A time capsule is buried at the site and a plaque on the sidewalk reads: "From the people of the Bicentennial to the Tricentennial – our mementos to be opened by the Mayor of Philadelphia on July 4, 2076."

Cross Front Street to the Irish Memorial ④, a memorial to those who suffered during the Irish Potato Famine (1845–50).

Detail of Irish Memorial Sculpture ④

Irish Memorial to Christopher Columbus Park

Pass over I-95 and enter Penn's Landing ⑤ *(see p66)*. Head down the curving walkway toward the river for great views of the Benjamin Franklin Bridge and the Camden Waterfront *(see p101)*, home to the Adventure Aquarium and the *Battleship New Jersey*. Walk past the RiverLink Ferry port and the Independence Seaport Museum ⑥ *(see pp64–5)*, where the museum's cruiser *Olympia* and submarine *Becuna* are berthed. A dead-end walkway stretches out into the Delaware River offering splendid views of the river and the Benjamin Franklin Bridge. Continue around the marina to Christopher Columbus Park ⑦, which has as its centerpiece a tribute dedicated in 1992 to the 500th anniversary of the explorer's voyage to America.

Across from the *Olympia* and *Becuna* is the Penn's Landing Visitor Center.

Christopher Columbus Park to Korean War Memorial

Continue south along the waterfront to the *Moshulu* ⑧, a 1904 four-masted sailing ship that is now a floating restaurant *(see p148)*. The *Spirit of Philadelphia*, a dinner cruise ship, is also berthed here. Then walk along Columbus

Camden Waterfront, across Penn's Landing and along the scenic Delaware River ⑤

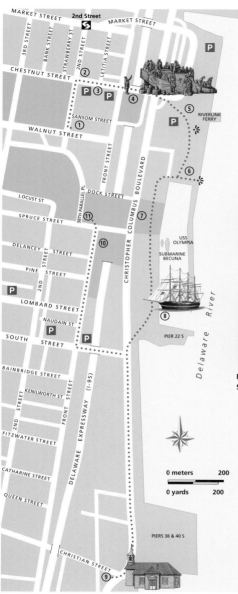

Market Street
2nd Street
Market Street
3RD STREET
BANK STREET
STRAWBERRY ST
2ND STREET
LETITIA STREET
CHESTNUT STREET
P
2
P 3 P
4
5 RIVERLINK FERRY
SANSOM STREET
1
WALNUT STREET
P
FRONT STREET
6
CHRISTOPHER COLUMBUS BOULEVARD
DOCK STREET
LOCUST ST
38TH PARALLEL PL
SPRUCE STREET
11
7
DELANCEY STREET
2ND STREET
10
USS OLYMPIA
SUBMARINE BECUNA
PINE STREET
P
LOMBARD STREET
Delaware River
NAUDAIN ST
P
8
SOUTH STREET
P
PIER 22 S
BAINBRIDGE STREET
DELAWARE EXPRESSWAY (I-95)
KENILWORTH ST
FRONT STREET
2ND STREET
FITZWATER STREET
0 meters 200
0 yards 200
CATHARINE STREET
QUEEN STREET
PIERS 38 & 40 S
CHRISTIAN STREET
9

TIPS FOR WALKERS

Starting point: *Welcome Park on 2nd St between Chestnut and Walnut Sts.*
Length: *2 miles (3 km).*
Getting there: *Philly Phlash.*
Stopping-off points: *Stop at the Irish Memorial, take in the views along the river at Penn's Landing, and relax under the trees at Christopher Columbus Park. Take time to explore the Gloria Dei Church and a few moments to reflect at the Vietnam War and Korean War memorials.*

Exterior of the restored Gloria Dei (Old Swedes') church, founded in 1677 ⑨

was completed in 1700, with the steeple added in 1703. Now an Episcopal parish, the church still contains the original marble baptismal font and carved wooden cherubim holding a bible, which were brought to the New World by the Swedish colonists. Among those buried in the church cemetery are soldiers of the Revolutionary War.

Head back up Columbus Boulevard and cross back over I-95 using the South Street overpass. Turn right on Front Street and continue to the Vietnam War Memorial ⑩. It pays tribute to the city's 80,000 veterans who served in the Vietnam War (1960–75), and has the names of more than 600 of those killed etched in stone. Cross Spruce Street and enter Foglietta Plaza, whose centerpiece is the Korean War Memorial ⑪ with the names of 603 local veterans killed or declared missing in action during the Korean War (1950–53).

KEY

• • • Suggested route

☀ Viewpoint

S SEPTA subway stop

P Parking

Boulevard past the old Municipal Piers 38 and 40. Cross the boulevard at Christian Street to reach the Gloria Dei (Old Swedes') Church ⑨, the oldest in the state. Swedish Lutherans, who settled here in 1643, founded the church in 1677, before the arrival of William Penn. The brick building standing today

A 90-Minute Walk of Historic Homes in Germantown

Once a small country town a few miles northwest of Old City, Germantown *(see p96)* is now one of Philadelphia's oldest neighborhoods. It was settled in 1683 by immigrants from the Rhine Valley in Germany, who were attracted by Penn's promise of religious freedom. Within a century it evolved into a retreat for wealthy Philadelphia families. The homes on this walk, along cobblestoned Germantown Avenue, have been well preserved by the active Germantown Historical Society and are National Historic Landmarks. The stop-offs should be made during the day, as the area is best avoided at night. The route can be easily driven through, and tourism markers make the homes easy to find.

The Deshler-Morris House, now a National Park Service property ③

Germantown Historical Society and Visitor Center ①

Germantown Historical Society Museum and Library to Deshler-Morris House

The walk starts at the Germantown Historical Society Museum and Library ①. This museum traces Germantown's history, in addition to selling maps of the region. The museum's rotating exhibits are culled from the society's 20,000-artifact collection of paintings, kitchenware, toys, and period clothing. Exit the center, turn left on Germantown Avenue, and walk a few blocks to

Grumblethorpe ②, built in 1744 and home of wine merchant John Wister. Sally, his daughter, lived here during the American Revolution and kept a diary recording her impressions of the turbulent times. British General James Agnew died here after being mortally wounded in the fierce Battle of Germantown in 1777 *(see p21)* and a bloodstain remains on the first floor. The Georgian Grumblethorpe displays items that belonged to the family and the gardens outside still retain their 19th-century appearance.

Head back up Germantown Avenue to one of the community's most famous homes, the Deshler-Morris House ③. The house is situated opposite the Visitor Center and Market Square, which has a Civil War monument as its centerpiece. Built in the mid-1700s by Quaker David Deshler, the home served as the headquarters of British General William Howe during the

Chelten Avenue
250m

Grumblethorpe, home to one family for 160 years ②

Battle of Germantown. After the Revolutionary War, the building became known as the Germantown "White House" when President Washington and his family lived here to escape the 1793 yellow fever epidemic. Today, the house exhibits period furnishings and original paintings by colonial artists Gilbert Stuart and Charles W. Peale.

Back parlor of the Wyck House and Garden [4]

TIPS FOR WALKERS

Starting point: *Germantown Historical Society Museum and Library.* ***Tel*** *(215) 844-1683.*
Length: *1.5 miles (2.5 km).*
Getting there: *Take the Chestnut Hill West SEPTA regional rail line to Chelten Avenue station.*
Stop-off points: *Visits to all homes are recommended, though these would be dependent on opening hours.*

Deshler-Morris House to Ebenezer Maxwell Mansion

Continue up Germantown Avenue several blocks to the Wyck House and Garden [4], owned for three centuries by nine generations of the same Quaker family. It contains the family's belongings, collected from 1689 until 1973, including antiques, books, and manuscripts that highlight the family's history and its devotion to the Quaker faith.

Turning left on Walnut Lane, walk two blocks to turn right on Greene Street to the Ebenezer Maxwell Mansion [5]. Built in 1859, it is the city's only authentically restored Victorian residence. It features original 19th-century stenciled designs in the upstairs rooms, Rococo furniture in the dining room and parlor, and various other period items that reflect life in the 1860s.

Ebenezer Maxwell Mansion to Cliveden

Turn right on Tulpehocken Street back to Germantown Avenue and turn left for the Johnson House [6], built in 1768. This stone house was owned by three generations of an abolitionist Quaker family, who made it into the city's only stop on the Underground Railroad that led slaves to freedom in Canada and the northern states *(see p60)*.

Continuing up Germantown Avenue, the next home on the walk is Upsala [7]. Built around 1740 and expanded in 1800, the home is an outstanding example of Federal architecture, with wooden and marble mantels inside *(see p28)*. This house is where the Continental Army made its stand during the Battle of Germantown on October 4, 1777. Across the street is Cliveden [8]. Built in 1767, it is one of the finest surviving colonial homes in the city. During the Battle of Germantown, British troops occupied the Georgian-style Cliveden and repulsed the colonial army. Chipped bricks from rifle shots are still evident on the home's façade, and one room has an original musket ball hole from the battle that raged in the street outside. Reenactments of the battle are held on the grounds on the first Saturday of every October.

Ebenezer Maxwell Mansion [5], a 19th-century Victorian house

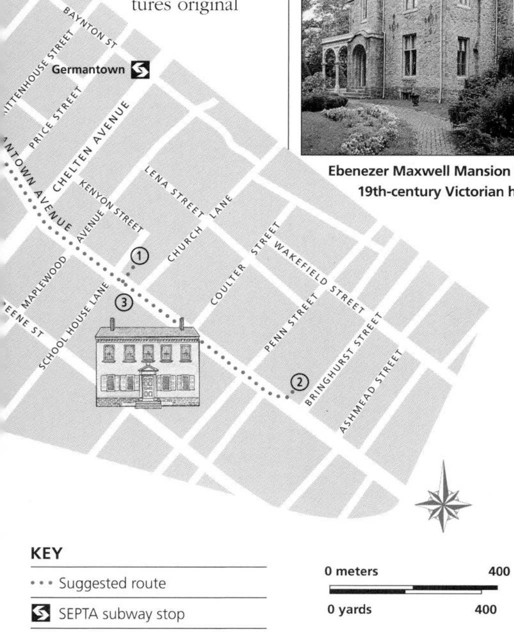
BAYNTON ST
RITTENHOUSE STREET
Germantown
PRICE STREET
CHELTEN AVENUE
GERMANTOWN AVENUE
KENYON STREET
AVENUE
LENA STREET
LANE
CHURCH
MAPLEWOOD
SCHOOL HOUSE LANE
GREENE ST
COULTER
STREET
WAKEFIELD STREET
PENN STREET
BRINGHURST STREET
ASHMEAD STREET
KEY
Suggested route
SEPTA subway stop
0 meters 400
0 yards 400

The study at Cliveden, an example of a colonial-era house [8]

A Three-Hour Drive Around Fairmount Park Historic Mansions

One of the many statues in Fairmount Park

Boathouse Row along Kelly Drive

Prominent colonial Philadelphia families took note of the trees and rolling hills in the landscape just west of the city along the Schuylkill River, and built mansions in what is today Fairmount Park *(see p97)*. Some of the homes had working farms with grazing lands and orchards, while others were upscale summer retreats. The park was established when the city began purchasing these properties in the mid-19th century, thus preserving scenic land and the homes in their architectural splendor. They are open for tours and are best seen as part of a driving tour. Those without vehicles can take a trolley tour during the Christmas holiday season.

Lemon Hill to Laurel Hill

Begin the drive from the parking lot at the Philadelphia Museum of Art's West Entrance ①. Turn left at the traffic light onto Kelly Drive, then drive straight on. At the seated statue of President Lincoln ②, take the fork to the right, and then make a sharp left to reach Lemon Hill ③. The house was named after the lemon trees that once grew here when Revolutionary War financier and signer of the Declaration of Independence Robert Morris owned the land. A later owner, Henry Pratt, built the mansion in 1800. The oval rooms, with curved doors, fanlights, and fireplaces on all three levels, are Federal elements, while the Palladian windows are Georgian remnants. Return to the Lincoln statue, and turning right, continue up Kelly Drive past Boathouse Row. At the statue of Ulysses S. Grant turn right onto Fountain Green Drive and then left for Mount Pleasant ④. Once described by President John Adams as "the most elegant seat in Pennsylvania," this Georgian house has ornate woodwork and classical motifs in the entrance hall and stairway. Returning to Fountain Green Drive, which merges with Reservoir Drive, continue to Ormiston ⑤. Built in the 1790s in Georgian style, the house has an original Scottish oven and an open fireplace. Events and rotating exhibits at Ormiston highlight the area's British heritage.

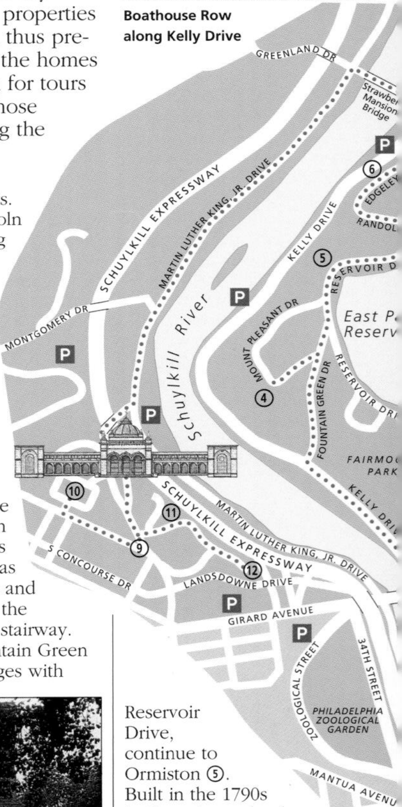

Drive down Reservoir Drive and turn left onto Randolph Drive. Continue to Edgeley Drive for Laurel Hill ⑥, a 1767 Georgian-style country house with a two-story octagonal wing, perched on a prominent bluff overlooking the river.

Mount Pleasant, built between 1762 and 1765 ④

Woodford, a National Historic Landmark ⑦

Laurel Hill to Memorial Hall

Continue through an intersection that has an equestrian statue of an American Indian, and onto Dauphin Drive. Turn left before 33rd Street onto Greenland Drive to reach Woodford ⑦, built in 1758 by William Coleman, a merchant and friend of Benjamin Franklin. The Georgian house has an array of exquisite colonial decorative arts and furniture, donated by Naomi Wood, a Philadelphian collector. Continue up Greenland Drive a short distance to Strawberry Mansion ⑧, with its Federal-style center

wing built by Judge William Lewis in 1789. Two large wings, in Greek Revival style, were added later. The house displays Empire and Federal period furnishings. Key exhibits include a doll collection and a well-preserved Victorian dollhouse. Drive down Strawberry Mansion Drive, turn right at Woodford Drive, and cross the Strawberry Mansion Bridge. Make a quick left onto West River Drive, continue for about a mile (1.6 km) and turn right onto Black Road toward the Smith Civil War Memorial ⑨. Turn right at the Memorial onto North Concourse Drive to reach Memorial Hall ⑩. Built in Beaux-Arts style, it was the city's first art museum and now houses the Please Touch Museum for children *(see p170)*. Guided tours of Memorial Hall allow visitors to view the building behind the scenes.

Memorial Hall to Sweetbriar

Returning to the Smith Civil War Memorial, turn left, and then make a quick right onto Cedar Grove Drive and head to Cedar Grove ⑪, a house that was built elsewhere and reassembled in Fairmount Park. This Georgian house has an unusual two-sided wall of closets on the second floor, and much of its original, early Pennsylvania furniture.

TIPS FOR DRIVERS

Starting point: *Philadelphia Museum of Art, West Entrance parking lot.*
Length: *5 miles (8 km) to visit homes, then another 2 miles (3 km) back to the museum.*
Stop-off points: *Homes open to the public can be visited, depending on opening hours and time.*
Trolley tour: *Tours during the Christmas holiday season leave from the Philadelphia Museum of Art and the Independence Visitor Center (6th & Market Sts). Tel (215) 925-8687. May–Dec 15: 10:30am & 1:45pm Wed–Sun.*

Sweetbriar, a three-story house built in Federal style ⑫

It is now maintained by the Philadelphia Museum of Art. For the last stop, turn right after Cedar Grove towards the Federal-style Sweetbriar ⑫, the home of merchant Samuel Breck, built in 1797. The Etruscan Room is decorated in keeping with Breck's interest in classical forms and ancient Etruscan wall painting.

0 meters 500 / 0 yards 500

KEY
••• Suggested route
P Parking

Cedar Grove, built as a summer home in 1750 ⑪

BEYOND
PHILADELPHIA

Exploring Beyond Philadelphia

Statue, Gettysburg

To the west of Philadelphia, the area encompassing Lancaster County is known as the Pennsylvania Dutch Country, and is made up of bucolic hills and farmland as far as the eye can see. The region is home to the Amish *(see p115)* who wear traditional clothing and are often seen riding in horse-drawn buggies. Farther west is the town of Hershey, home of the chocolates, and Gettysburg, site of the American Civil War's bloodiest battle. To the east, the glitzy casinos of Atlantic City are just over an hour's drive away, and a little farther is the idyllic beach resort of Cape May.

Fountains at Longwood Gardens

SIGHTS AT A GLANCE

Williamsport · Sunbury
Selinsgrove
Shamokin
15
209 · Lykens
Millersburg
322
New Bloomfield
Linglestown
81
Palm
HARRISBURG 11 **12**
Pittsburgh 81 HERSHEY
76 Middletown
Carlisle Elizabethtown
81
PENNSYLVANIA
83
YORK 10
Red
30
9 GETTYSBURG
Hanover
15 New Freedom
Taneytown
Frederick
83
Westminster
Cockeysville
Reisterstown
Towson
Baltimore
Washington DC Dund

SEE ALSO

KEY

▬▬	Highway
▬▬	Major road
▬	Other roads
—	Major rail
—	Minor rail
▬	State boundary

Boy outside a candy and ice cream store in Strasburg

◁ Farmers using horse-drawn wagons and traditional implements in Lancaster County, Pennsylvania *(see p114)*

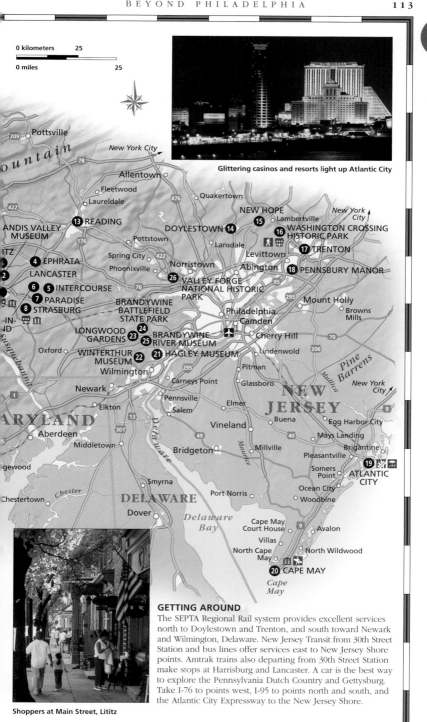

0 kilometers 25

0 miles 25

Glittering casinos and resorts light up Atlantic City

Pottsville

New York City

Allentown

Fleetwood

Laureldale

Quakertown

13 READING

DOYLESTOWN **14**

NEW HOPE **15**

Lambertville

WASHINGTON CROSSING HISTORIC PARK **16**

17 TRENTON

Pottstown

Lansdale

Levittown

Spring City

4 EPHRATA

Norristown

Abington

LANCASTER

Phoenixville

18 PENNSBURY MANOR

6 **5** INTERCOURSE

26 VALLEY FORGE NATIONAL HISTORIC PARK

7 PARADISE

8 STRASBURG

BRANDYWINE BATTLEFIELD STATE PARK

Philadelphia

Mount Holly

Camden

Browns Mills

LONGWOOD GARDENS **23** **24**

BRANDYWINE RIVER MUSEUM

Cherry Hill

Oxford

25

22 **21** HAGLEY MUSEUM

Lindenwold

WINTERTHUR MUSEUM

Wilmington

Pitman

Pine Barrens

Carneys Point

Glassboro

New York City

Newark

Pennsville

NEW JERSEY

Elkton

Salem

Elmer

Buena

Egg Harbor City

Aberdeen

Vineland

Mays Landing

Middletown

Bridgeton

Millville

Brigantine

Pleasantville

Somers Point

19 ATLANTIC CITY

Smyrna

Port Norris

Ocean City

Woodbine

Chestertown

DELAWARE

Dover

Delaware Bay

Cape May Court House

Avalon

Villas

North Cape May

North Wildwood

20 CAPE MAY

Cape May

MARYLAND

Aberdeen

gewood

Chester

GETTING AROUND

The SEPTA Regional Rail system provides excellent services north to Doylestown and Trenton, and south toward Newark and Wilmington, Delaware. New Jersey Transit from 30th Street Station and bus lines offer services east to New Jersey Shore points. Amtrak trains also departing from 30th Street Station make stops at Harrisburg and Lancaster. A car is the best way to explore the Pennsylvania Dutch Country and Gettysburg. Take I-76 to points west, I-95 to points north and south, and the Atlantic City Expressway to the New Jersey Shore.

Shoppers at Main Street, Lititz

For additional map symbols see back flap

Soldiers and Sailors Monument in
Penn Square, Lancaster

Lancaster **❶**

Lancaster County, PA. 🏠 55,000. 🚊
🚌 ℹ *Pennsylvania Dutch Country
Visitors Center: Route 30 at Greenfield
Exit, 501 Greenfield Rd; 1-800-PA-
DUTCH.* **www**.padutchcountry.com

Founded by John Wright in
1730 and named after his
birthplace in England, today
Lancaster is the county seat.
Its tree-shaded streets are still
lined with 18th- and 19th-
century buildings. In the heart
of downtown is Penn Square
with its centerpiece Soldiers
and Sailors Monument, dedicated in 1874 to local men
who fought in the American
Civil War between 1861 and
1865. On the square's northwest corner, three adjoining
buildings dating from the
1790s house the **Lancaster
Heritage Center Museum**. Its
collection includes striking
colonial grandfather clocks.
A Renaissance-style mural
adorns the vaulted ceiling
of one of the buildings.
   At the **Lancaster Central
Market**, next to the museum,
vendors and Amish farmers
sell cheeses, meats, flowers,
fresh produce, and treats such
as homemade cider. Nearby,
in a Beaux Arts-style building
modeled after New York's
Penn Station, is the **Lancaster
Quilt & Textile Museum** with
a collection of 82 Amish and
Mennonite quilts.
   Located west of downtown
is **Wheatland**, the estate of

the 15th president of the US,
James Buchanan, who served
during the tumultuous years
leading up to the Civil
War. The house,
named for the wheat
fields it once over-
looked, features
most of Buchanan's
original belongings,
and has a beautiful
19th-century garden.

An old-fashioned
pretzel

🏛 **Lancaster Heritage Center
Museum**
5 W King St. **Tel** *(717) 299-6440.*
◯ *9am–5pm Mon–Sat; first Fri of
month: 5–9pm; Dec: noon–4pm
Sun.* 🅿

🏛 **Lancaster Quilt
& Textile Museum**
37 Market St. **Tel** *(717) 397-2970.*
◯ *10am–5pm Mon, Wed & Thu,
9am–5pm Tue, Fri & Sat, 5–9pm first
Fri of month.* 🅿

🏚 **Wheatland**
1120 Marietta Ave. **Tel** *(717) 392-
4633.* ◯ *Apr–Oct: 10am–4:30pm
Mon–Sat, noon–4pm Sun; Nov & Dec:
10am–4:30pm Fri & Sat.* ◼ *Jan–Mar,
Thanksgiving, Dec 25.* 🅿

Landis Valley
Museum **❷**

See pp116–17.

Lititz **❸**

Lancaster County, PA. 🏠 9,000. 🚌
ℹ *Lititz Welcome Center: 18 N Broad
St, (717) 626-7960.* **www**.lititzpa.com

Named after a town in
Bohemia, Lititz was founded
by Moravians in 1756 and

remained a closed settlement
for nearly a century. The town
boasts 18th-century buildings
and a quaint Main Street,
and features the Lititz
Springs Park, which
has a natural
spring-fed creek.
Moravian Church
Square today
includes the center-
piece church. Nearby
is the **Lititz Historical Museum**
with its star exhibit, the
Johannes Mueller House, a
restored 1792 Moravian stone
house named for a local
tanner and dyer. A room in
the museum is dedicated to
General John Sutter, founder
of Sacramento and a Lititz
resident. It was the discovery
of gold on his land that led to
the 1849 California Gold Rush.
   The **Sturgis Pretzel House**,
dating from 1861, offers visitors pretzel tours. The **Wilbur
Chocolate Candy Store and
Museum** displays 19th-century
chocolate molds and recipe
cards that highlight the company's history since 1884.

🏛 **Lititz Historical Museum**
137–145 East Main St. **Tel** *(717) 627-
4636.* ◯ *Memorial Day–Oct: 10am–
4pm Mon–Sat; special weekends in
May, Nov, & Dec.* 🅿 ◼

🏚 **Sturgis Pretzel House**
219 East Main St. **Tel** *(717) 626-
4354.* ◯ *9am–5pm Mon–Sat (Jan–
mid-May: until 4pm Mon–Fri).* 🅿

🏛 **Wilbur Chocolate Candy
Store and Museum**
48 N Broad St. **Tel** *(717) 626-3249.*
◯ *10am–5pm Mon–Sat.*
www.wilburbuds.com

Lititz's historic Main Street shopping district

The Amish, Mennonites, and Brethren

The Mennonites and the Amish trace their roots to the Swiss Anabaptist ("New Birth") movement of 1525, an offshoot of the Protestant Reformation, whose creed rejected the formality of the established churches. Lured by the promise of religious freedom held out to them by William Penn, the Mennonites were the first to arrive in Germantown in the late 17th century. They were soon followed by the Amish

Detail from an Amish quilt

who settled in what is now Lancaster County in the early 18th century. However, not all Pennsylvania Dutch are Amish or Mennonites; Brethren and other sub-groups are also part of the community. The mostly German heritage of these groups has given rise to a popular myth about the name "Pennsylvania Dutch" – it is thought that it came from other early colonists mispronouncing "Pennsylvania Deutsch."

Amish farms *have changed little since the 17th century. Farming is usually done with horsedrawn equipment with bare metal wheels.*

AMISH
The Amish sect began in the 1690s when Jacob Amman, a Swiss bishop, split from the Mennonites. The conservative Old Order Amish disdain any device that would connect them to the larger world, including electricity, cars, modern farm tools, and telephones.

Amish families *dress in plain, dark attire, with women in white caps and men in straw hats.*

Buggies are used even today

MENNONITES
Taking their name from Menno Simons, a young Dutch priest who advocated adult baptism by faith in the 1530s, Mennonites are pacifists and believe in simple living. However, they do not segregate themselves from society, and in recent years, urbanization has lured many to the cities.

Mennonites in traditional dress

Old Order Brethren at a Pennsylvania Dutch Country covered bridge

BRETHREN
Alexander Mack founded this movement in 1708, breaking away from the established and reformed faiths of the time and following the German Pietists in espousing worship on a more personal level. The pacifist Brethren migrated to America in the late 1720s. They believe in adult baptism and adhere only to the teachings of the New Testament.

The Brethren church *is where the community worships and baptizes adults by "dunking" them thrice in the name of the Holy Trinity.*

Landis Valley Museum ❷

Wares at the Country Store

The descendents of German settlers, brothers George and Henry Landis, started the Landis Valley Museum in the 1920s. At that time, it included more than 75,000 objects from the 18th and 19th centuries, featuring the traditions and farming culture of the Pennsylvania German community. Now supported and run by the state Historical and Museum Commission, Landis Valley is a living history village of Pennsylvania German life and home to nearly 100,000 artifacts such as quilts, rugs, leather goods, carriages, kitchen utensils, baskets, and lace. More than 30 homes, barns, sheds, shops, and other structures highlight the trades and crafts of earlier generations, complemented by regular demonstrations by craftspeople.

Maple Grove School
This late 1800s school features authentic wooden desks.

★ **Landis Collections Gallery**
Items like this silver lamp are displayed in the museum's historic collection, which dates from 1740 to 1940.

Country Store
A wide range of items, including farm tools, saddles, phonograph records, and glass-jarred licorice, stock the shelves of this reconstructed store.

STAR SIGHTS

★ Landis Collections Gallery

★ Transportation Building

★ Landis House and Stable

★ Gun Shop

Firehouse and Surveyor Shop
The larger firehouse, which has original pumpers inside, resembles a late 19th-century fire company.

★ Transportation Building

An assortment of late 19th-century sleighs is one of the displays in this building, which also houses horse-drawn buggies, carriages, wagons, and hand-drawn carts once used for light chores.

VISITORS' CHECKLIST

Route 272, 2451 Kissel Hill Road, Lancaster, PA. **Tel** (717) 569-0401; Weathervane Museum Store (717) 569-9312. 🚇 Amtrak from 30th St Station to Lancaster. ⬤ 9am–5pm Mon–Sat, noon–5pm Sun. ⬤ Jan 1, Thanksgiving, Dec 25. 📷 ♿ call to arrange. 📷 www.landisvalleymuseum.org

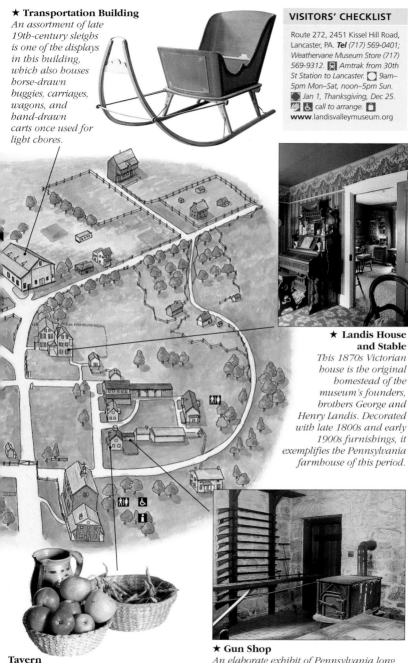

★ Landis House and Stable

This 1870s Victorian house is the original homestead of the museum's founders, brothers George and Henry Landis. Decorated with late 1800s and early 1900s furnishings, it exemplifies the Pennsylvania farmhouse of this period.

Tavern

The spacious brick-paved kitchen of the inn, with its enormous walk-in fireplace and displays of baskets, utensils, and stoneware jugs, reflects 18th-century cooking methods.

★ Gun Shop

An elaborate exhibit of Pennsylvania long rifles, powder horns, and gunsmithing tools sits within this stone structure. Early settlers used such shops to perfect the accuracy of their weapons.

Austere interior of the Saal, the meetinghouse in Ephrata Cloister

Ephrata ❹

Lancaster County, PA. 🏠 13,000. 🚌
i 16 E Main St, Suite 1; (717) 738-9010. **www**.ephrata-area.org

This northern Lancaster County community was settled in 1732 by a German religious order led by Conrad Beissel, who founded one of America's earliest communal societies. The order built the medieval-style buildings that make up the **Ephrata Cloister**. Today, nine structures from the mid-1700s remain. The Sisters' House, next to the meetinghouse, has rows of windows for each small chamber where members slept on narrow benches. Other buildings include a schoolhouse, bakery, woodshop, and print shop. The visitor center displays artifacts, such as the Mennonites' 1,500-page *Martyrs' Mirror*. Just north of town, vendors at the Green Dragon Farmers' Market sell antiques, Pennsylvania Dutch treats, and crafts every Friday.

🏛 **Ephrata Cloister**
632 W Main St. **Tel** (717) 733-6600. 🕐 9am–5pm Mon–Sat, noon–5pm Sun. 📷
www.ephratacloister.org

Intercourse ❺

Lancaster County, PA. 🏠 900.
🚌 **i** 3551 Old Philadelphia Pike; (717) 768-3231. **www**.intercoursevillage.com

Theories abound on how the village acquired its interesting name, including it coming from the intersection of the two main roads, from an old racecourse, or even from Intercourse being a center for social interaction. Founded in 1754, the village is one of the main centers for Amish business. Key to its success are the extensive gift shops and stores that lure tourists by the busloads. For instance, Kitchen Kettle Village, a mini-shopping center, has over 30 restaurants and country shops selling everything from quilts and baskets to woodcraft. One store delights customers with homemade jellies and relishes bottled on the spot by Amish women. In the center of town, along Old Philadelphia Pike, is the **People's Place Quilt Museum**. Opened in 1988, the museum displays antique Mennonite and Amish quilts through rotating exhibitions.

West of the town center is the **Amish Experience at Plain & Fancy Farm**, where visitors can tour a modern Amish home and view the multimedia show, *Jacob's Choice*,

Exhibit detail at the People's Place Quilt Museum

which chronicles an Amish family's efforts to preserve its lifestyle.

🏛 **People's Place Quilt Museum**
3510 Old Philadelphia Pike.
Tel (800) 828-8218.
🕐 9am–5pm Mon–Sat. ♿
www.ppquiltmuseum.com

🏛 **Amish Experience at Plain & Fancy Farm**
3121 Old Philadelphia Pike, Route 340, Bird-In-Hand.
Tel (717) 768-3600 ext 210.
🕐 Times vary by tour type. Visit the website or call for details.
www.amishexperience.com

Bird-In-Hand ❻

Lancaster County, PA. 🏠 300. 🚌
i 2727 Old Philadelphia Pike; (800) 665-8780. **www**.bird-in-hand.com

This village is said to have received its unusual name from a historic 1734 inn *(see p141)* that once dangled a tavern sign depicting a man with a perched bird in his hand. The village contains a cluster of restaurants, stores, hotels, and quaint farmhouses.

The **Farmers' Market** bustles with stalls packed with foods ranging from farm vegetables to fresh bacon and sausage. Across the street, the **Americana Museum** displays antiques from 1890 through 1930, which depict important professions and trades, and include an early 20th-century toy store, apothecary, print shop, wheelwright shop, and milliner's. Set up in 1877, the Weavertown One-Room School showcases a typical

Amish boys ride a buggy into the village of Intercourse

schoolhouse still attended by
Amish children today.

▣ Farmers' Market
2710 Old Philadelphia Pike. *Tel (717)
393-9674.* ◯ *Apr–Jun & Nov:
8:30am–5:30pm Wed, Fri, & Sat; Jul–
Oct: 8:30am–5:30pm Wed–Sat;
Dec–Mar: 8:30am–5:30pm Fri & Sat.*

🏛 Americana Museum
2709 Old Philadelphia Pike. *Tel (717)
391-9780.* ◯ *Apr–Nov: 10am–5pm
Tue–Sat; winter tours by request.* 📷

Paradise ❼

Lancaster County, PA. 🚌 *1,000.*
🚌 ℹ *Pennsylvania Dutch Country
Visitors Center: 501 Greenfield
Rd; (717) 299-8901.*
www.800padutch.com

The origins of this small
village along Route 30 date
from colonial times when the
road served as a link between
Lancaster and Philadelphia.
Paradise grew as the number
of inns and taverns increased
along Route 30. One of them,
the Historic Revere Tavern,
was built in 1740 and is still a
working restaurant *(see p153).*
President James Buchanan
purchased it in 1841 as a
home for his brother, a
reverend, whose wife was the
sister of songsmith Stephen
Foster, writer of such
American favorites as "Oh!
Susanna" and "My Olde
Kentucky Home".

A short drive
east is the one-
of-a-kind
**National
Christmas
Center**, where
the spirit of
Yuletide is
always in the air.
Spread over 20,000
sq ft (1,860 sq m)
are life-sized scenes
depicting Christmas feasts
and snowy villages, toy train
and nativity displays, and
several versions of St. Nicholas
from around the globe.

🏛 National Christmas Center
3427 Lincoln Hwy East.
Tel (717) 442-7950. ◯ *May 1–Jan 1:
10am–6pm daily; Mar & Apr:
10am–6pm Sat & Sun.* ⬛ *Jan–Feb,
Thanksgiving, Dec 25.* **www.**
nationalchristmascenter.com

An Amish house and buggy in Strasburg

**Signage at the National
Christmas Center**

Strasburg ❽

Lancaster County, PA. 🚌 *2,800.*
ℹ *Pennsylvania Dutch Country Visitors
Center: 501 Greenfield Rd; (717)
687-0405.* **www**.strasburgpa.com

Initially settled by French
Huguenots in the early 18th
century, Strasburg is named
after the cathedral city of
Strasbourg in France. The first
structures, built in 1733, are
now part of the historical
district along with numerous
colonial stone and log homes.
The town developed as an
educational and cultural center
as followers of different faiths
chose to settle here.
But by the mid-
19th century, it
had become
home to the
railroads that
are today its
most popular
attraction. Set
up in 1832, the
**Strasburg
Railroad** offers
45-minute rides in
refurbished railcars pulled by
early 20th-century coal-fired,
smoke-belching locomotives.
Directly across the highway is
the **Railroad Museum of Pennsylvania**, with spacious hang-
ars housing one of the nation's
largest collections of classic
railroad cars, locomotives,
and colorful cabooses. The
National Toy Train Museum has
exhibitions of collector-item
locomotives and exquisite

model train layouts. The **Choo
Choo Barn**, meanwhile, has
one of the most unique model
railroads in the world, with
22 trains running through
scenes of Lancaster County.

North of town is the **Amish
Village** with an 1840s Amish
house, smokehouse, black-
smith shop, and operational
water wheel. The majestic
Millennium Theater nearby is
home to inspirational, Biblical-
themed stage productions.

🚂 Strasburg Railroad
301 Gap Rd Ronks, Rte 741, E
of Strasburg. *Tel (717) 687-7522.*
◯ *Feb–Dec; check website or call
for times.* ⬛ *Jan.* **www.**
strasburgrailroad.com

**🏛 Railroad Museum
of Pennsylvania**
300 Gap Rd. *Tel (717) 687-8628.*
◯ *Apr–Oct: 9am–5pm Mon–Sat,
noon–5pm Sun; Nov–Mar: 9am–5pm
Tue–Sat, noon–5pm Sun.* ⬛ *Jan 1,
Easter, Nov 11, Thanksgiving, Dec
24, 25, & 31.*

🏛 National Toy Train Museum
300 Paradise Lane, off Rte 741, E of
Strasburg. *Tel (717) 687-8976.* ◯
*Apr–Dec: 10am–4:30pm Mon–Fri
(also Sat & Sun in Dec).* ⬛ *Jan–Mar.*

🏛 Choo Choo Barn
Rte 471, E of Strasburg. *Tel (717)
687-7911.* ◯ *Mar–Dec: 10am–
4:30pm.* ⬛ *Jan–Mar, Easter,
Thanksgiving, Dec 25.* **www.**
choochoobarn.com

🚂 Amish Village
Rte 896, N of Strasburg. *Tel (717)
687-8511.* ◯ *spring, summer &
fall: 9am–5pm Mon–Sat, 10am–
5pm Sun.* **www**.800padutch.com/
avillage.html

Gettysburg

This south-central Pennsylvania town amidst gently sloping hills is home to the greatest military encounter ever fought in North America, the Battle of Gettysburg in 1863, during the Civil War (1861–65). Shaded streets are lined with well-preserved Civil War-era buildings, which served as makeshift hospitals during the conflict. Many of these have today been converted into museums, restaurants, and hotels. Shops sell Civil War souvenirs and artifacts, including authentic rifles and a seemingly unending supply of cannon balls and bullets unearthed from the battleground. Other attractions include museums with dioramas – some with waxwork figures – depicting events of the Gettysburg battle and the Civil War.

Lincoln's chair at Wills House

The *Gettysburg Cyclorama*, a 360-degree painting of Pickett's Charge

🏛 Gettysburg Museum and Visitor Center

1195 Baltimore Pike. *Tel* (717) 334-6274. ◯ 8am–6pm daily (to 7pm Jun–Aug). ● Jan 1, Thanksgiving, Dec 25. ◪ www.gettysburg foundation.org

The Gettysburg Museum and Visitor Center opened in 2008 at the Gettysburg National Military Park. The 139,000 sq ft (12,900 sq m), awe-inspiring facility houses a modern visitor center that serves to navigate visitors around the park. A 20-minute film, introducing the Battle of Gettysburg, is repeated here every 30 minutes throughout the day. The facility also houses the Museum of Civil War with wide-ranging military artifacts, including an impressive display of artillery shells and fuses, are on display. Also on view is the *Gettysburg Cyclorama*. First exhibited in Boston in 1883, this colossal panoramic painting depicts Pickett's Charge, the conflict's climactic moment *(see pp122–3)*.

🏚 Dobbin House Tavern

89 Steinwehr Ave. *Tel* (717) 334-2100. ◯ 11:30am onward. www.dobbinhouse.com

Built in 1776, this stone house is Gettysburg's oldest standing structure. An upstairs museum displays a secret crawl space that once hid runaway slaves as part of the Underground Railroad *(see p60)*. Now a restaurant, the building has original fireplaces, hand-carved woodwork, and a colonial wooden bar in the downstairs tavern *(see p152)*.

🏚 Eisenhower National Historic Site

250 Eisenhower Farm Drive. *Tel* (717) 338-9114. ◯ 9am–4pm. ● Jan 1, Thanksgiving, Dec 25. ◪ ◪ mandatory. www.nps.gov/eise

Before being elected president in 1952, Dwight D. Eisenhower had served as Supreme Commander of the Allied Forces during World War II. While president, he and his wife Mamie owned this farm on the outskirts of Gettysburg and used it for weekend retreats. Inside are original furnishings and exhibits highlighting his career as general and president.

🏚 Farnsworth House Inn

401 Baltimore St. *Tel* (717) 334-8838. ◯ hours vary. www.farnsworthhouseinn.com

Dating from 1810, this historic home sheltered Confederate sharpshooters, one of whom is thought to have shot Jennie Wade. Most impressive are the more than 100 bullet piercings still evident on the house's brick façade from Union soldiers returning fire. Now an inn *(see p152)*, the house offers ghost tours and an interesting Mourning Theatre in the cellar with Civil War-related ghost tales told around a coffin by candlelight.

🏚 General Lee's Headquarters Museum

401 Buford Ave. *Tel* (717) 334-3141. ◯ mid-Feb–Nov: 9am–5pm, longer summer hours (call for details). ● Dec–mid-Feb.

Confederate General Robert E. Lee spent the night of July 1, 1863, at this house so he could see the Union line with his fieldglasses. Inside are war artifacts and the wooden table on which he dined.

General Lee's Headquarters, today a museum

Entrance to the Pennsylvania Memorial in Gettysburg

VISITORS' CHECKLIST

🛈 *Gettysburg Convention & Visitors Bureau: inside David Will's House, 8 Lincoln Square.* **Tel** *(866) 486-5735.* ◯ *8:30am–5pm Mon–Fri, 10am–3pm Sun.* 🎏 *Apple Blossom Festival (May), Gettysburg Anniversary Civil War Battle Reenactments (Jul), Apple Harvest Festival (Oct), Remembrance Day (Nov).* **www**.gettysburg.travel

🏛 Jennie Wade House

528 Baltimore St. **Tel** *(717) 334-4100.* ◯ *Mar–Sep: 9am–5pm.* 🖼
www.jennie-wade-house.com
Twenty-year-old Jennie Wade was the only civilian killed during the Battle of Gettysburg. A sharpshooter's bullet pierced two doors and struck her while she baked bread for Union soldiers. The home contains original furnishings, and a statue of her stands outside.

🏛 Lincoln Railroad Station

35 Carlisle St. ◯ *10am–5pm; extended hours in summer.*
This 1858 Italianate-styled railroad depot is where President Lincoln stepped off the train from Washington, a day before delivering the Gettysburg Address. Inside is an interpretive center, with exhibits about the train station and town history, and information on sights, attractions, and tours.

🏛 Soldiers' National Cemetery

Taneytown Rd, across Visitor Center.
www.nps.gov/gett/gncem.htm
This peaceful and shaded cemetery contains the graves of 6,000 US servicemen killed in various conflicts in America's history, from the Civil War to the Vietnam War. More than 3,500 are Union soldiers killed at the three-day Battle of Gettysburg. They are buried in a semi-circle around the Soldiers' National Monument, which marks the spot where President Lincoln delivered his moving Gettysburg Address. The now-famous address is commemorated by the nearby Lincoln Speech Memorial, which contains an inscription of his speech and his bust.

Soldiers' National Monument

🏛 Shriver House Museum

307 Baltimore St. **Tel** *(717) 337-2800.* ◯ *Mar: 10am–5pm Sat, 10am–2pm Sun; Apr–Nov: 10am–5pm Mon–Sat, noon–5pm Sun.* ● *Jan.* 🖼 🖼
This 19th-century home portrays the life of a family under the three-day Confederate occupation. The third-floor attic has original holes in the brick wall where rebel sharpshooters stood poised. A small museum displays artifacts, including three unfired bullets discovered during restoration.

🏛 Wills House and Lincoln Room Museum

8 Lincoln Square. **Tel** *(866) 486-5735.* ◯ *9am–5pm; extended hours on some weekends.*
President Abraham Lincoln slept in this corner house on the town's center square the night before he delivered the Gettysburg Address. His bedroom, where he made final revisions to his speech, is part of the Lincoln Room Museum. It houses copies of the letter sent by attorney and home-owner David Wills inviting Lincoln to visit the town.

LINCOLN'S GETTYSBURG ADDRESS

Four months after the battle, President Abraham Lincoln visited Gettysburg to dedicate a cemetery for Union soldiers. Although not the main speaker, and asked only to make "a few appropriate remarks," Lincoln's 272-words, two-minute speech on November 19, 1863 not only gave new meaning to the war's losses, but was an inspiration to preserve a nation divided. His words conferred significance on the sacrifice of the thousands who died during the battle, urging for the "resolve that these dead shall not have died in vain."

Lincoln's bust at Soldiers' National Cemetery

A Tour of Gettysburg National Military Park

The Battle of Gettysburg was fought on the first three days of July 1863. Not only was it the turning point of the American Civil War between the North and South, it was also the war's largest battle, leaving more than 51,000 Union and Confederate soldiers killed, wounded, captured, or missing. Although the Union army won this critical battle, it took a further two years for them to decisively win the Civil War on April 26, 1865. This self-guided tour traces the course of the three-day battle.

Eternal Light Peace Memorial (2)
From Oak Hill, Confederates attacked Union forces on the first day. This memorial to "Peace Eternal in a Nation United" was built in 1938.

McPherson's Ridge (1)
This quiet farm with McPherson's barn is where the Battle of Gettysburg began early in the morning on July 1, 1863. Confederate infantry advanced eastward and engaged in heavy fire with Union Cavalry.

Oak Ridge (3)
Union troops held this ridge but retreated to Cemetery Hill on July 1 as their defenses collapsed.

North Carolina Memorial (4)
On the second day, the Confederates stood on Seminary Ridge. Union troops held Culp's and Cemetery Hills.

Virginia Memorial (5)
This monument on Seminary Ridge overlooks the field where, on July 3, 12,000 Confederates launched their last major assault, known as "Pickett's Charge." In less than an hour, 10,000 of them were dead or wounded.

Pitzer Woods (6)
Confederates occupied these woods on the second day. An observation tower offers grand views of the "Pickett's Charge" battlefield.

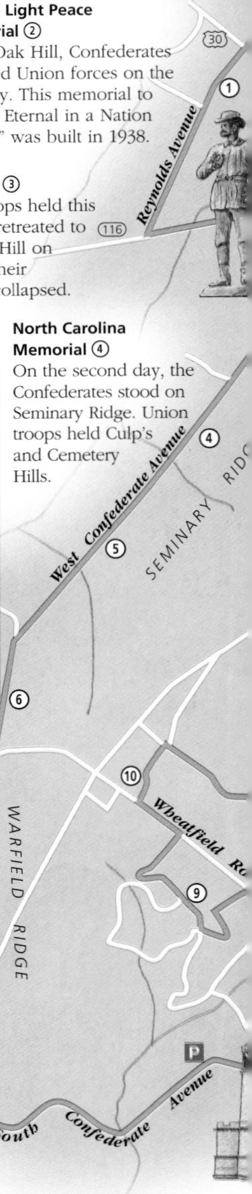
30
Reynolds Avenue
116
West Confederate Avenue
SEMINARY RIDGE
EISENHOWER NATIONAL HISTORIC SITE
West Confederate Avenue
WARFIELD RIDGE
Wheatfield Ro
BR 15
Emmitsburg
South Confederate Avenue
0 meters 500
0 yards 500

Warfield Ridge (7)
On the battle's second day, Confederates charged Union troops at Devil's Den and Little and Big Round Tops.

KEY

- Suggested route
- Other roads
- ℹ Visitor information
- [P] Parking

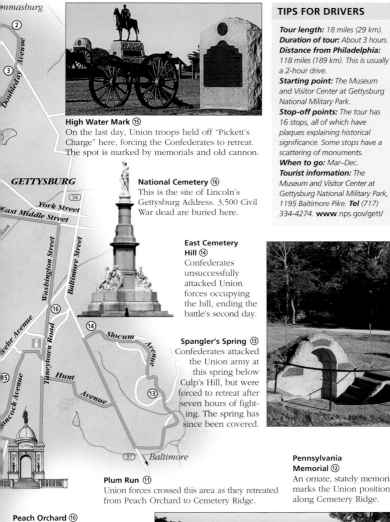

High Water Mark ⑮
On the last day, Union troops held off "Pickett's Charge" here, forcing the Confederates to retreat. The spot is marked by memorials and old cannon.

TIPS FOR DRIVERS
Tour length: 18 miles (29 km).
Duration of tour: About 3 hours.
Distance from Philadelphia: 118 miles (189 km). This is usually a 2-hour drive.
Starting point: The Museum and Visitor Center at Gettysburg National Military Park.
Stop-off points: The tour has 16 stops, all of which have plaques explaining historical significance. Some stops have a scattering of monuments.
When to go: Mar–Dec.
Tourist information: The Museum and Visitor Center at Gettysburg National Military Park, 1195 Baltimore Pike. **Tel** (717) 334-4274. **www**.nps.gov/gett/

National Cemetery ⑯
This is the site of Lincoln's Gettysburg Address. 3,500 Civil War dead are buried here.

East Cemetery Hill ⑭
Confederates unsuccessfully attacked Union forces occupying the hill, ending the battle's second day.

Spangler's Spring ⑬
Confederates attacked the Union army at this spring below Culp's Hill, but were forced to retreat after seven hours of fighting. The spring has since been covered.

Pennsylvania Memorial ⑫
An ornate, stately memorial marks the Union position along Cemetery Ridge.

Plum Run ⑪
Union forces crossed this area as they retreated from Peach Orchard to Cemetery Ridge.

Peach Orchard ⑩
On the second day, Confederate soldiers overran this position despite heavy Union cannon fire.

The Wheatfield ⑨
Charges and countercharges here on the second day left over 4,000 men dead and wounded.

Little Round Top ⑧
At first undefended on the second day, this position was reinforced when an alert Union general called for help. Monuments, such as this one to the 155th Pennsylvania Volunteer Infantry, dot the hill.

Map labels: mmasburg · ② · ③ · Doubleday Avenue · GETTYSBURG · ㉞ · York Street · East Middle Street · Washington Street · Baltimore Street · ⑯ · ⑭ · Slocum Avenue · Taneytown Road · ⑬ · Hunt · Avenue · ㉙⑦ · Baltimore · ⑮ · Hancock Avenue

The Golden Plough Tavern, one of York's historic establishments

York ⑩

York County, PA. 🏘 40,500. 🚊 🚌
ℹ️ 1425 Eden Rd, (717) 852-9675.
www.yorkpa.org

The first Pennsylvania town west of the Susquehanna River, York was laid out in 1741, with inhabitants that were mainly tavern-keepers and craftspeople catering to pioneers heading west. Since then, manufacturing has been the town's economic strength.

East of York is the **Harley-Davidson Final Assembly Plant**, noisy, colorful, and the size of two football fields. Its giant presses mold steel while motorcycles fly overhead. A small museum depicts Harley Davidson's history from its 1903 inception as a motorized bike company to the present.

🏛 Harley-Davidson Final Assembly Plant
1425 Eden Rd. **Tel** (717) 848-1177.
⏰ 8am–4:30pm Mon–Fri. 🎫 9am–2pm Mon–Fri; some Saturdays in summer; under 12 not allowed.

Harrisburg ⑪

Dauphin County, PA. 🏘 47,000. 🚊
🚌 ℹ️ Hershey Harrisburg Regional Visitors Bureau: (877) 727-8573.
www.pacapitalregions.com

First settled in the early 18th century by Englishman John Harris, Harrisburg is situated along the Susquehanna River. The city was not planned until the 1780s and became the capital of Pennsylvania in 1812. Today, the state government is the biggest employer in the city, which has the impressive **State Capitol** as a focal point. The Renaissance-style building was dedicated in 1906 by President Theodore Roosevelt.

The **National Civil War Museum** tells the story of the war through permanent displays of artifacts, photographs, manuscripts, and documents from its 24,000-item collection. City Island, located in the middle of the Susquehanna, offers panoramic views of the city. It includes marinas, parks and nature areas, riverboat rides and dinner cruises, and a replica of John Harris's 18th-century trading post.

🏛 State Capitol
3rd & State Sts. **Tel** (717) 787-6810.
⏰ 8:30am–4:30pm Mon–Fri.
🎫 8:30am–4:30pm Mon–Fri, 9am,

11am, 1pm, 3pm Sat–Sun & hols.
⛔ Jan 1, Easter, Thanksgiving, Dec 25. ♿

🏛 National Civil War Museum
Lincoln Circle (Reservoir Pk). **Tel** (717) 260-1861. ⏰ 10am–5pm Mon–Sat, noon–5pm Sun. ⛔ Mon, Jan–Mar.
♿
www.nationalcivilwarmuseum.org

Hershey ⑫

Dauphin County, PA. 🏘 12,800.
🚊 🚌 www.hersheypa.com

This factory town, now a tourist destination, revolves around chocolate, so much so that even its streetlights are shaped like silver-foil-wrapped Hershey Kisses. The town's main attraction is **Hershey Park**, an amusement park that has 80 rides on offer, and a fine, four-row carousel. There are also two resort hotels in the park. Nearby is Chocolate World, which features a 15-minute ride through animated tableaux that reveal Hershey's chocolate-making process. A free sample awaits at the end of the tour.

Hershey's Chocolate World signage

🎢 Hershey Park
100 W Hersheypark Drive.
Tel 1-800-HERSHEY. ⏰ May 21–Sep 1: 10am–8pm daily (for other times check website). 🎫 www.hersheypark.com

State Capitol complex in Harrisburg, the seat of Pennsylvania's government

The towers and parapets of Mercer Castle, Doylestown

Reading ⑬

Berks County, PA. 👥 80,000. 🚂 🚌
🅸 Greater Reading Convention &
Visitors Bureau, 2525 N 12th St, (610)
375-4085. **www**.readingberkspa.com

Once a center of industry,
Reading has reinvented itself
as a discount-store capital
(see p157), with more than
80 name-brand stores, from
Brooks Brothers to Mikasa
and Wedgewood. The
Reading Pagoda, on the outskirts of the town, is the main
attraction here. Built in the
early 20th century, it is modeled after a Shogun structure.
  The **Mid-Atlantic Air
Museum**, located at Reading
Regional Airport, includes a
selection of over 60 different
military and civilian aircraft.

🏛 Mid-Atlantic Air Museum
11 Museum Drive. **Tel** (610) 372-
7333. 🕙 9:30am–4pm.
www.maam.org

Doylestown ⑭

Bucks County, PA. 👥 9,200. 🚂 🚌
🅸 Bucks County Visitors Center: 3207
Street Road, Bensalem, (800) 836-2825.

Doylestown's origins date to
1745, when William Doyle built
a tavern here. The town later
developed as a cultural and
commercial center, and today
it is also the Bucks County seat.
  The biggest attractions in
town are the castle-like museums that tower over shaded
grassy areas close to the town
center. The **Mercer Museum**,
built by archaeologist Henry

Mercer in 1916, displays his
collection of folk art, woodwork, textiles, and furnishings. After his death in 1930,
his 44-room home, **Fonthill**,
was turned into a tile museum.
  Named after a famous writer
from this area, the **James A.
Michener Art Museum**,
located in a 19th-century
county jail, has a world-class
collection of Pennsylvania
Impressionist paintings.

🏛 Mercer Museum
84 S Pine St. **Tel** (215) 345-0210.
🕙 10am–5pm Mon–Sat, noon–5pm
Sun, until 9pm Tue.
www.mercermuseum.org

🏛 Fonthill Museum
E Court St and Rt 313. **Tel** (215) 348-
9461. 📷 mandatory; reservations
advised. **www**.mercermuseum.org

**🏛 James A. Michener Art
Museum**
138 S Pine St. **Tel** (215) 340-9800.
🕙 10am–4:30pm Tue–Fri, 10am–
5pm Sat & Sun. 📷
www.michenerartmuseum.org

New Hope ⑮

Bucks County, PA. 👥 2000. 🅸 Visitor
Center: Main & Mechanic Sts, (215)
862-5030. **www**.newhopepa.com

This delightful waterfront
village and shoppers' paradise
teems with upscale boutiques
and restaurants. Tracing its
roots to the early 18th century, it gained its name when
Benjamin Parry's gristmill,
which ground grain, burned
down in 1790. He rebuilt it
and named it "New Hope
Mills" with a promise of
prosperity for the town.
  Today, that prosperity is
evident with more than 200 art
galleries, boutiques, and craft
and antiques shops, including
a branch of the **James A.
Michener Art Museum**. Train
rides aboard restored 1920
passenger cars, horse-drawn
carriages, and mule-drawn
barge trips down the scenic
19th-century canal add to the
town's ambience.
  Parry, who also helped
finance the first bridge across
the Delaware, built a house
in 1784 that was occupied
by successive generations of
his family until 1966. Today,
the **Parry Mansion Museum**
showcases its separate rooms,
decorated according to different periods of its history.

🏛 Parry Mansion Museum
45 S Main St. **Tel** (215) 862-5652.
🕙 late Apr–early Dec: 1–5pm Sat &
Sun. 📷 by appointment. 📷

**🏛 James A. Michener Art
Museum – New Hope**
500 Union Square Dr, New Hope.
Tel (215) 862-7633. 📷 **www**.
michenerartmuseum.org

Storefronts line New Hope's old-world, picturesque streets

Delaware River at Washington Crossing Historic Park

Washington Crossing Historic Park ⓰

Washington Crossing, PA. **Tel** (215) 493-4076. ☐ 9am–5pm Tue–Sat, noon–5pm Sun. ⬤ public hols except Jul 4, Memorial Day, Labor Day, Dec 25. ⬙

This waterfront park, set up in 1917 to commemorate Washington's historic crossing of the Delaware River, is divided into two sections. The McConkey's Ferry section, named after a local 18th-century inn, includes the riverbank from which Washington and his army departed in Durham boats. A monument marks this area outside the visitor center. Nearby is a 19th-century boathouse containing replicas of the boats, which are now used for the annual Christmas Day crossing reenactment.

About 4 miles (6 km) upstream is the Thompson's Mill section, which includes historic buildings, a gristmill, an observation tower, and a cemetery along the peaceful Delaware Canal containing the graves of Revolutionary War soldiers.

On the New Jersey side of the river, Washington Crossing State Park marks the site where Washington landed. This forested area includes historic homes, a visitor center and museum, and miles of hiking, riding, and biking trails.

Trenton ⓱

Mercer County, NJ. 🚶 85,000. 🚉 🚌 ℹ️ Lafayette at Barrack St, (609) 777-1770. **www**.trentonnj.com

The capital of New Jersey, Trenton's origin dates to 1679 when Quaker Mahlon Stacy built a gristmill along the Delaware. In 1714, his son sold land to merchant William Trent who laid out a new city called "Trent's Town" in 1721. Today, a big attraction is the Trenton Battle Monument. It pays tribute to the Battle of Trenton, in which General Washington and 2,400 men crossed the ice-clogged Delaware River on December 25, 1776, to launch an attack on British and Hessian soldiers. The latter were defeated and this battle was the turning point in the Revolutionary War. Prior to this, the Continental Army had suffered many defeats, and a win was badly needed

Plaque marking the river crossing

to boost morale in the fight for independence. The Old Barracks, dating to 1758, were occupied by Hessian soldiers during the encounter, and now house a museum.

🏛 **Old Barracks Museum**
Barrack St. **Tel** (609) 396-1776. ☐ 10am–5pm. ⬤ Jan 1, Easter, Thanksgiving, Dec 24–25. ⬙
www.barracks.org

Pennsbury Manor ⓲

400 Pennsbury Memorial Rd, Morrisville, PA. **Tel** (215) 946-0400. ☐ 9am–5pm Tue–Sat, noon–5pm Sun. 🎫 📷 **www**.pennsbury manor.org

An elegant brick Georgian house 26 miles (42 km) north of Philadelphia, this manor is a re-creation of William Penn's country home and estate from the 1680s. The plantation sits on the site chosen by Penn, and this manor was built in 1939 on original foundations, where some 17th-century bricks are the only remnants of Penn's initial home. Inside, a hall served as a waiting room between the family's quarters and governor's parlor, while the second floor had three bedrooms and a nursery.

The estate today includes farm animals similar to those owned by Penn. Other recreated structures include a blacksmith shop, brew house, smokehouse, and horse shelter. The $3.5 million visitor center offers activities for schools, a gallery, office space, an auditorium and facilities for video conferencing.

Gardens at Pennsbury Manor, Penn's country estate

Atlantic City's glamorous resorts by night – lighting up the Jersey coast

Atlantic City ⑲

Atlantic County, NJ. 🏛 40,000. 🚉
🚌 ⓘ *Atlantic City Convention &
Visitors Authority: 2314 Pacific Ave.*
Tel *(609) 348-7100, (888) 222-4748.*
www.atlanticcitynj.com

Called the "Queen of the
Coast" by generations of
beachgoers, Atlantic City has
been a favored vacation spot
since the mid-1800s. The first
casino opened on the
famous Board-
walk in 1978,
and since
then the
town has
become one of
the most popular
destinations on the
eastern seaboard. All
gambling – referred
to as "gaming" – takes place in
the large, ostentatious casino
hotels that lie within a block
of the beach and Boardwalk,
which is lined with shops and
amusement arcades.

More than a dozen casino
resorts – with their towers
shooting up along the Boardwalk – make up the dazzling
city skyline. They include
Caesars, Bally's, Harrah's,
Showboat, Resorts, Tropicana,
and the properties owned by
billionaire developer Donald
Trump, such as the 51-story
Trump Taj Mahal *(see p139)*.
Among the flashier hotels are
the Borgata Hotel Casino and
Spa, a $1-billion, 2,000-room
hotel, and its companion
property, The Water Club.
Many resorts include spas,
several restaurants each, convention facilities, nightclubs,
and concert halls with popular
comedy and musical acts.

Visitors not enchanted by the
casinos instead head for the
lively local attractions. Amusement parks with roller coasters
jut out over the ocean on the
Central Pier Arcade and
Speedway, and the famous
Steel Pier. Another attraction
is the Absecon Lighthouse,
the tallest lighthouse in New
Jersey, which offers splendid
views of the city and waterfront. Atlantic City also hosts
the prestigious annual
Miss America
Pageant, held
here since
1928.
Shopping
is also a big
draw, with the
arrival of Atlantic
City Outlet – The
Walk – housing
stores like Banana Republic,
Nautica, and Coach.

In nearby Margate City,
Lucy the Elephant stands tall
in celebration of American
marketing ingenuity. Built by
a real estate developer
in 1881 to draw pro-
spective buyers to his
holdings, "Lucy" has
served as a residence
and a tavern over the
years. Today, guided
tours take visitors into
the structure that has
become instantly recog-
nizable as part of the
Jersey shoreline.

**Playing cards used
in gaming**

🐘 Lucy the Elephant
3200 Atlantic Ave, Margate.
Tel *(609) 823-6473.* ⃝ *mid-
Jun–Labor Day: 10am–8pm
Mon–Sat, 10am–5pm Sun;
weekends in spring and fall;
Nov–Dec: hours vary.* ⃞
www.lucytheelephant.org

Cape May ⑳

Cape May County, NJ. 🏛 4,000.
ⓘ *Cape May Welcome Center: 609
Lafayette St, (609) 884-5508.*

First explored by Cornelius
Mey for the Dutch West India
Company in 1621, Cape May
is one of the oldest resorts on
the Atlantic coast. Popular
with Philadelphia socialites
during the late 1800s, it has,
since then, continued to enjoy
a fine reputation among beach
lovers. The building boom of
the Victorian era characterizes
Cape May today. **Historic Cold
Spring Village** is a living
history museum showcasing
25 restored buildings, with
costumed actors portraying
19th-century lifestyles.

**🏛 Historic Cold Spring
Village**
720 US 9. **Tel** *(609) 898-2300.* ⃝ *mid-
Jun–Labor Day: 10am–4:30pm Tue–
Sun; only weekends Labor Day–mid-
Sep & Memorial Day–mid-Jun.* ⃞ ⃞

**Brightly painted façade of a house at Cape
May, America's largest Victorian district**

Hagley Museum 21

200 Hagley Rd, Rte 141, Wilmington, DE. *Tel (302) 658-2400.* ☐ *Jan–mid-Mar: 9:30am– 4:30pm Sat & Sun, mid-Mar–Dec: 9:30am–4:30pm daily.* ● *Thanksgiving, Dec 25 & 31.* ☑ *Jan–mid-Mar: 1:30pm Mon–Fri.* ☐ ✍ *www.hagley.org*

Not a museum in the conventional sense, this forested site along the rocky Brandywine River is where the DuPont Company was founded. In 1802, French immigrant Eleuthere Irenee du Pont built a factory to manufacture gunpowder and "black powder" used in explosives. The earliest buildings included the first du Pont family home, gardens, and company office. Through its 119-year-history, overseen by five generations of du Ponts, the mill expanded downriver, with waterwheels powering production facilities that sifted, mixed, and crushed raw materials into fine powder.

Today, only the façades of the original buildings remain. Some have working exhibitions, such as a rolling mill using safe charcoal. Staff members demonstrate the workings of a steam engine and the operations in a machine shop, but most impressive is the ignition of a powder sample. Some buildings house artifacts, original furniture, and rare du Pont cars, including a 1911 electric car and a 1928 Phaeton.

View of the Brandywine River at Hagley Museum

Interior of the conservatory at Longwood Gardens

Winterthur Museum 22

5105 Kennett Pike, Rte 52, Winterthur, DE. *Tel (302) 888-4600.* ☐ *10am–5pm Tue–Sun.* ● *Mon (except hols), Jan 1, Thanksgiving, Dec 25.* ✍ ☑ ☐ *www.winterthur.org*

Once the home of Henry Francis du Pont, great-grandson of Eleuthere Irenee du Pont, this vast estate contains an extraordinary 175-room mansion. The original home, the core of the current mansion, dates to 1839. It was built by J.A. Bidermann and his wife, Evelina, Eleuthere du Pont's daughter. Henry Francis inherited the estate in 1926, expanding it during the two-decade-long conversion of his home into a museum. Today, it houses 85,000 items from the 17th to the 19th centuries, including paintings, textiles, furniture, ceramics, and Chinese porcelain. The main dining room features original silver tankards crafted by Paul Revere, and works of art by Gilbert Stuart and Benjamin West. The parlor features a unique oval Mont Morency staircase and is elegantly decorated with Chippendale furniture. The estate contains meadows, streams, and woods, including a tulip-poplar tree, which has been around since William Penn's days, and the fairy-filled Enchanted Woods.

Longwood Gardens 23

Rte 1, Kennett Square, PA. *Tel (800) 737-5500, (610) 388–1000.* ☐ *Apr–Oct: 9am–6pm; Nov–Mar: 9am–5pm.* ● *Mon (except hols), Jan 1, Thanksgiving, Dec 25.* ✍ ♿ *www.longwoodgardens.org*

This well-manicured horticultural wonderland consists of colorful gardens, woodlands, lush meadows, greenhouses, and spectacular fountains amid idyllic bucolic scenery. Settler George Pierce acquired the land in 1700, and in 1798, his descendants established an arboretum that, by the mid-19th century was one the nation's finest.

Industrialist Pierre S. du Pont bought it in 1906 and it is his design that remains today. It includes over 11,000 plant varieties in both indoor and outdoor displays, whimsical topiaries, and a children's garden. The massive main greenhouse and conservatory are engineering marvels that shelter an array of exotic plant life. But the most breathtaking sights are the fabulous fountains with choreographed eruptions highlighted at night by colored lights, which create dazzling displays that are often the backdrop of musical events.

Brandywine Battlefield State Park ㉔

878 Baltimore Pike, Rte 1, Chadds Ford, PA. **Tel** (610) 459-3342.
9am–5pm Tue–Sat, noon–5pm Sun. Mon.

The Battle of Brandywine, fought on these rolling hills on September 11, 1777, was the biggest engagement of the American Revolution. General Washington stationed his troops atop this high ground at Chadds Ford along the Brandywine River in an attempt to stop the advancing British. The Americans were outmaneuvered as the British crossed the Brandywine River at an unguarded ford to the north of Washington's troops, forcing them to retreat.

Today, the battlefield is a state park with a visitor center and two historic houses, both restored to the way they were in 1777. The Benjamin Ring House was owned by a Quaker farmer and served as Washington's headquarters on the eve of the battle. The French patriot and American Revolution hero, Marquis de La Fayette, stayed in the farmhouse of Quaker Gideon Gilpin. The visitor center includes a small museum.

Revolutionary War hero La Fayette's quarters at Brandywine Park

Brandywine River Museum ㉕

1 Hoffman's Mill Road, Chadds Ford, PA. **Tel** (610) 388-2700.
9:30am– 4:30pm. Dec 25.
Apr–mid-Nov: timed tours of N.C. Wyeth House & Studio, and Kuerner Farm Wed–Sun.
www.brandywinemuseum.org

Located in a Civil War-era gristmill along Brandywine River, this museum is best known for housing artworks by three generations of the Wyeths – N.C., Andrew, and Jamie. Galleries showcase landscapes inspired by the Brandywine River Valley, and paintings and illustrations by the Wyeths and other artists.

N.C. Wyeth (1882–1945) was a famous illustrator of the early 20th century, completing more than 1,000 illustrations, including some for classics such as *Treasure Island* and *Robin Hood*. N.C.'s son Andrew is known for mastering dry-brush watercolor and egg tempura mediums. His son Jamie painted portraits of figures such as President John F. Kennedy and artist Andy Warhol.

Tours are organized to the N.C. Wyeth House and Studio, and the Kuerner Farm, which inspired Andrew for over 70 years. A farmhouse and barn display his works related to the farm.

National Memorial Arch at Valley Forge

George Washington's restored headquarters at Valley Forge

Valley Forge National Historic Park ㉖

Rte 23 & North Gulph Rd, Valley Forge, PA. **Tel** (610) 783-1077.
Visitor Center: 9am–5pm.
Jan 1, Thanksgiving, Dec 25.
www.nps.gov/vafo

George Washington and his soldiers spent the harsh winter of 1777–78 at Valley Forge, retreating to these hills after losing to British forces at Brandywine and Germantown (*see p107*). No battles were fought here, but nearly 2,000 soldiers died of typhus, typhoid, pneumonia, and dysentery. Today, reconstructed cabins, statues, and cannon are scattered through the park. Key exhibits are the National Memorial Arch, designed by Paul Cret, and built in 1917 in the memory of those who died in the winter of 1777–78, and stone farmhouses that once served as officers' quarters. The park has miles of fields and woods crisscrossed by hiking paths, and a visitor center with artifacts such as muskets and powder horns.

The American Revolution Center is the country's first museum dedicated to that conflict. Built within a quarry bluff, the vast space will showcase the largest collection of Revolutionary artifacts, information, and experiences ever assembled.

Cloth Angels
HAndmyde by
an Amish girl
12.00 plus tx.

TRAVELERS' NEEDS

WHERE TO STAY

The Philadelphia area offers a wide selection of hotel rooms to fit every style and budget. More expensive hotels include towers overlooking scenic Center City and riverfront views, boutique hotels, upscale chain hotels, and smaller but luxurious bed-and-breakfasts – some with colonial themes. The more budget-conscious traveler will find a wide range of comfortable chain hotels, motels, inns, and bed-and-breakfasts within the city and beyond. Hotel rates are quite reasonable, though they tend to be higher in the more popular business district and tourist areas.

Doorman at Westin

LOCATIONS

The Center City district has the highest concentration of hotel rooms in the Philadelphia metropolitan area with over 10,000 rooms available. Business travelers prefer to stay in one of the many Center City properties, which include high-end names, such as the Four Seasons Hotel and the Ritz Carlton. In particular, hotels are clustered near Logan Square and on Market, Chestnut, and Walnut Streets, with many in and around Rittenhouse Square, the Pennsylvania Convention Center, and along the Avenue of the Arts in the theater district.

A few hotels can be found in Old City and Society Hill, while some are also located along the Delaware River waterfront. Quality hotels are also concentrated in University City, along City Line Avenue on the city's north-western edge, at the airport, and in the suburbs of Valley Forge and King of Prussia.

FACILITIES AND AMENITIES

All hotels in Philadelphia have standard air con-ditioning, cable TV, and other conveniences. Upscale prop-erties and some chain hotels have in-room business services and centers, including com-puter and fax facilities, though only a few smaller hotels or bed-and-breakfasts offer Internet access to guests.

Chain hotels, in particular, offer fitness facilities and some of the larger hotels have pools. Sometimes, hotels make arrangements with nearby health clubs for the use of their facilities by hotel guests. Additional charges may apply for certain amenities, and some may be costly. It is best to call and clarify when booking accommodation.

RESERVATIONS

Most larger chain hotels have toll-free reservation numbers, or visitors can make reservations through their Internet sites, with some offering discounts for online bookings. Prices quoted are often for double occupancy and do not include taxes or parking charges. Online hotel reservation service companies offer reduced rates for rooms, but often add hidden fees and taxes. A good resource is the website of the **Greater Philadelphia Tourism and Marketing Corporation**, with current hotel packages that may include tours, show performance tickets, and other offers.

HIDDEN COSTS

If you are traveling solo, always make sure you are quoted the rate for one per-son, as hotels usually quote room rates assuming double occupancy. Room taxes in Philadelphia amount to around 14 percent, while parking rates range anywhere from $10 to $30 per day. Rooms with a view can also cost more – the splendid panoramas of the waterfront, skyline, and neighborhoods can be seen from the higher floors of many hotels in the city.

View of the First Bank of the US from a Ritz Carlton room *(see p136)*

◁ Jars of traditional Amish jams, jellies, preserves, and pickles at Reading Terminal Market

Entrance to the Radisson Plaza-Warwick Hotel Philadelphia *(see p136)*

DISCOUNTS

Discounts are often available when booking packages. The "Philly's More Fun When You Sleep Over" promotion runs at different times in the year and offers free parking, gifts, and other discounts on two weekend hotel nights for two. It is also available through the website of the **Greater Philadelphia Tourism and Marketing Corporation**.

BED-AND-BREAKFASTS

Accommodations at places offering bed-and-breakfast (B&Bs) are found within quiet and shaded neighborhoods, with some housed in quaint 18th- and 19th-century buildings and Victorian homes. Prices vary depending on services, amenities, and location. B&Bs include breakfast, but tend not to have restaurants, business facilities or exercise areas. Most B&Bs in the city are located in the neighborhoods of University City, Chestnut Hill, Center City, and near City Line Avenue. To find out more and make reservations, contact **A Bed and Breakfast Connection of Philadelphia**.

HOSTELS

Younger travelers and students often stay in hostels, which offer much cheaper accommodation than hotel rooms. Some good hostels are: the **Bank Street Hostel**, in a renovated 19th-century building, has modern amenities and is located near Independence Mall; and the **Hosteling International Chamounix Mansion**, which is situated in one of Fairmount Park's historic homes.

TRAVELING WITH CHILDREN

With Philadelphia's many historic attractions and science-oriented museums, children are warmly welcomed at most city hotels. Younger children can usually stay for free in their parents' rooms, but it is best to check when making reservations. Ask about family rates and suites that might better accommodate kids. Hotels often supply cots at an additional cost. Family hotel packages are available through the **Greater Philadelphia Tourism and Marketing Corporation** website. These may include accommodations, meals, tickets for different historic tours, or free child meals and free parking.

DISABLED TRAVELERS

Most of the larger hotels accommodate wheelchairs, while smaller establishments, such as B&Bs, may not have full amenities for the disabled as they are housed in 18th- and 19th-century homes. For more information, contact the hotels or call the **Mayor's Commission on People with Disabilities**.

Bedroom at Rittenhouse 1715, a boutique hotel *(see p136)*

Choosing a Hotel

Hotels have been selected across a wide price range for facilities, good value, and location. All rooms have private bath, TV, air conditioning, and have disabled access unless otherwise indicated. Most have Internet access, and in some cases, fitness facilities may be offsite. The hotels are listed by area. For map references, *see pp194–7.*

PRICE CATEGORIES
The price ranges are for a standard double room per night, including tax, during the high season. Breakfast is not included, unless specified.
$ $60–$105
$$ $106–$145
$$$ $146–$185
$$$$ $186–$240
$$$$$ Over $240

OLD CITY

Comfort Inn Downtown/Historic Area $$
100 N Columbus Blvd, Philadelphia **Tel** *(215) 627-7900* **Fax** *(215) 238-0809* **Rooms** *185*   **Map** *4 E2*

This budget-priced, high-rise hotel has no frills but is in a great location within walking distance of historic sites. It offers clean, comfortable rooms, as well as a free Continental breakfast. In addition, children under 18 stay free with parents. It offers easy access to the I-95 and good views of the Delaware River. **www.choicehotels.com**

The Thomas Bond House $$
129 S 2nd St, Philadelphia **Tel** *(215) 923-8523* **Fax** *(215) 923-8504* **Rooms** *12*   **Map** *4 E3*

Once the home of prominent colonial physician, Thomas Bond, this historic inn dates back to 1769. Rooms are decorated with period furniture that create an ambience of colonial warmth and quiet luxury. Guests can make use of fitness facilities at an establishment close to the inn. **www.thomasbondhousebandb.com**

Best Western Independence Park Hotel $$$
235 Chestnut St, Philadelphia **Tel** *(215) 922-4443* **Fax** *(215) 922-4487* **Rooms** *36*   **Map** *4 E3*

Small, historic hotel dating back to 1856 with exquisitely decorated rooms, located within the heart of Old City and just a few blocks from Independence Mall and Penn's Landing. The hotel offers complimentary breafast and free wired or wireless high-speed Internet access. **www.independenceparkhotel.com**

Holiday Inn Historic District $$$
400 Arch St, Philadelphia **Tel** *(215) 923-8660* **Fax** *(215) 829-1796* **Rooms** *364*   **Map** *4 E2*

Comfortable chain hotel with reasonably priced rooms. Its excellent and convenient location – one block from Independence Mall and within walking distance of the Market Street shopping area – make it a popular destination for tourists. Children love the rooftop pool during the warmer months. **www.holidayinn.com/phlhistoric**

Morris House Hotel $$$
225 S 8th St, Philadelphia **Tel** *(215) 922-2446* **Fax** *(215) 922-2466* **Rooms** *15*   **Map** *3 C3*

This 1787 home is now a luxury boutique hotel and is one of the city's best hotels to experience colonial ambience. It has the coziness of a B&B and unique features such as a private garden, colonial-style reading room, two dining rooms with fireplaces, and rooms with hardwood floors. **www.morrishousehotel.com**

Omni Hotel $$$$
401 Chestnut St, Philadelphia **Tel** *(215) 925-0000* **Fax** *(215) 925-1263* **Rooms** *150*   **Map** *4 D3*

This four-star, four-diamond hotel has large-sized rooms with marble bathrooms. It is just a few blocks from key restaurants and nightlife spots, and within walking distance of shopping stores and Jewelers' Row. The rooms offer views of the Independence Mall area. **www.omnihotels.com**

Penn's View Hotel $$$$
14 N Front & Market Sts, Philadelphia **Tel** *(215) 922-7600* **Fax** *(215) 922-7642* **Rooms** *51*   **Map** *4 E3*

Cozy and family owned, this European-style hotel features murals and marble throughout the property. Its superb Italian restaurant and the unique "Il Bar" offers over 120 wines by the glass *(see p147)*. Situated across from Penn's Landing, it is just a block away from excellent restaurants and nightlife. **www.pennsviewhotel.com**

SOCIETY HILL AND PENN'S LANDING

Sheraton Society Hill $$$
1 Dock St, Philadelphia **Tel** *(215) 238-6000* **Fax** *(215) 238-6652* **Rooms** *365*   **Map** *4 E4*

The Sheraton Society Hill is another excellent hotel for the business traveler. There is a 24-hour business center, computer rentals, and a secretarial service. Situated on cobblestoned Dock Street, the hotel is also ideal for tourists as it is just a block or two from Penn's Landing. **www.sheraton.com/societyhill**

Key to Symbols *see back cover flap*

Hyatt Regency Philadelphia at Penn's Landing

$$$$

201 S Columbus Blvd, Philadelphia **Tel** *(215) 928-1234* **Fax** *(215) 521-6543* **Rooms** *348* **Map** *4 F3*

This upscale property on Penn's Landing is Philadelphia's only waterfront hotel. Twenty-two stories overlook the Delaware River, and also offer superb views of Society Hill and Center City. Elegant rooms with a full range of amenities make it ideal for the business traveler. **www.hyattregencyphiladelphia.com**

CENTER CITY

Alexander Inn

$$

12th & Spruce Sts, Philadelphia **Tel** *(215) 923-3535* **Fax** *(215) 923-1004* **Rooms** *48* **Map** *3 B3*

This boutique hotel has modern decor that adds a touch of European charm. It has an excellent Center City location, just a couple of blocks from the theater district. The restaurant only serves a breakfast buffet, and the business center allows guests to access emails. **www.alexanderinn.com**

Hampton Inn Convention Center

$$

1301 Race St, Philadelphia **Tel** *(215) 665-9100* **Fax** *(215) 665-9200* **Rooms** *250* **Map** *3 B1*

Located right next to the Convention Center, this property is ideal for people attending conventions. It is situated a few blocks from Chinatown and the Market Street shopping area and within walking distance of historic sights. The clean rooms have modern amenities, including high-speed Internet access. **www.hershahotels.com**

Hilton Garden Inn Philadelphia Center City

$$

1100 Arch St, Philadelphia **Tel** *(215) 923-0100* **Fax** *(215) 925-0800* **Rooms** *279* **Map** *3 C2*

This popular and fashionable chain hotel has newly renovated rooms and is located near the Pennsylvania Convention Center, a block or two from Chinatown. All rooms are outfitted with modern amenities, such as microwaves and refrigerators. The rooftop restaurant and lounge offer city views. **www.philadelphiacentercity.stayhgi.com**

Holiday Inn Express Midtown

$$

1305 Walnut St, Philadelphia **Tel** *(215) 735-9300* **Fax** *(215) 732-2593* **Rooms** *166* **Map** *3 B3*

A comfortable budget chain hotel, this Holiday Inn has a convenient location just a few blocks from the theater district and the Market Street shopping area. Complimentary Continental breakfast is served and the hotel gives passes for a nearby fitness center to those guests who wish to keep in shape. **www.himidtown.com**

La Reserve

$$

1804 Pine St, Philadelphia **Tel** *(215) 735-1137* **Fax** *(215) 735-0582* **Rooms** *7* **Map** *2 D5*

A luxurious and cozy B&B in a Philadelphia townhouse, La Reserve has elegant rooms with antiques and beautiful lamps. The establishment has an all-you-can-eat gourmet breakfast and free wireless Internet access. Parking is available at nearby lots. **www.lareservebandb.com**

Travelodge

$$

1227 Race St, Philadelphia **Tel** *(215) 564-2888* **Fax** *(215) 564-2700* **Rooms** *50* **Map** *3 B1*

This budget chain hotel has clean rooms and serves a complimentary Continental breakfast. Located directly across from the Pennsylvania Convention Center and just one block from Chinatown, it is within walking distance of historic sights and the Market Street shopping district. **www.travelodge.com**

Courtyard by Marriott Philadelphia Downtown

$$$

21 N Juniper St, Philadelphia **Tel** *(215) 496-3200* **Fax** *(215) 496-3696* **Rooms** *498* **Map** *2 F4*

This is a comfortable Marriott-brand hotel housed in the historic, former City Hall Annex building. Located across the street from the Masonic Temple and the Pennsylvania Academy of the Fine Arts, it is just a few blocks from the Convention Center. Lobby and lounge areas are expansive. **www.philadelphiadowntowncourtyard.com**

Doubletree Hotel Philadelphia

$$$

237 S Broad St, Philadelphia **Tel** *(215) 893-1600* **Fax** *(215) 893-1664* **Rooms** *427* **Map** *2 F5*

A high-rise hotel in the heart of Philadelphia on the Avenue of the Arts, this property is across from the Kimmel Center, the Academy of Music, and the Merriam Theater. The lobby has a comfortable lounge area and sports bar and bistro, and the roof garden sports a jogging track. **www.philadelphia.doubletree.com**

Latham Hotel

$$$

135 S 17th St, Philadelphia **Tel** *(215) 563-7474* **Fax** *(215) 563-4034* **Rooms** *139* **Map** *2 D4*

This small, European-style boutique hotel is in the heart of the fashionable Rittenhouse Row shopping district. Rooms are decorated in Victorian style. It offers all modern amenities, including free wireless Internet access in all rooms. It also boasts a hip bar and restaurant *(see p148)*. **www.lathamhotel.com**

The Independent Hotel

$$$

1234 Locust St, Philadelphia **Tel** *(215) 772-1440* **Fax** *(215) 772-1022* **Rooms** *24* **Map** *3 B3*

This sophisticated boutique hotel is housed in a restored Georgian Revival building in Center City's hip, midtown village district. The rooms are stylish and well equipped; single and double rooms have queen size beds while the executive room beds are king size. A complimentary breakfast is served in the hotel's fireside lounge. **www.theindependenthotel.com**

Rodeway Inn Center City

1208 Walnut St, 19107 **Tel** *(215) 546-7000* **Fax** *(215) 546-7573* **Rooms** *32*

Map *3 B3*

No-frills accommodations, but shortcomings in luxury are compensated for by the location, blocks from City Hall, theaters, and an exciting restaurant and bar scene along 13th Street. Rooms are small, and parking is at an independent lot across the street. **www.rodewayinn.com**

Crowne Plaza Philadelphia Center City

1800 Market St, Philadelphia **Tel** *(215) 561-7500* **Fax** *(215) 561-7500* **Rooms** *445*

Map *2 E4*

Located within the city's cluster of skyscrapers, this chain hotel is ideal for business travelers. It offers modern, comfortable rooms. Just a few blocks from Rittenhouse Square with its many fine restaurants and boutiques, it is within walking distance of the theater and museum districts. **www.crowneplaza.com/philadelphia**

Hotel Palomar

117 S 17th St, 19103 **Tel** *(215) 563-5006* **Fax** *(215) 563-5007* **Rooms** *230*

Map *2 E4*

A modernist renovation of a historical building has resulted in an eye-catching, stylish, and eco-friendly boutique hotel. A well-regarded restaurant and hip lobby bar add to the appeal. The location is only steps away from Center City shopping areas, the upscale Rittenhouse Park, and an array of dining choices. **www.hotelpalomar-philadelphia.com**

Loews Philadelphia

1200 Market St, Philadelphia **Tel** *(215) 627-1200* **Fax** *(215) 231-7205* **Rooms** *581*

Map *3 B2*

This high-rise luxury hotel is housed in the landmark PSFS building, a 1932 former bank office. It has been renovated with elegant decor and Art Deco accents, including exotic woods and carved glass. Rooms offer astounding views. A spa and fitness center encompass the entire fifth floor of the hotel. **www.loewshotels.com/philadelphia**

Hyatt at the Bellevue

Broad & Walnut Sts, Philadelphia **Tel** *(215) 893-1234* **Fax** *(215) 732-8518* **Rooms** *172*

Map *2 E5*

A residential-style hotel with international flair, the Hyatt is perched on the upper floors of the 100-year-old Bellevue Building, which was once nicknamed the "Grand Dame of Broad Street." Marble staircases and chandeliers highlight the old world elegance. The property has upscale shops on its premises. **www.parkhyattphiladelphia.com**

Philadelphia Marriott Downtown

1201 Market St, Philadelphia **Tel** *(215) 625-2900* **Fax** *(215) 625-6000* **Rooms** *1,410*

Map *3 B2*

A world-class convention hotel connected to the Convention Center and Reading Terminal Market, the Philadelphia Downtown Marriott offers upgraded amenities on concierge-level floors. Located in the heart of the Market Street shopping area and within walking distance of historic sights and the theater district. **www.philadelphiamarriott.com**

Radisson Plaza-Warwick Hotel Philadelphia

1701 Locust St, Philadelphia **Tel** *(215) 735-6000* **Fax** *(215) 790-7788* **Rooms** *300*

Map *2 E5*

One block from fashionable Rittenhouse Square, this is a prestigious hotel whose guests have included celebrities and presidents. Built in 1926 in English Renaissance style, it has a majestic two-story lobby with a sweeping staircase, and an upscale steakhouse, The Prime Rib *(see p149)*. **www.radisson.com/philadelphiapa**

Sofitel Philadelphia

120 S 17th St, Philadelphia **Tel** *(215) 569-8300* **Fax** *(215) 569-1492* **Rooms** *306*

Map *2 E4*

An elegant, four-diamond hotel with a distinctive French flair in design and embellishments, the Sofitel houses a chic French restaurant, and the lobby has a bar with dramatic floor-to-ceiling windows. The spacious rooms have elegant and modern decor. Rittenhouse Row shopping areas and restaurants are only a block away. **www.philadelphiasofitel.com**

The Westin Philadelphia

99 S 17th St, Philadelphia **Tel** *(215) 563-1600* **Fax** *(215) 564-9559* **Rooms** *294*

Map *2 E4*

This is an elegant chain hotel with luxuriously decorated lobby, lounge areas, and restaurants. The hotel is connected to Liberty Place, which has trendy shops and boutiques. It has a great location just a few blocks from the Rittenhouse Row shopping hub, and the theater and museum districts. **www.westin.com/philadelphia**

AKA Rittenhouse Square

135 S 18th St, Philadelphia **Tel** *(215) 825-7000* **Fax** *(215) 563-8486* **Rooms** *80*

Map *2 D5*

This luxury development, overlooking Rittenhouse Square, is one of a new generation of extended stay hotel residences that offer the comfort of a furnished apartment with the amenities of a hotel. Accommodations comprise contemporary studios, one and two bedroom apartments, and penthouse suites. Minimum one week stay. **www.hotelaka.com**

Le Meridien Philadelphia

1421 Arch St, 19102 **Tel** *(215) 422-8200* **Fax** *(215) 422-8277* **Rooms** *202*

Map *2 F3*

A classic stone Georgian-revival building, this hotel features a striking atrium lobby and a mix of antiques and contemporary style. Overlooking City Hall, it is centrally located near the Convention Center, museums, and major business headquarters. Off-site valet parking means planning ahead to retrieve your car. **www.lemeridien.com/philadelphia**

Rittenhouse 1715

1715 Rittenhouse Sq, Philadelphia **Tel** *(215) 546-6500* **Fax** *(215) 546-8787* **Rooms** *23*

Map *2 D5*

This 16-room boutique hotel offers posh accommodation in a refurbished 1900s Philadelphia carriage house. It boasts a private, elegant, and luxurious lobby, serves a complimentary Continental breakfast in a Parisian-like breakfast room, and has a 24-hour concierge service. Parking is available at nearby lots. **www.rittenhouse1715.com**

Key to Price Guide *see p134* **Key to Symbols** *see back cover flap*

The Rittenhouse Hotel

$$$$$

210 W Rittenhouse Sq, Philadelphia **Tel** *(215) 546-9000* **Fax** *(215) 732-3364* **Rooms** *98* **Map** *2 D5*

This top-of-the-line luxury hotel is one of the city's finest and boasts two award-winning restaurants, the Lacroix and the Smith & Wollensky steakhouse *(see p149)*. A five-diamond property with lavishly decorated rooms and marble bathrooms, the hotel also has an upscale spa and salon. **www.rittenhousehotel.com**

The Ritz Carlton Philadelphia

$$$$$

10 S Broad St, Philadelphia **Tel** *(215) 523-8000* **Fax** *(215) 568-0942* **Rooms** *273* **Map** *2 F4*

This exquisite, five-diamond luxury hotel sits directly across from City Hall in the former Girard/Mellon Bank Building. It has an impressive columned façade entrance and the lobby is situated in the expansive rotunda. The rooms are lavishly decorated and have superb city views. **www.ritzcarlton.com/philadelphia**

LOGAN SQUARE AND THE MUSEUM DISTRICT

Best Western Center City Hotel

$$$

501 N 22nd St, Philadelphia **Tel** *(215) 568-8300* **Fax** *(215) 557-0259* **Rooms** *183* **Map** *2 D1*

A four-story budget hotel, this Best Western has the advantage of a good location within walking distance of the museum district. Some rooms offer excellent views of the Philadelphia skyline. Children who are 18 and younger can stay free with a paying adult. **www.bestwestern.com/centercityhotel**

Embassy Suites Hotel Philadelphia Center City

$$$

1776 Benjamin Franklin Pkwy, Philadelphia **Tel** *(215) 561-1776* **Fax** *(215) 561-1850* **Rooms** *288* **Map** *2 E3*

Popular hotel in a landmark cylindrical building opposite Logan Square. This chain features only suites – every room has an adjacent living room and a balcony. Situated in the museum district and close to the Museum of Art and Rittenhouse Square. The fitness room has a jogging track. **www.embassysuites.com**

Sheraton Philadelphia City Center Hotel

$$$

17th & Race Sts, Philadelphia **Tel** *(215) 448-2000* **Fax** *(215) 448-2853* **Rooms** *760* **Map** *2 E3*

This upscale, high-rise hotel is ideal for both the business and vacation traveler. Located four blocks from the Convention Center, it has a fabulous seafood restaurant and an impressive modern design with a four-story high lobby atrium. The comfortable and gracious rooms have all the modern amenities. **www.sheraton.com/philadelphiacitycenter**

The Windsor Suites

$$$$

1700 Benjamin Franklin Pkwy, Philadelphia **Tel** *(215) 981-5678* **Fax** *(215) 981-5609* **Rooms** *148* **Map** *2 E3*

Specialty hotel that offers furnished suites and unfurnished apartments. All rooms have complimentary high-speed Internet access and kitchens. Some suites have living rooms, separate sleeping areas, and private balconies. The hotel has two restaurants on its premises. **www.thewindsorsuites.com**

Four Seasons Hotel

$$$$$

1 Logan Sq, Philadelphia **Tel** *(215) 963-1500* **Fax** *(215) 963-9507* **Rooms** *364* **Map** *2 E3*

One of Philadelphia's most elegant hotels, the Four Seasons is luxuriously decorated with Federal-style furnishings. It features one of the city's best restaurants *(see p150)*, as well as a courtyard café with decorative water fountains. It is located close to the financial, commercial, and museum districts. **www.fourseasons.com/philadelphia**

FARTHER AFIELD

Howard Johnson Inn and Conference Center

$

2389 Rt 70 W, Cherry Hill, NJ, 08002 **Tel** *(856) 317-1900* **Fax** *(856) 317-0800* **Rooms** *90*

This budget hotel is located within 5 miles (8 km) of Center City in Philadelphia. It is also well-placed to visit other sights, such as the Adventure Aquarium and the Camden Waterfront. The hotel offers a complimentary Continental breakfast and there is an Indian restaurant on the premises. **www.hojo.com**

Mount Laurel Marriott

$

915 Rt 73, Mount Laurel, NJ, 08054 **Tel** *(856) 234-7300* **Fax** *(856) 802-3912* **Rooms** *283*

This pleasant suburban hotel is excellent for both business travelers and tourists. The hotel features a new premier steakhouse and a heated pool. Concierge-level rooms have upgraded amenities and balconies. There is also a game room for children and tennis courts. **www.mtlaurelmarriott.com**

Ramada Inn Philadelphia Airport

$

76 Industrial Hwy, Essington, PA, 19029 **Tel** *(610) 521-9600* **Fax** *(610) 521-9388* **Rooms** *292*

Located 3 miles (5 km) south of Philadelphia Airport, this comfortable hotel has a complimentary, 24-hour shuttle service to the airport. Each room has its own balcony. Special discounts are available for groups of ten or more people. **http://ramadaphl.com**

Chestnut Hill Hotel
 $$

8229 Germantown Ave, Philadelphia, PA, 19118 **Tel** *(215) 242-5905* **Fax** *(215) 242-8778* **Rooms** *36*

Built in 1891, this historic hotel is situated along the cobblestoned streets of Germantown Avenue. Although furnished with 18th-century decor, it offers all modern amenities. Within walking distance of Fairmount Park's Wissahickon Gorge and a short drive from historic Germantown. **www.chestnuthillhotel.com**

Clarion Hotel & Conference Center
$$

1450 Rt 70 E and I-295, Cherry Hill, NJ, 08034 **Tel** *(856) 428-2300* **Fax** *(856) 354-7662* **Rooms** *197*

Across the Delaware River, this hotel and conference center is ideal for both the business and leisure traveler. An in-house café serves breakfast, entrées, and pastries, and a neighborhood-like pub and restaurant is next door. The hotel is a short drive from the Camden Waterfront and central Philadelphia. **www.clarionofcherryhill.com**

Conwell Inn at Temple University
$$

1331 Polett Walk, Philadelphia, PA, 19122 **Tel** *(215) 235-6200* **Fax** *(215) 235-6235* **Rooms** *22*

A small hotel, Conwell Inn lies within the heart of the Temple University campus. A deluxe historic landmark hotel, it has cozy and comfortable rooms and suites that have been decorated very tastefully. The hotel provides a complimentary European breakfast. **www.conwellinn.com**

Hampton Inn Philadelphia Airport
$$

8600 Bartram Ave, Philadelphia, PA, 19158 **Tel** *(215) 966-1300* **Fax** *(215) 966-1313* **Rooms** *152*

The Hampton Inn is a quality budget hotel with clean and comfortable rooms. The hotel offers a shuttle service to the airport, which is about 2 miles (3 km) away. A short drive away are professional sports stadiums and south Philadelphia sights, including the Italian Market. **www.hamptoninn.com**

Fairfield Inn Philadelphia Airport
$$

8800 Bartram Ave, Philadelphia, PA, 19153 **Tel** *(215) 365-2254* **Fax** *(215) 365-2254* **Rooms** *109*

Located just half a mile away from the airport, this comfortable, high-end budget property by Marriott offers full amenities and conveniences at superior value for the dollar. Complimentary Continental breakfast. 3 miles (5 km) from professional sports venues in south Philadelphia. **www.marriott.com**

Quality Inn & Conference Center
$$

531 Rt 38 W, Maple Shade, NJ, 08052 **Tel** *(856) 235-6400* **Fax** *(856) 727-1027* **Rooms** *109*

This three-diamond hotel and conference center is ideal for both the business and leisure traveler and features Jacuzzi suites. The bar by the poolside is open only on the weekends. About 10 miles (16 km) from central Philadelphia, it is also close to a number of entertainment areas. **www.qualityinn.com/hotel/nj129**

Cornerstone Bed & Breakfast
 $$$

3300 Baring St, Philadelphia, PA, 19104 **Tel** *(215) 387-6065* **Fax** *(215) 387-0590* **Rooms** *6*   **Map** *1 A2*

This intimate urban inn sits in a restored 1870s church-stone mansion, and has a wrap-around porch and stained glass windows. Its lavishly decorated rooms and lounge areas have original wood floors and high ceilings. The inn is situated close to the Philadelphia Zoo and the Museum of Art. **www.cornerstonebandb.com**

Crowne Plaza Hotel Philadelphia – Cherry Hill
 $$$

2349 W Marlton Pike, Cherry Hill, NJ, 08002 **Tel** *(856) 665-6666* **Fax** *(856) 662-1414* **Rooms** *408*

Located in suburban Cherry Hill, this upscale and full-service Hilton property features modern rooms with full amenities, dark oak furniture, and marble countertops. It is convenient for visiting the Adventure Aquarium and the Camden Waterfront, while the Atlantic City beaches and casinos are just an hour away. **www.crowneplaza.com/cherryhillnj**

Embassy Suites Hotel – Philadelphia International Airport
 $$$

9000 Bartram Ave, Philadelphia, PA, 19153 **Tel** *(215) 365-4500* **Fax** *(215) 365-4803* **Rooms** *263*

This recently renovated three-diamond, modern chain hotel is an all-suites establishment. It has a unique tropical atrium lobby, which is filled with ducks and fishponds. The hotel offers a complimentary cook-to-order breakfast. Just one mile (1.6 km) from the Philadelphia Airport. Free airport shuttle. **www.philadelphiaairport.embsuites.com**

Hilton Philadelphia Airport
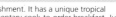 $$$

4509 Island Ave, Philadelphia, PA, 19153 **Tel** *(215) 365-4150* **Fax** *(215) 937-6382* **Rooms** *331*

The Hilton chain offers comfort and a touch of elegance with this full-service hotel, located just one mile (1.6 km) from the airport. The Landing Restaurant and Grill is highly recommended, as are its bar and indoor pool. A complimentary 24-hour airport shuttle service is offered. Close to the city's sports stadiums. **www.hilton.com**

Hilton Philadelphia City Avenue
 $$$

4200 City Ave, Philadelphia, PA, 19131 **Tel** *(215) 879-4000* **Fax** *(215) 879-9020* **Rooms** *209*

An upscale chain hotel on the outskirts of the city, this Hilton hotel is a short drive from Fairmount Park and the Barnes Foundation. It has comfortable and elegantly furnished rooms. Guests can indulge in plenty of shopping and culinary delights in the shops and restaurants on City Avenue. **www.philadelphiacityavenue.hilton.com**

Holiday Inn Philadelphia Stadium
  $$$

900 Packer Ave, Philadelphia, PA, 19148 **Tel** *(215) 755-9500* **Fax** *(215) 339-0842* **Rooms** *238*

This newly renovated property is a hotel ideal for fans taking in a game at one of nearby professional sports venues in south Philadelphia. Comfortable rooms with a full range of amenities for leisure and business travelers as well. There is a sports bar and restaurant on the premises. **www.ichotelsgroup.com**

Key to Price Guide *see p134* **Key to Symbols** *see back cover flap*

Sheraton University City Hotel
3549 Chestnut St, Philadelphia, PA, 19104 **Tel** *(215) 387-8000* **Fax** *(215) 387-7920* **Rooms** *332*

This is a large and efficient full-service chain hotel on the University of Pennsylvania campus. Rooms have modern decor with plush beds and oversized chairs. Ideal for visiting Philadelphia Zoo and the Museum of Archaeology and Anthropology. The lobby features complimentary, wireless Internet access. **www.philadelphiasheraton.com**

The Inn at Penn
3600 Sansom St, Philadelphia, PA, 19104 **Tel** *(215) 222-0200* **Fax** *(215) 222-4600* **Rooms** *238*

Just across the Schuylkill River from Center City, this upscale Hilton hotel sits in the heart of the University of Pennsylvania campus. Also close to the Drexel University, Philadelphia Zoo, 30th Street Amtrak Station, and the University of Pennsylvania's Museum of Archaeology and Anthropology. **www.theinnatpenn.com**

Renaissance Hotel Philadelphia Airport
500 Stevens Dr, Philadelphia, PA, 19113 **Tel** *(610) 521-5900* **Fax** *(610) 521-8954* **Rooms** *350*

This four-diamond, modern, and upscale chain hotel is on I-95, close to the airport. It is tastefully decorated with the Renaissance's signature European flair. There is an expansive lobby atrium and the rooms have high-speed Internet access. It is in a convenient location for a quick drive into the city on the interstate. **www.renaissancehotels.com**

Philadelphia Airport Marriott
Arrivals Rd, Philadelphia, PA, 19153 **Tel** *(215) 492-9000* **Fax** *(215) 492-4799* **Rooms** *419*

This upscale and full-service Marriott Hotel is the only one in Philadelphia connected to the airport via a skybridge to Terminal B. Nearby is the convenient R1 commuter train linking the airport with Center City. Terrific in-hotel dining and lounge at Riverbend Bar and Grille. **www.philadelphiaairportmarriott.com**

BEYOND PHILADELPHIA

ATLANTIC CITY Bally's Atlantic City Hotel & Casino
1900 Pacific Ave, Atlantic City, NJ, 08401 **Tel** *(609) 340-2000* **Fax** *(609) 340-4713* **Rooms** *1,246*

One of the few remnants of historic Atlantic City, the 1860s Dennis Hotel has been restored as part of this mega-resort complex, which also includes a modern 45-story tower. Fans of the board game Monopoly will know that the hotel stands on the city's most valuable corner. The hotel's casino features a Wild West theme. **www.ballysAC.com**

ATLANTIC CITY Caesars Atlantic City Hotel Casino
2100 Pacific Ave, Atlantic City, NJ, 08401 **Tel** *(609) 348-4411* **Fax** *(609) 343-2405* **Rooms** *1,144*

A premier destination on the New Jersey shore, Caesars is a luxurious hotel and casino on the Boardwalk with an "Ancient Rome" theme. The hotel's lobby is done up to look like a Roman temple, and there are 11 restaurants and 3 lounges. The 1,100-seat Circus Maximus Theater offers the best in entertainment. **www.caesarsac.com**

ATLANTIC CITY Trump Taj Mahal Hotel Casino and Resort
1000 Boardwalk at Virginia Ave, Atlantic City, NJ, 08401 **Tel** *(609) 449-1000* **Rooms** *1,250*

One of Atlantic City's landmark casinos, this luxury five-diamond resort has all the opulence that lives up to the Trump name. A 51-story tower hovers over the Boardwalk, and the themed hotel and casino has 9 in-house restaurants *(see p152)* and a 5,000-seat arena for concerts and sports events. **www.trumptaj.com**

BRANDYWINE VALLEY Brandywine River Hotel
Rts 1 & 100, Chadds Ford, PA, 19317 **Tel** *(610) 388-1200* **Rooms** *40*

A Victorian-style country B&B, the Brandywine River Hotel has elegantly decorated rooms with fireplaces and Jacuzzis. It is a short drive from Longwood Gardens, Brandywine Battlefield, Brandywine River Museum, Chadds Ford, and Winterthur. The hotel is surrounded by several award-winning restaurants. **www.brandywineriverhotel.com**

CAPE MAY The Chalfonte Hotel
301 Howard St, Cape May, NJ, 08204 **Tel** *(609) 884-8409* **Fax** *(609) 884-4588* **Rooms** *70*

This whitewashed Victorian-era hotel was built in 1874 and offers old-fashioned charm with rocking chairs on the wrap-around front porch. Chalfonte has always been unconventional – rooms have no televisions or phones, and the hotel is just two blocks from the beach. **www.chalfonte.com**

CAPE MAY Queen Victoria Bed and Breakfast
102 Ocean St, Cape May, NJ, 08204 **Tel** *(609) 884-8720* **Rooms** *32*

Built in the 1870s and fully restored in 1995, this mansard-roofed Victorian inn is located in the heart of Cape May, just a block from the beach, antiques shops, gourmet dining, and historic tours. Bicycles to tour the area are available for free, and the hotel provides a complimentary European breakfast buffet. **www.queenvictoria.com**

DELEWARE Hotel du Pont
11th & Market Sts, Wilmington, DE, 19801 **Tel** *(302) 594-3100* **Fax** *(302) 594-3108* **Rooms** *217*

Dating back to 1913, this four-diamond, four-star hotel is the ultimate in luxury in Delaware. Each room is lavishly furnished with mahogany furniture and brass bathroom fixtures. Close to most of the region's attractions, including the Brandywine River Museum, Winterthur, Hagley Museum, and Longwood Gardens. **www.hoteldupont.com**

DOYLESTOWN Hargrave House [P] ❄ $$$

50 S Main St, Doylestown, PA, 18901 ***Tel*** *(215) 340-1814* ***Fax*** *(215) 340-2234* ***Rooms*** *7*

This historic inn is within walking distance of the Mercer Museum and the James A. Michener Art Museum. Many rooms overlook Doylestown Historical Society Park. The rooms are decorated with 19th-century furnishings, but have all modern conveniences. A full country breakfast is offered on weekends. **http://hargravehouse.net**

GETTYSBURG Quality Inn at General Lee's Headquarters [P] 🍴 🏊 🏋 🍸 ❄ $

401 Buford Ave, Gettysburg, PA, 17325 ***Tel*** *(717) 334-3141* ***Fax*** *(717) 334-1813* ***Rooms*** *45*

Quaint inn with renovated rooms next to Confederate General Robert E. Lee's former headquarters. The three-diamond inn has spacious, bright, and clean rooms with antique furniture. Two-story suites are also available. Free Continental breakfast and admission to General Lee's Headquarters Museum. **www.thegettysburgaddress.com**

GETTYSBURG Farnsworth House Inn [P] 🍴 $$

401 Baltimore St, Gettysburg, PA, 17325 ***Tel*** *(717) 334-8838* ***Fax*** *(717) 334-5862* ***Rooms*** *16*

This B&B is housed in one of Gettysburg's most historic buildings, with walls that still have bullet holes from the Civil War, and a small open-air garden. The lavish rooms have period decor, and the B&B conducts ghost tours of some of the "haunted" rooms. It also has quaint dining rooms *(see p152)*. **www.farnsworthhouseinn.com**

GETTYSBURG Gettystown Inn [P] 🍴 ❄ $$

89 Steinwehr Ave, Gettysburg, PA, 17325 ***Tel*** *(717) 334-2100* ***Fax*** *(717) 334-6905* ***Rooms*** *9*

Victorian B&B consisting of three separate Civil War-era houses near where President Lincoln delivered his famous Gettysburg Address *(see p121)*. Rooms are lavishly decorated with 19th-century antiques and furnishings. A complimentary breakfast is served at the adjacent Dobbin House Tavern *(see p152)*. **www.dobbinhouse.com**

GETTYSBURG The Brafferton Inn [P] $$$

44 York St, Gettysburg, PA, 17325 ***Tel*** *(717) 337-3423, (866) 337-3423* ***Rooms*** *17*

This elegant and lovely B&B is located in a 1786 fieldstone house – the oldest residence in Gettysburg. All rooms are furnished with 18th- and 19th-century family antiques, elaborate stencils, and family portraits. A two-night stay is the minimum on weekends from April to November. **www.brafferton.com**

GETTYSBURG Hilton Garden Inn Gettysburg ⇅ [P] 🍴 🏊 🏋 🍸 ❄ $$$

1061 York St, Gettysburg, PA, 17325 ***Tel*** *(717) 334-2040* ***Fax*** *(717) 334-2073* ***Rooms*** *88*

A pleasant hotel focused on both business and leisure travelers. All the rooms are beautifully appointed, with a refrigerator, microwave, and complimentary Internet access. The hotel is located a short distance away from the historic battlefield, museums, and the town center. **www.hiltongardeninn.com**

HARRISBURG Hilton Harrisburg ⇅ [P] 🍴 🏊 🍸 ❄ $$$

1 N 2nd St, Harrisburg, PA, 17101 ***Tel*** *(717) 233-6000* ***Fax*** *(717) 233-6830* ***Rooms*** *341*

This upscale, full-service Hilton hotel is just three blocks from the State Capitol. It has elegant rooms; "Tower Level" guest rooms are accorded enhanced amenities, including a complimentary Continental breakfast and evening hors d'ouevres. The hotel has four restaurants on its premises. **www.harrisburg.hilton.com**

HERSHEY Hampton Inn & Suites Hershey ⇅ [P] 🏊 🍸 ❄ $$$$

749 East Chocolate Ave, Hershey, PA, 17033 ***Tel*** *(717) 533-8400* ***Fax*** *(717) 520-1892* ***Rooms*** *110*

A comfortable chain hotel in downtown Hershey, the Hampton Inn & Suites is only 1 mile (1.6 km) from the renowned attractions of the area, including Hershey Chocolate World and Hershey Park. The hotel offers a complimentary Continental breakfast and high-speed Internet access. **www.hamptoninn.com**

HERSHEY The Hotel Hershey ⇅ [P] 🍴 🏊 🏋 🍸 ❄ $$$$$

100 Hotel Rd, Hershey, PA, 17033 ***Tel*** *(717) 533-2171* ***Fax*** *(717) 534-8887* ***Rooms*** *232*

This grand hotel with its majestic gardens and fountains sits atop a hill overlooking the town. Luxurious and lavishly decorated rooms and common areas have old-world charm, and historic photographs and original artworks line the walls. Turndown service at night with Hershey's "Kisses" chocolates. **www.thehotelhershey.com**

PENNSYLVANIA DUTCH COUNTRY General Sutter Inn [P] 🍴 $

14 E Main St, Lititz, PA, 17543 ***Tel*** *(717) 626-2115* ***Fax*** *(717) 626-0992* ***Rooms*** *15*

The General Sutter Inn is one of the oldest in Pennsylvania, dating back to 1764. Spacious rooms and suites are decorated with antiques in Victorian style. It is home to two fine restaurants and a lively bar, and has a delightful courtyard that is used for outdoor dining and cocktails. **www.generalsutterinn.com**

PENNSYLVANIA DUTCH COUNTRY Revere Inn & Suites ⇅ [P] 🍴 🏊 🍸 ❄ $

3063 Lincoln Hwy, Paradise, PA, 17562 ***Tel*** *(717) 687-8601* ***Fax*** *(717) 687-6141* ***Rooms*** *95*

This unique hotel has comfortable and tastefully decorated rooms and suites in three different buildings, including the 18th-century Revere House. All rooms have modern amenities and the historic Revere Tavern restaurant is situated on the property. Located on Route 30 in the heart of the Pennsylvania Dutch Country. **www.revereinn.com**

PENNSYLVANIA DUTCH COUNTRY Bird-In-Hand Family Inn ⇅ [P] 🍴 🏊 🏋 🍸 $$

2740 Old Philadelphia Pike, Bird-In-Hand, PA, 17505 ***Tel*** *(717) 768-8271* ***Fax*** *(717) 768-1117* ***Rooms*** *125*

This large, three-diamond property is an ideal getaway for a family holiday. Facilities such as tennis courts, mini-golf, a playground, game room, and even a petting zoo keep the kids busy. It has a family restaurant with an all-you-can-eat buffet. **www.bird-in-hand.com/familyinn**

PENNSYLVANIA DUTCH COUNTRY Bird-In-Hand Village Inn & Suites [P] ≋ $$

2695 Old Philadelphia Pike, Bird-In-Hand, PA, 17505 ***Tel*** *(717) 293-8369* ***Fax*** *(717) 768-1117* ***Rooms*** *24*

This 1734 inn is responsible for the unique naming of this small town. Four well-preserved historic buildings house rooms and suites. The complimentary Continental breakfast includes local freshly baked treats. Guests can take a 2-hour complimentary bus tour of the area. **www.bird-in-hand.com/villageinn**

PENNSYLVANIA DUTCH COUNTRY Fulton Steamboat Inn ⇅ [P] 🍴 ≋ 🏃 👪 ♿ $$

Rt 30 at Rt 896, Lancaster, PA, 17602 ***Tel*** *(717) 299-9999* ***Fax*** *(717) 299-9992* ***Rooms*** *97*

This unique hotel is shaped like a 19th-century steamboat in honor of inventor Robert Fulton, who was born nearby in 1765. Family-oriented, with three "decks" of spacious guest rooms and"cabins" with bunk beds for kids, the inn is not far from the Strasburg Railroad and the Amish Village. Two-night minimum stay. **www.fultonsteamboatinn.com**

PENNSYLVANIA DUTCH COUNTRY The Inn at Kitchen Kettle Village [P] 🍴 $$

Rt 340, Intercourse, PA, 17534 ***Tel*** *(717) 768-8261* ***Rooms*** *11*

Located among Pennsylvania Dutch Country farms, 11 tastefully decorated rooms and suites are tucked amidst the specialty shops at Kitchen Kettle Village, which comprises 32 shops, restaurants, and lodging. The rooms are comfortable and offer all modern amenities. **www.kitchenkettle.com**

PENNSYLVANIA DUTCH COUNTRY Strasburg Village Inn [P] $$

1 W Main St, Strasburg, PA, 17579 ***Tel*** *(717) 687-0900* ***Fax*** *(717) 687-3650* ***Rooms*** *10*

Dating back to the late 1780s, this historic inn is situated on one corner of Strasburg's center square. Ten rooms in "Williamsburg" style are warmly furnished in Victorian-style decor with canopy beds and antiques. The inn sits next door to the old-style Strasburg Creamery, an ice cream and sandwich shop. **www.strasburg.com**

PENNSYLVANIA DUTCH COUNTRY Amishview Inns & Suites ⇅ [P] 🍴 ≋ 👪 ♿ $$$

Rt 340, 3125 Old Philadelphia Pike, Bird-In-Hand, PA, 17505 ***Tel*** *(717) 768-1162* ***Rooms*** *50*

This country inn has scenic views of cornfields and silos. It is located halfway between Intercourse and Bird-In-Hand on the Plain and Fancy Farm, which is also home to Lancaster's first family-style restaurant *(see p153)*. Adjacent to the Amish Experience Theater and the Amish Homestead. **www.amishviewinn.com**

PENNSYLVANIA DUTCH COUNTRY Historic Strasburg Inn [P] 🍴 ≋ 🏃 👪 ♿ $$$

1400 Historic Dr, Strasburg, PA, 17579 ***Tel*** *(717) 687-7691* ***Fax*** *(717) 687-5290* ***Rooms*** *102*

The Historic Strasburg Inn sits on 18 acres (7 ha) of beautifully landscaped grounds with views of Amish farmland and is just a short walk from popular shops and restaurants. The accommodation ranges from traditional doubles to multi-room family options to luxury Jacuzzi suites. **www.historicinnofstrasburg.com**

PENNSYLVANIA DUTCH COUNTRY The Inn & Spa at Intercourse Village [P] $$$

Rt 340, Main St, Intercourse, PA, 17534 ***Tel*** *(717) 768-1162* ***Rooms*** *12*

This 1909, Victorian-style B&B is a four-diamond facility with traditional fireplaces in suites with beamed ceilings and private baths with Jacuzzis. Enjoy candlelit gourmet breakfasts in the ornate dining room. The B&B is located close to antiques and craft shops in the heart of Intercourse's main shopping street. **www.amishcountryinns.com**

TRENTON Trenton Marriott at Lafayette Yard ⇅ [P] 🍴 👪 ♿ $$

1 W Lafayette St, Trenton, NJ, 08608 ***Tel*** *(609) 421-4000* ***Fax*** *(609) 421-4002* ***Rooms*** *197*

An upscale and modern three-diamond hotel in downtown Trenton, the hotel has elegant guest rooms. It is adjacent to the Trenton War Memorial, and is just one block from the tourist information center and Old Barracks Museum. A short drive away are Washington Crossing State Park and New Hope. **www.marriott.com**

VALLEY FORGE Dolce Valley Forge 🍴 ≋ 👪 $$

215 West Dekalb Pike, King of Prussia, PA, 19406 ***Tel*** *(610) 337-1200* ***Fax*** *(610) 337-1959* ***Rooms*** *348*

This hotel provides lodging just minutes from Valley Forge National Historic Park and the King of Prussia Mall. Each guest room artfully combines traditional touches with modern facilities and amenities. The hotel's executive and luxury suites are ideal for extended stays. **www.dolce-valley-forge-hotel.com**

VALLEY FORGE Crowne Plaza Valley Forge ⇅ [P] 🍴 ≋ 👪 ♿ $$$

260 Mall Blvd, King of Prussia, PA, 19406 ***Tel*** *(610) 265-7500* ***Fax*** *(610) 265-4076* ***Rooms*** *225*

This upscale hotel is walking distance from the colossal King of Prussia Mall. The property has tastefully decorated rooms with many amenities, including Jacuzzis. It also offers complete business facilities. The hotel is 2 miles (3 km) from the Valley Forge National Historic Park. **www.cpvalleyforge.com**

VALLEY FORGE Homewood Suites Valley Forge ⇅ [P] ≋ 🏃 👪 ♿ $$$

681 Shannondell Blvd, Audubon, PA, 19403 ***Tel*** *(610) 539-7300* ***Fax*** *(610) 539-2970* ***Rooms*** *123*

This spacious, all-suite hotel is located near Valley Forge National Historic Park and the King of Prussia Mall. Suites are available for short and extended stays; all have fully equipped kitchens and free Internet access. Breakfast (daily) and light evening meals (Monday through Thursday) are complimentary. **www.homewoodsuitesvalleyforge.com**

VALLEY FORGE Wayne Hotel ⇅ [P] 🍴 $$$

139 E Lancaster Ave, Wayne, PA, 19087 ***Tel*** *(610) 687-5000* ***Fax*** *(610) 687-8387* ***Rooms*** *40*

Dating back to 1906, this century-old hotel along Philadelphia's fashionable Main Line has been restored to its former Victorian elegance. Tudor Revival-style architecture adds to the old-world charm. It is a just a few miles from the King of Prussia Mall. Fitness facilities and pool can be used at nearby establishments. **www.waynehotel.com**

RESTAURANTS AND CAFES

Though the city is perhaps traditionally best known for the Philadelphia cheesesteak, its culinary repertoire has expanded widely and is today home to some of the country's top-rated restaurants. In addition to superb American fare, some of the city's best dining rooms specialize in international cuisine, including French, Italian, Thai,

Typical Dutch Country pretzel

Moroccan, Chinese, and more. Excellent bistros, seafood restaurants, and steakhouses that feature cooking styles from Southern home cooking and colonial fare to Pennsylvania Dutch can be found in Center City. Modest restaurants and eateries, many serving traditional cheesesteak sandwiches, can be found in every city neighborhood and beyond.

Park-side alfresco dining at Rouge in Rittenhouse Square *(see p149)*

PHILLY FARE

For breakfast, the locals love to order grilled pork rolls along with their eggs and hash brown potatoes. At noon, cheesesteaks and lunchmeat-filled "hoagies" or "grinders" are favorites, and these can be found at the many food courts, pizzerias, and sandwich shops dotted around the city. Hoagies are Italian rolls filled with fresh meats and cheeses, as well as lettuce, tomatoes, and onions, topped off with a dash of oregano. Philly cheesesteaks consist of finely-sliced grilled beef along with onions, which are topped off with thick cheese sauce served up in a foot-long roll.

In Pennsylvania Dutch Country, meals are influenced by the traditional cooking of the Amish and Mennonites *(see p115)*. Family-style restaurants usually offer a good selection of this distinctive food, while staple and favorite treats are readily available at local farmers' markets scattered throughout the area *(see p144)*.

RESTAURANTS, BISTROS, AND CAFES

Many of Philadelphia's best restaurants are in Center City. Fine dining rooms can also be found in Center City hotels and near the theater district, home to the Kimmel Center and other performing arts venues. In Old City, head to the area around Market and Chestnut Streets, between Front and 4th Streets, where some popular establishments can be found. Chinatown is home to several excellent restaurants, while some of the best family-owned trattorias are located in the Italian Market in south Philadelphia.

Numerous restaurants in the city's popular outdoor areas, such as Rittenhouse Square, Manayunk, and Chestnut Hill are stylish with upscale bistros and cafés. There are more than 200 restaurants here offering outdoor dining. Many are small, cozy establishments serving cocktails and trendsetting dishes in an ambience reminiscent of a Parisian café. Several restaurants and comfortable neighborhood bars are also located along Fairmount Avenue, close to the Museum of Art.

Cuba Libre in Old City recreates 1940s Havana *(see p146)*

Geno's Steaks on Philadelphia's 9th Street *(see p150)*

HOURS AND PRICES

Luncheonettes and coffee shops open early for breakfast and may stay open through lunch only, catering to office workers. Finer restaurants open for lunch and dinner, with lunch served from 11:30am to 2:30pm or 3pm, and dinner from 5:30pm until 10pm or 10:30pm, and often later on weekends. Late-night restaurants that are also nightclubs stay open until 2am, but may stop serving food earlier.

Breakfast at diners and eateries can cost anywhere from $5 to $10 with a tip, while hotel buffet breakfasts can cost from $10 to $20. Full Sunday brunches at upscale restaurants and hotels can range from around $20 to $30 or more per person.

A typical lunch ranges from on-the-go sandwiches and sodas, from $5 to $9, to sit-down meals at restaurants that will cost $8 to $15 with a tip. Dinner is usually the big meal of the day. Starters and salads cost $5 to $10. Entrées can run $12 to $28, and up to $40 or more at high-end steakhouses and restaurants. Desserts and wine by the glass usually cost $5 to $12.

Some ethnic restaurants offer great quality food at less expensive costs. Greek, Chinese, Indian, Mexican, and Middle Eastern restaurants serve very generous portions at reasonable prices, with meals costing up to $15 or more per person.

EATERIES AND FAST FOOD

Good pizza, salads, and sandwiches abound in Philadelphia. Many pizza shops sell individual slices, as well as "hoagies" and cheesesteaks. *Taquerias* near the Italian Market in South Philly offer authentic Mexican dishes at low prices. The Reading Terminal Market, at 11th and Arch Streets, offers a wide variety of inexpensive food.

ALCOHOL AND SMOKING

Many restaurants serve wine by the glass or bottle. Simple eateries and fast-food restaurants generally do not serve alcohol. Philadelphia is known for its "BYOB" restaurants that do not sell alcohol but allow patrons to "Bring Your Own Bottle" at no extra charge. Few restaurants that sell liquor allow diners to bring their own wine. Most will impose daunting "corkage" fees for the privilege.

Restaurants and bars in Pennsylvania and New Jersey must stop serving alcohol by 2am. The legal drinking age is 21, and ID may be required when entering a bar. All restaurants and bars are non-smoking.

RESERVATIONS AND DRESS

Reservations for dining at upscale restaurants are recommended, and are often required on weekend nights. Nonetheless, some popular spots may not reserve tables, and use waiting lists. Even if you have reservations, you might have to wait for up to an hour on busy days.

Casual wear is accepted at most city restaurants, although there are some trendy and fine-dining establishments that expect patrons to wear smart-casual styles or business attire, so it is best to check when making reservations.

TIPPING

At most restaurants, your wait-person will bring you your bill. A 15 percent tip is considered a minimum, with up to 20 percent or more for excellent service.

CHILDREN

Well-behaved children are usually welcome in restaurants. It is not recommended, however, to bring young children to establishments that have late-night crowds and a large bar area, as patrons aged 21 or younger may not be allowed inside.

A classy French restaurant interior in Philadelphia

Flavors of the Pennsylvania Dutch Country

Philadelphians savor the broad range of American and ethnic tastes from the many cultures that call the city home. Nearby Pennsylvania Dutch Country has its own unique flavors, comprising basic, hearty foods prepared from simple recipes. Amish and Mennonite cooks take advantage of the plentiful harvests to prepare dishes often characterized as good home cooking. To preserve the excess from the harvests, fresh country produce is both canned and jarred in homes and small shops, with much of it turned into tangy relishes and sweet jams. Such treats are available at various farmers' markets.

Corn-on-the-cob

Fresh produce at a farmer's market in Lancaster County

BOUNTIFUL HARVESTS

Amish and Mennonite food stems from the cultural tastes that the settlers brought from their home countries of Germany and Switzerland – recipes later adapted to the available crops that could be cultivated in the New World. Throughout the generations, the Amish have continued to nurture their gardens and fields through traditional methods with horse-drawn farming equipment. They grow all manner of fresh vegetables including corn, string beans, carrots, beets, onions, tomatoes, peppers, lettuce, potatoes, sweet potatoes, cauliflower, and more. Fruits include apples, cherries, plums, peaches, and sweet watermelon, with many used as ingredients for the delicious desserts that have made the Pennsylvania Dutch Country famous.

MEATS AND DELIS

Amish delis and restaurants feature a wide variety of cheeses, meats, and poultry, including fresh country sausages, sweet bologna, bacon, ham, dried beef and jerky, and smoked turkey. Cuts of fresh beef, pork, and chicken are favorites among the locals, who serve them up as part of tasty recipes such as scrapple, a dish that is made of pork, onions, cornmeal, and spices.

Molasses cookies · **Whoopie pie** · **Mincemeat cookies** · **Apple pie** · **Shoofly pie**

A selection of Pennsylvania Dutch Country cakes and desserts

LOCAL DISHES AND SPECIALITIES

Pennsylvania Dutch restaurants are known for their family-style buffets with meat dishes such as golden fried chicken, roast beef, chicken pot pie, and spicy sausage. Staples include mashed potatoes, home-made noodles and breads, and a choice of vegetables. Popular jellies and relishes include smooth apple butter, and Chow Chow, a mixture of sweet pickled vegetables. Amish recipes are handed down from mother to daughter to granddaughter, making for unique tastes. Dishes include Amish bean soup, corn fritters, spare ribs and sauerkraut, baking powder biscuits, cornmeal mush, and "Schnitz and Knepp," made with dried apples and ham. Popular desserts include Whoopie pie – chocolate cake surrounding white icing – and Shoofly pie, which has a coffeecake-like topping with a thick molasses bottom.

Fresh green apples

Chicken pot pie *comprises tender chicken pieces with vegetables and noodles, cooked in a pot of broth.*

Choosing a Restaurant

The restaurants in this guide have been selected for value, quality of food, atmosphere, and location. They are listed by area, starting with Philadelphia's Old City and moving on to restaurants farther away and beyond the city. All restaurants are non-smoking. For map references, *see pp194–97*.

PRICE CATEGORIES
The price ranges represent a three-course evening meal for one, a glass of house wine, tax, and service charges.

$ under $25
$$ $26–$35
$$$ $36–$50
$$$$ $51–$70
$$$$$ Over $70

OLD CITY

Ariana Restaurant $

134 Chestnut St, Philadelphia, PA, 19106 **Tel** *(215) 922-1535*   **Map** 4 E3

This small and cozy restaurant serves authentic Afghan cuisine featuring Kabuli *pulao* (rice with vegetables and meat), marinated lamb kebabs, and dishes scented with spices such as cinnamon and cumin. The decor includes ethnic photographs, creating a unique atmosphere. There is bay window seating for groups in traditional Afghan style.

Aromatic House of Kebob $

113 Chestnut St, Philadelphia, PA, 19106 **Tel** *(215) 923-4510*   **Map** 4 E3

A family-owned eatery in historic Old City, this restaurant features a comfortable café-like setting. It specializes in traditional Persian cooking, but also offers other popular fare such as *souvlaki* and *gyros* (Greek meat dishes) and kebabs. The restaurant usually stays open for patrons visiting the Old City in the late hours.

Franklin Fountain $

116 Market St, Philadelphia, PA, 19106 **Tel** *(215) 627-1899*   **Map** 4 E3

This ice-cream parlor seems to have time-traveled from a hundred years ago. Home-made ice creams, sodas, and other desserts are treats from another era. Prices are high but so is the quality; brave the lines and lack of air-conditioning for excellent sundaes (especially hot fudge), unique beverages, and old-fashioned decor. Cash only.

Q BBQ & Tequila $

207 Chestnut St, Philadelphia, PA, 19106 **Tel** *(215) 625-8605*   **Map** 4 E3

Credible versions of a variety of American barbecue cuisines are available here: Southern-style ribs, North Carolina pulled pork, Texas brisket. Also Tex-Mex specialties, good burgers, and a wide selection of tequilas. A small patio provides pleasant outdoor seating. Reasonable prices and a location near historical sights make this a popular spot.

The Bourse $

111 S Independence Mall E, Philadelphia, PA, 19106 **Tel** *(215) 625-0300*   **Map** 4 D3

The lobby of the Bourse, a historic 19th-century commodities exchange building *(see p156)*, is home to a food court and several souvenir shops. Its many eateries offer Chinese food, pizzas, cheesesteaks, sandwiches, burgers, and more. The food court is an ideal lunch venue for sightseers in Independence National Historic Park.

Aqua Malaysian & Thai Restaurant $$

705 Chestnut St, Philadelphia, PA, 19106 **Tel** *(215) 928-2838*   **Map** 4 D3

Malaysian and Thai cuisines are both represented here. The *Roti Canai*, a thin pancake-like bread served with a curry sauce for dipping, is a special treat. Classic Thai curries and noodle dishes are good choices as are the stew-like Malaysian Beef *Rendang* and (chicken) *Kari Ayam*. Plenty of options for vegetarians. BYOB.

Café Spice $$

35 S 2nd St, Philadelphia, PA, 19106 **Tel** *(215) 627-6273*   **Map** 4 E3

A trendy, vibrant bistro which gives a contemporary edge to traditional fare from all over India, such as kebabs and chicken tikka. Spacious interiors with modern decor and warm colors add to the chic and elegant atmosphere. The bar offers an extensive martini list. A DJ spins on weekends.

Han Dynasty $$

108 Chestnut St, Philadelphia, PA, 19106 **Tel** *(215) 922-1888*   **Map** 4 E3

Traditional Sichuan Chinese food, featuring the famous combination of chili heat and numbing peppercorn tingle. A long way from westernized Chinese-style food, this is authentic cooking. Spicy Dan Dan Noodles with ground pork, wontons in chili oil, lamb with cumin, and "Fish in Dry Pot" stand out. Some tamer dishes are available too.

Kabul Afghan Cuisine Restaurant $$

106 Chestnut St, Philadelphia, PA, 19106 **Tel** *(215) 922-3676*   **Map** 4 E3

This popular ethnic restaurant near the heart of Old City has traditional Afghan decor and a warm and welcoming atmosphere. The menu is replete with meat kebab and vegetarian specialties cooked with exotic Afghan spices. Call in advance to dine in traditional Afghan style on a platform with rugs and pillows. No lunch service.

Key to Symbols *see back cover flap*

The Continental Restaurant and Martini Bar

138 Market St, Philadelphia, PA, 19106 **Tel** *(215) 923-6069*

$$ Map *4 E3*

With its imaginative interior, the Continental is one of the hippest and most popular after-dark spots in the Old City's lively nightlife district. It serves contemporary cuisine with a pan-Asian flair, and has extensive martini, champagne, and wine lists. Latin and lounge music is played. Weekday lunch, weekend brunch, and daily dinner service.

Amada

217 Chestnut St, Philadelphia, PA, 19106 **Tel** *(215) 625-2450*

$$$ Map *4 E3*

A Spanish restaurant serving authentic tapas based on the earthy Mediterranean flavors that have long been the passion of founder and executive chef Jose Garces. The impressive menu of inspired creations gives guests the opportunity to mix and share multiple dishes. Signature tapas include octopus, garlic shrimps, and tortilla.

Chifa

707 Chestnut St, Philadelphia, PA, 19106 **Tel** *(215) 925-5555*

$$$ Map *4 D3*

`This offering from Ecuadorian-American chef Jose Garces puts a unique spin on traditional favorites and modern Asian-Fusion trends, while emphasizing Chinese and Peruvian cuisines. Don't miss the excellent *ceviches*, pork belly buns, or crisp roast chicken, accompanied by a Pisco Sour from the bar.

City Tavern

138 S 2nd St, Philadelphia, PA, 19106 **Tel** *(215) 413-1443*

$$$ Map *4 E3*

Authentic colonial-style cuisine, such as West Indies pepperpot soup, is served at this historically accurate reconstruction of the original 1773 tavern. Colonial ales brewed according to George Washington's and Thomas Jefferson's original recipes are also served. Three floors with colonial decor and staff in period costume.

Cuba Libre Restaurant and Rum Bar

10 S 2nd St, Philadelphia, PA, 19106 **Tel** *(215) 627-0666*

$$$ Map *4 E3*

Trendy and happening, this restaurant's spacious atrium reaches out onto the sidewalk for alfresco dining in warmer months. Bright colors and balconies evoke memories of 1940s Havana. Two bars and four dining rooms serve up contemporary Cuban and inventive Latin cuisine. Brunch is on offer on the weekend.

DiNardo's Famous Crabs

312 Race St, Philadelphia, PA, 19106 **Tel** *(215) 925-5115*

$$$ Map *4 E2*

A favorite since 1976, this seafood restaurant serves up excellent crabs in a casual and friendly atmosphere. Specialties include steamed Louisiana crabs served "hot and dirty" Baltimore-style, jumbo shrimp, stuffed flounder, and more. Located one block from St. George's Church and Fireman's Hall. No lunch service on Sunday.

Eulogy Belgian Tavern

136 Chestnut St, Philadelphia, PA, 19106 **Tel** *(215) 413-1918*

$$$ Map *4 E3*

This cozy pub and restaurant features an enormous selection of 185 international and Belgian beers. Traditional Belgian fare, including fish, meatballs, fries, and mussels, is prepared in five different sauces. The restaurant has limited wheelchair access and does not allow children after 8pm.

Serrano-Tin Angel

20 S 2nd St, Philadelphia, PA, 19106 **Tel** *(215) 928-0770*

$$$ Map *4 E3*

This stylish restaurant sits in a 1820s townhouse-like building with the popular folk music café, Tin Angel, on the second level. It offers international cooking, with specialties such as Malaysian pork chop, vegetable *kung pao*, and calamari. No lunch service.

Spasso Italian Grille

34 S Front St, Philadelphia, PA, 19106 **Tel** *(215) 592-7661*

$$$ Map *4 E3*

This old world-style trattoria is located across from Penn's Landing and features traditional Italian cuisine with dishes from both southern and northern Italy. Popular dishes include home-made pastas, fresh seafood, veal, and chicken. The restaurant sports a warm and casual atmosphere. No lunch service on the weekend.

The Plough & The Stars

207 Chestnut St, Philadelphia, PA, 19106 **Tel** *(215) 735-0300*

$$$ Map *4 E3*

This trendy Irish pub is housed in the Corn Exchange Building. The restaurant plays traditional Irish music on Sundays and has plenty of Guinness on tap. The fare, however, is not necessarily traditional but instead gourmet and creative. The pub has some outdoor seating in the warmer months.

Buddakan

325 Chestnut St, Philadelphia, PA, 19106 **Tel** *(215) 574-9440*

$$$$ Map *4 E3*

An Asian-Fusion restaurant, Buddakan has a traditonal menu with some more contemporary items. The *edamame* (soy bean) ravioli, wasabi tuna pizza, and miso-glazed black cod are enduring classics. A giant Buddha statue gazes over a dramatically illuminated communal table. This persists as one of the most striking dining rooms in the city.

Fork

306 Market St, Philadelphia, PA, 19106 **Tel** *(215) 625-9425*

$$$$ Map *4 E3*

Located in the heart of the Old City nightlife district, Fork offers a mix of casual sophistication and an urban, upscale style. It serves new American, bistro-style cuisine with an international flavor. Decor includes delicately painted velvet curtains and chandeliers. It also has a unique center bar. No lunch service on Saturday.

Key to Price Guide *see p145* **Key to Symbols** *see back cover flap*

Jones ☾ ♿ 🚸 🍸 $$$$

700 Chestnut St, Philadelphia, PA, 19106 ***Tel*** *(215) 223-5663* ***Map*** *4 D3*

Buffed-up versions of old-fashioned American comfort food served in a fun, retro setting and accompanied by goofy cocktails and a lively pop music soundtrack. Indulge your cravings for a Thanksgiving turkey dinner, mac and cheese, or chicken and waffles. Finish with a big piece of chocolate cake served with a glass of milk. Weekend brunch.

Ristorante Panorama and Il Bar 🚸 ♿ 🍸 $$$$

Front and Market Sts, Philadelphia, PA, 19106 ***Tel*** *(215) 922-7800* ***Map*** *4 E3*

This is an exquisite family-owned hotel *(see p134)* and restaurant near Penn's Landing. The bustling trattoria decorated with Florentine tiles and hand-painted murals features Italian food – home-made pastas and the finest cuts of veal. The unique "Il Bar" features the world's largest wine dispensing system and offers 120 wines by the glass.

Morimoto 🚸 ♿ ☾ 🍸 $$$$$

723 Chestnut St, Philadelphia, PA, 19106 ***Tel*** *(215) 413-9070* ***Map*** *4 D3*

This renowned restaurant's dining room is elegant and upscale with modern decor. One of the best fusion restaurants in Philadelphia, it brings contemporary Japanese cuisine to the table through Chef Morimoto's blending of traditional Japanese cooking with Western flair.

SOCIETY HILL AND PENN'S LANDING

Jim's Steaks 💳 🚸 ♿ ☾ $

400 South St, Philadelphia, PA, 19147 ***Tel*** *(215) 928-1911* ***Map*** *4 D4*

With its distinctive Art Deco storefront, Jim's is undoubtedly one of Philadelphia's busiest and most popular eateries. Long lines often stretch onto hip South Street as visitors and locals alike flock here for authentic Philly cheesesteaks with mounds of onions and dripping hot cheese. It also serves excellent hoagies.

South Street Souvlaki 🚸 ♿ 🍸 $

509 S St, Philadelphia, PA, 19147 ***Tel*** *(215) 925-3026* ***Map*** *4 D4*

One of the town's oldest and most popular Greek restaurants, this South Street icon recently celebrated its 25th anniversary. Specialties include classic Greek and Mediterranean cuisine, including lamb, seafood, and vegetarian dishes. Pleasant dining room and streetfront takeout window as well.

Marrakesh ♿ 🍸 $$

517 Leithgow St, Philadelphia, PA, 19147 ***Tel*** *(215) 925-5929* ***Map*** *4 D5*

At Marrakesh you can sit on cushioned pillows and enjoy an authentic seven-course Moroccan feast beginning with a hand-washing ritual and ending with a tea ceremony. The restaurant has a number of private dining rooms for hire, and belly dancers are available upon request.

Percy Street Barbecue ☾ ♿ 🚸 🍸 $$

600 S 9th St, Philadelphia, PA, 19147 ***Tel*** *(215) 625-8510* ***Map*** *3 C5*

A Texas-style barbecue joint right down to the red oak in the smokers, and the roadhouse feel of the room. The highlight is beef brisket: moist and tender with an assertive smoke flavor. Also on offer are pork ribs, chicken, and pork belly. Everything's served simply on butcher paper. Side dishes are good, and desserts are not to be missed.

Bridget Foy's 🚸 ♿ ☾ 🍸 $$$

200 South St, Philadelphia, PA, 19147 ***Tel*** *(215) 922-1813* ***Map*** *4 E5*

An American grill in the South Street district, it faces New Market and Head House Square. The menu offers American cuisine, with old standards such as steaks, fresh fish, burgers, and sandwiches. An outdoor café makes this great spot to break for lunch on bustling South Street.

Dark Horse Pub 🚸 ♿ ☾ 🍸 $$$

421 S 2nd St, Philadelphia, PA, 19147 ***Tel*** *(215) 928-9307* ***Map*** *4 E4*

A popular watering hole that doubles up as a restaurant. This colonial inn-style restaurant serves hearty pub fare, including steak and mushroom pie, as well as gourmet cuisine. It has five bars with a range of beers and wines. No lunch service on Monday.

Downey's 🚸 ♿ 🎵 ☾ 🍸 $$$

526 S Front St, Philadelphia, PA, 19147 ***Tel*** *(215) 625-9500* ***Map*** *4 E5*

Blessed with its great location at South and Front Streets, Downey's – a "drinking house and dining saloon" – has been a neighborhood mainstay since 1976. Pub decor includes antiques and Irish memorabilia, while the menu features hearty Irish stews and American fare. It is also a vibrant night spot.

Horizons 🚸 🍸 $$$

611 S 7th St, Philadelphia, PA, 19147 ***Tel*** *(215) 923-6117* ***Map*** *3 C4*

Horizons is an entirely vegan restaurant, yet the food here is so creative and hearty that even omnivores will leave satisfied. This is not austere good-for-you food based on deprivation; it's indulgent cuisine with big flavors. An extensive beer and wine list has also been vetted to be free of animal products.

Pizzeria Stella

$$\text{\$}\text{\$}\text{\$}$$

420 S 2nd St, Philadelphia, PA, 19147 **Tel** *(215) 320-8000*   **Map** *4 E4*

Neapolitan-style pizzas with creative toppings are the focus here. A traditional dome-shaped wood-burning oven is the centerpiece, and its high heat creates crisp pizza crusts in minutes. A few starters and salads balance the menu. Italian wine can be ordered by the glass. Save room for *gelato* (ice cream) for dessert.

Xochitl

$$\text{\$}\text{\$}\text{\$}$$

408 S 2nd St, Philadelphia, PA, 19147   **Map** *4 E4*

Contemporary Mexican cuisine, based on the traditions of the state of Puebla. Enticing snacks, vibrant *ceviches*, creative tacos and sandwiches, and a few fancier dishes show more sophistication than you'll find at the corner *taqueria*. The best margaritas in town are made from hand-squeezed limes and excellent tequila.

Southwark

$$\text{\$}\text{\$}\text{\$}\text{\$}$$

701 S 4th St, Philadelphia, PA, 19147 **Tel** *(215) 238-1888*   **Map** *4 D5*

The chef here has long-standing relationships with local farms, and serves only the freshest seasonal products. Vibrant flavors from the kitchen show the virtues of taking the farm-to-table movement seriously. At its handsome bar, housing a good selection of gin and rye whiskey, Southwark's bartenders concoct the best classic cocktails in town.

Zahav

$$\text{\$}\text{\$}\text{\$}\text{\$}$$

237 St James Pl, Philadelphia, PA, 19106 **Tel** *(215) 625-8800*   **Map** *4 E3*

Israeli street food given a gourmet spin. Modern techniques and excellent ingredients add extra gloss (and expense) to traditional snacks, salads, and kebabs. The chef's tasting menus offer an easy overview and good value. Don't miss the various types of hummus with freshly baked *laffa* bread, and lamb shoulder marinated in pomegranate juice.

Moshulu

$$\text{\$}\text{\$}\text{\$}\text{\$}\text{\$}$$

401 S Columbus Blvd, Philadelphia, PA, 19106 **Tel** *(215) 923-2500*   **Map** *4 F4*

Lovely fine-dining restaurant aboard a restored, century-old sailing ship moored off Penn's Landing. The four-masted vessel is ablaze with lights at night, and offers excellent river and skyline views from indoor dining rooms and from atop the deck in warmer months. Bar and deck menu also available.

CENTER CITY

Penang

$$\text{\$}$$

117 N 10th St, Philadelphia, PA, 19107 **Tel** *(215) 413-2531, (215) 413-2532*   **Map** *3 C2*

This trendy, storefront restaurant in the heart of Chinatown is always buzzing with activity. It has a predominantly Malaysian cuisine offering spicy curry and seafood dishes, along with some Thai, Indian, and Indonesian specialties as well. Also serves beer and wine.

Reading Terminal Market

$$\text{\$}$$

12th and Arch Sts, Philadelphia, PA, 19107 **Tel** *(215) 922-2317*   **Map** *3 C2*

Part farmers' market and part food court, the RTM offers everything from fresh produce to prepared meals. Highlights include DiNic's roast pork sandwich, Miller's Twist soft pretzels, Bassett's Ice Cream, and traditional Amish fare (Thu–Sat). Ethnic food stands are a good bet, or sample a classic "hoagie" (sandwich). Closes 5pm; some stands closed Sun.

Sakura Mandarin

$$\text{\$}$$

1038 Race St, Philadelphia, PA, 19107 **Tel** *(215) 873-8338*   **Map** *3 C2*

Regional Chinese food that rises above the watered-down Chinatown cliches. Specialties of Shanghai, such as *xiao long bao* (soup dumplings) and "lion's head" (pork) meatballs are joined by spicy Szechuan dishes and crowd-pleasing Cantonese favorites. Try the unusual thin scallion pancake. Surprisingly good sushi and other Japanese dishes, too.

El Vez

$$\text{\$}\text{\$}$$

121 S 13th St, Philadelphia, PA, 19103 **Tel** *(215) 928-9800*   **Map** *2 F3*

Dine on delicious, modern versions of traditional Mexican classics at this fashionable Center City restaurant. The made-to-order guacamole and the Mahi-Mahi tacos are highly recommended. There is also an extensive selection of drinks, including wonderful pomegranate margaritas.

Zavino

$$\text{\$}\text{\$}$$

112 S 13th St, Philadelphia, PA, 19107 **Tel** *(215) 732-2400*   **Map** *3 B3*

A large portion of the menu at this tiny casual wine bar is taken up by pizza, and these Neapolitan-style creations are a highlight. The domed oven creates a charred, puffy crust minimally topped with high-quality ingredients. But don't miss the chef's other offerings including vibrant salads, pastas, and daily specials of hearty country-style Italian fare.

The Black Sheep Irish Pub

$$\text{\$}\text{\$}\text{\$}$$

247 S 17th St, Philadelphia, PA, 19103 **Tel** *(215) 545-9473*   **Map** *2 E5*

Dine on hearty Irish stews and other favorites, including shepherd's pie, sandwiches, crab cakes, and more. Just one block from Rittenhouse Square, this pub and restaurant offers a relaxed atmosphere and has friendly staff. There are three floors with antique bars, and a drink selection from around the world. Wheelchair access limited to first level.

Key to Price Guide *see p145* **Key to Symbols** *see back cover flap*

Matyson
37 S 19th St, Philadelphia, PA, 19103 Tel (215) 564-2925 $$$ **Map 2 D4**

A consistent highlight of the Philly BYOB scene, this restaurant delivers interesting New American cuisine. Thematic, often whimsical, chef's tasting menus are available Mon–Thu at dinner and offer a wide variety of dishes and good value. The regular menu features fresh, high-quality, local ingredients. Open for lunch and dinner.

McCormick and Schmick's Seafood Restaurant
1 S Broad St, Philadelphia, PA, 19102 Tel (215) 568-6888 $$$ **Map 2 F4**

This upbeat and lively restaurant is an upscale fish house, located just across from historic City Hall. Features over 40 varieties of fresh fish that are flown in daily from both the Atlantic and Pacific Oceans. The two-story restaurant has a dark wood-paneled dining room accented by stained glass ceilings and mosaic floor.

Rouge
205 S 18th St, Philadelphia, PA, 19103 Tel (215) 732-6622 $$$ **Map 2 D5**

A hip bistro and popular late night spot in the swanky Rittenhouse Square area. They have wines of exquisite vintage and a trendsetting menu that is a cross between Continental, American, and French fare with contemporary seafood, poultry, and beef dishes. The biggest draw is the location, with outdoor seating facing the square.

Alma de Cuba
1623 Walnut St, Philadelphia, PA, 19103 Tel (215) 988-1799 $$$$ **Map 2 E5**

This cutting-edge restaurant, bar, and lounge brings modern Cuban cuisine to Philadelphia. Festive Cuban cocktails such as Mojitos and Daiquiris perfectly compliment the flavors, brilliant colors, and textures of the spectacular cuisine. Dishes include red bean soup with pumpkin and chorizo, and octopus *Escabeche* (pickled).

Amis
412 S 13th St, Philadelphia, PA, 19147 Tel (215) 732-2647 $$$ **Map 3 B4**

A relaxed neighborhood *trattoria* from acclaimed chef Marc Vetri. House-cured meats and terrines are a highlight, as are the tender meatballs based on the chef's father's recipe. The pastas are not to be missed. Thoughtful Italian wine list and full bar. Prices are expensive considering the casual feel, but the high caliber of cooking makes it good value.

Devon Seafood Grill
225 S 18th St, Philadelphia, PA, 19103 Tel (215) 546-5940 $$$$ **Map 2 D5**

A much-visited and comfortable restaurant, the Devon Seafood Grill serves fresh fish specialties, including Maryland crab cakes, pan-roasted Alaskan halibut, live Maine lobsters, Block Island swordfish, and more. The dining room is elegant. It is particularly popular in the warmer months with sidewalk seating facing Rittenhouse Square.

Oyster House
1516 Sansom St, Philadelphia, PA, 19102 Tel (215) 567-7683 $$$$ **Map 3 A3**

A classic Philadelphia fish house, The Oyster House offers modern versions of old favorites like clam chowder, snapper (turtle) soup, lobster rolls, and crabcakes. But the main attraction is the broad selection of fresh oysters, expertly shucked to order. Try an innovative cocktail or an Oyster House Punch on the side. Closed Sun.

Parc
227 S 18th St, Philadelphia, PA, 19103 Tel (215) 545-2262 $$$$ **Map 2 D5**

This stylish addition to Rittenhouse Square pays tribute to French café culture. Ideal for a light snack or a more leisurely meal, this French bistro offers many classics such as onion soup and escargots, as well as meat and fish platters and a choice of baguettes. Inside are red leather banquettes backed with panels of frosted glass for privacy.

The Prime Rib
1701 Locust St, Philadelphia, PA, 19103 Tel (215) 772-1701 $$$$ **Map 2 E5**

This upscale steakhouse is one of Philadelphia's best. Housed in the prestigious Radisson-brand Warwick Hotel *(see p136)*, its decor is reminiscent of a 1940s Manhattan supper club. Its specialties include aged prime rib, blue-ribbon steaks, extra thick chops, and fresh seafood. Children are allowed only on request. Formal dress required. No lunch service.

Tinto
116 S 20th St, Philadelphia, PA, 19103 Tel (215) 665-9150 $$$$ **Map 2 D4**

Tapas-style dining with a Basque flavor from chef Jose Garces. More elegant (and expensive) than the *pintxos* (snacks) you'd find at bars in northern Spain, these flavors still have a rustic power. Village Whiskey, Garces' speakeasy bar next door, offers an unmatched selection of spirits, skilled bartenders, and the best hamburgers in town.

Lacroix at the Rittenhouse
210 W Rittenhouse Square, Philadelphia, PA, 19103 Tel (215) 790-2533 $$$$$ **Map 2 D5**

Elegant restaurant on the second floor of the Rittenhouse Hotel *(see p136)* with stunning views of Rittenhouse Square. Decorated with minimalist and Asian theme, it serves French-American cuisine with options of three, four, or five courses, and diners can also create their own menus. Dessert complimentary as a gift from the chef.

Smith & Wollensky
210 W Rittenhouse Square, Philadelphia, PA, 19103 Tel (215) 545-1700 $$$$$ **Map 2 D5**

One of the top steakhouses Philadelphia has to offer. *The New York Times* referred to this high-end restaurant chain as "a steakhouse to end all arguments." Patrons are treated to up to 18 and 28-ounce cuts, good chops, salads, seafood, and an excellent wine list too. Located in the posh Rittenhouse Hotel *(see p136)*.

LOGAN SQUARE AND THE MUSEUM DISTRICT

Brigid's $\text{\textcircled{S}}\text{\textcircled{S}}$

726 N 24th St, Philadelphia, PA, 19130 **Tel** *(215) 232-3232*   **Map** *1 C1*

A friendly neighborhood pub with a rotating selection of local beers on tap, and an amazing list of bottled Belgian ales. A small dining room in the back serves affordable, comforting food from many cuisines, posted on blackboard menus. Mussels are a long-time favorite, as is the half a crispy duck *Chambord*, drizzled with raspberry sauce.

Illuminare $\text{\textcircled{S}}\text{\textcircled{S}}$

2321 Fairmount Ave, Philadelphia, PA, 19130 **Tel** *(215) 765-0202*   **Map** *2 D1*

From brick oven pizza to veal chops and filet mignon, this upscale restaurant serves wide-ranging Italian cuisine, which also includes fresh pastas and seafood. Housed in a renovated rowhouse, it has elegant decor that showcases stunning handcrafted woodwork, tile-work, and stained glass.

The Bishop's Collar $\text{\textcircled{S}}\text{\textcircled{S}}\text{\textcircled{S}}$

2349 Fairmount Ave, Philadelphia, PA, 19130 **Tel** *(215) 765-1616*   **Map** *2 D1*

This friendly corner watering hole and restaurant serves creative pub fare, along with a wide-ranging selection of beers and ales. Tables are set up outdoors in the warmer months. Situated a couple of blocks from the Philadelphia Museum of Art and the Kelly Drive walking path along Boathouse Row.

Jack's Firehouse $\text{\textcircled{S}}\text{\textcircled{S}}\text{\textcircled{S}}$

2130 Fairmount Ave, Philadelphia, PA, 19130 **Tel** *(215) 232-9000*   **Map** *2 D1*

This unique restaurant sits within a former firehouse building that still retains its original interiors – complete with a firemen's sliding pole and an expansive arched doorway. Popular chef-owner Jack McDavid uses fresh local ingredients for "down home" American fare, often accenting Southern cooking styles. Live music on the first Friday of each month.

London Grill $\text{\textcircled{S}}\text{\textcircled{S}}\text{\textcircled{S}}$

2301 Fairmount Ave, Philadelphia, PA, 19130 **Tel** *(215) 978-4545*   **Map** *2 D1*

Trendy and comfortable, this corner restaurant combines the coziness of a neighborhood pub with the elegance of fine dining. The menu changes daily, and dishes such as roasted chicken with garlic mashed potato cake, broccoli rosemary jus, and honey glazed grilled salmon are on offer. No lunch service on Saturday.

Rembrandt's $\text{\textcircled{S}}\text{\textcircled{S}}\text{\textcircled{S}}$

741 N 23rd St, Philadelphia, PA, 19130 **Tel** *(215) 763-2228, (800) 736-2726*   **Map** *2 D1*

Located near the Philadelphia Museum of Art, this elegant restaurant is known for its fine dining, accented by fabulous views of the city skyline. Specialties include creative seafood, meat, pasta, and vegetarian dishes. It also has a full tavern menu and eight draught beers on tap.

Zorba's Tavern $\text{\textcircled{S}}\text{\textcircled{S}}\text{\textcircled{S}}$

2230 Fairmount Ave, Philadelphia, PA, 19130 **Tel** *(215) 978-5990*   **Map** *2 D1*

Discover sumptuous Greek food at this family-owned restaurant. Paintings depicting old-world Greece add a special ambience to the authentic cuisine. It offers a full menu with lamb and seafood specialties, and all the traditional dishes. Located within walking distance of the Philadelphia Museum of Art and Boathouse Row. Closed Monday.

Water Works Restaurant and Lounge $\text{\textcircled{S}}\text{\textcircled{S}}\text{\textcircled{S}}\text{\textcircled{S}}$

640 Water Works Dr, Philadelphia, PA, 19130 **Tel** *(215) 448-2700*   **Map** *1 B1*

Built in 1812, the Fairmount Water Works building is now a national historic landmark overlooking the Schuylkill River. The restaurant's superb location and innovative American fusion cuisine makes for a fine dining experience and reservations are recommended. Wines are available by the glass.

Fountain Restaurant $\text{\textcircled{S}}\text{\textcircled{S}}\text{\textcircled{S}}\text{\textcircled{S}}\text{\textcircled{S}}$

1 Logan Sq, Philadelphia, PA, 19103 **Tel** *(215) 963-1500*   **Map** *2 E2*

Living up to the reputation of the posh Four Seasons Hotel *(see p137)*, this restaurant has been repeatedly rated as one of the city's best restaurants, serving Continental cuisine with delicate international influences. Elegant dining room with rich fabrics and warm woods. The restaurant offers splendid views of the Swann Fountain. Formal dress required.

FARTHER AFIELD

Geno's Steaks $\text{\textcircled{S}}$

1219 S 9th St, Philadelphia, PA, 19147 **Tel** *(215) 389-0659*

Geno's is one of Philadelphia's cheesesteak giants on the outskirts of the Italian Market. Founded in 1966 opposite Pat's King of Steaks, it serves delicious, piping hot cheesesteak sandwiches 24 hours a day, 7 days a week from a bright, neon-lit corner storefront.

Key to Price Guide *see p145* **Key to Symbols** *see back cover flap*

Pat's King of Steaks

1301 S 9th St, Philadelphia, PA, 19147 **Tel** *(215) 468-1547*

Founded in and family-owned since 1930, Pat's is known as the originator of the Philly cheesesteak with its sliced rib-eye steak, onions, cheese, and fresh Italian bread. In fact, locals will tell you it makes the city's best. Outside vendor windows and outside seating only. It is located at the Italian Market. Open 24 hours a day.

Chickie's and Pete's Café

1526 Packer Ave, Philadelphia, PA, 19145 **Tel** *(215) 218-0500*

This casual, south Philadelphia hotspot near the city's sports venues is always busy when the home teams play. Sightings of local personalities is common. The menu features crab fries, sandwiches, and cheesesteaks. Children have to be accompanied by adults after 10pm. A DJ plays recorded music.

Cantina Dos Segundos

931 N 2nd St, Philadelphia, PA, 19123 **Tel** *(215) 629-0500*

"Dos" and its older sibling in South Philadelphia, Cantina Los Caballitos, have developed reputations as fun places for pitchers of affordable specialty margaritas, but don't overlook the well-prepared Mexican food. Some dishes serves include hearty goat tacos, vegan fajitas, and authentic *moles*. Kitchen open until 1am. Brunch daily.

Cochon

801 E Passyunk Ave, Philadelphia, PA, 19147 **Tel** *(215) 923-7675*   **Map** *4 D5*

Unsurprisingly Cochon, French for pig, focuses its menu around pork. Indeed you can find tender braised pork shoulder with lentils and brussels sprouts, a variety of home-made sausages, and bacon flavoring almost everything. Large portions and bold flavors prevail. It's BYOB, so bring a hearty red from the Rhone, or perhaps a bright white from Alsace.

Jake's and Cooper's Wine Bar

4365-67 Main St, Manayunk, Philadelphia, PA, 19127 **Tel** *(215) 483-0444*

Choose from either the pioneering fine-dining restaurant Jake's or the casual and less expensive Cooper's Wine Bar to enjoy chef Bruce Cooper's creative cuisine. Pizzas covered with unconventional toppings, excellent burgers, and a thoughtful and affordable selection of wines by the glass make this a great place for a light dinner or a late-night bite.

Ralph's Italian Restaurant

760 S 9th St, Philadelphia, PA, 19147 **Tel** *(215) 627-6011*

Cozy, comfortable, and classy restaurant at the Italian Market. Owned and operated by four generations of the same family since 1900, this neighborhood restaurant is one of the city's most popular Italian eateries. It serves up classic red sauce and pastas, veal, poultry, seafood, and meat dishes, including the likes of Pork Chops Pizzaiola.

Standard Tap

901 N 2nd St, Philadelphia, PA, 19123 **Tel** *(215) 238-0630*

The original Philadelphia gastropub, this loud but cozy bar is great for sampling local beer on tap - it's the only kind they serve. Blackboard menus lack detail, but the food is artfully prepared. The burgers and pork sandwich are legendary. Their duck confit salad puts most French restaurants to shame. Finding a seat can be chaotic but it's worth the wait.

White Dog Café

3420 Sansom St, Philadelphia, PA, 19104 **Tel** *(215) 386-9224*

An eclectic University City café housed in three adjacent Victorian brownstones. On the menu is an unusual blend of contemporary American cuisine that uses fresh ingredients from local, self-reliant farmers. Music is played in the smoke-free piano parlor. The bar offers happy hours from 10pm to midnight Sunday through Thursday.

Distrito

3945 Chestnut St, Philadelphia, PA, 19104 **Tel** *(215) 386-1072*

Mexican food is given the tapas treatment by chef Jose Garces. Meticulous preparation and quality ingredients, like Kobe beef, elevate even the humble taco to new heights. Be sure to try the intense *moles*, vibrant *ceviches*, and creative cocktails. Prices can be high but the amusing decor (wrestling masks) and friendly service lighten the mood.

Pod

3636 Sansom St, Philadelphia, PA, 19104 **Tel** *(215) 387-1803*

Asian-Fusion cuisine and reliably good sushi served in a fun, futuristic setting. Color-changing seating pods, and a screen projecting Japanese cartoons set the scene for modern food. Japanese, Thai, and Chinese flavors predominate, with elaborate sushi platters and favorites like wasabi-crusted filet mignon.

BEYOND PHILADELPHIA

ATLANTIC CITY White House Sub Shop

2301 Arctic Ave, Atlantic City, NJ, 8401 **Tel** *(609) 345-1564*

An establishment in Atlantic City since 1946. Expect long lines, but it's worth the wait for classic submarine sandwiches. The "Special" (a large portion of various Italian cold cuts), tuna, and meatball subs are legendary. Some say their cheesesteak is better than those in Philadelphia. A half sandwich is huge, a whole sub could feed a family. Cash only.

ATLANTIC CITY Atlantic City Bar and Grill 🧒 ♿ 🌙 🍸 $$

1219 Pacific Ave, Atlantic City, NJ, 08401 ***Tel*** *(609) 348-8080, (609) 449-1991*

This family-owned restaurant opened more than 25 years ago and has become a favorite among locals, tourists, and even visiting celebrities and sports figures. Steaks, crabs, shrimp cocktail, lobsters, mussels, home-made pastas, pizzas, and sandwiches all feature on the menu. The spacious dining room has sports programming and is open until 4:30am.

ATLANTIC CITY Izakaya ♿ 🌙 🍸 $$$$

1 Borgata Way, Atlantic City, NJ, 08401 ***Tel*** *(609) 317-1000*

An ornate restaurant whose menu is inspired by the casual drinking and snacking culture of Japan. Chef Michael Shulson adds an elegant gloss to these simple foods. Try the gourmet dumplings, exotic meats cooked on a *robatayaki* grill, elaborate sushi rolls, and luxurious main dishes like Kobe sirloin or whole *branzino* (sea bass).

ATLANTIC CITY Primavera 🧒 ♿ 🌙 🍸 $$$$$

Caesars Casino, 2100 Pacific Ave, Atlantic City, NJ, 08401 ***Tel*** *(609) 348-4411, (800) 223-7272*

Fine dining with a range of northern Italian specialties and an extensive wine list in one of Atlantic City's best-known casino hotels, Caesars *(see p139)*. Try out the appetizer of oversized prawns with lemon-caper sauce. Intimate tables amidst artworks and murals of Venice enhance the ambience. Service is formal and reservations are required.

BRANDYWINE VALLEY Buckley's Tavern 🧒 ♿ 🍸 $$

5812 Kennett Pike, Centreville, DE, 19807 ***Tel*** *(302) 656-9776*

A favorite meeting place for locals in the Brandywine Valley, this tavern serves a variety of fine food, from the likes of Maryland crab cakes to Vietnamese shrimp salad. There is a popular outdoor dining patio. It is close to Longwood Gardens, Winterthur, and other attractions such as the Brandywine River Museum and Brandywine Battlefield.

BRANDYWINE VALLEY Chadds Ford Tavern and Restaurant 🧒 ♿ 🍸 $$$

US Rt 1 (1 mile south of Rt 202), Chadds Ford, PA, 19317 ***Tel*** *(610) 459-8453*

Family-owned and operated since 1968, this quaint country restaurant offers a menu ranging from home-made pub fare to fine food dishes. Housed in an 1830s tavern, the dining room is lit with hurricane candles and Tiffany lamps. Sample the crab cakes, a best-selling entrée. Reservations are recommended.

CAPE MAY The Black Duck ♿ $$$

1 Sunset Blvd, Cape May, NJ, 08204 ***Tel*** *(609) 898-0100*

Ask to dine on the patio if the weather's good. The sophisticated cooking here can feel a little dated, yet delicious. There's a wide array of seafood, much of it local, and plenty of other choices, including roast duck. Prices are high, but in line with comparable restaurants in the area. The BYO wine policy can save a few dollars.

CAPE MAY The Lobster House 🧒 ♿ 🍸 $$

Fisherman's Wharf, Cape May Harbor, Cape May, NJ, 08204 ***Tel*** *(609) 884-8296*

Feast on the region's freshest seafood in a picturesque dining room overlooking Cape May harbor, with many of the ingredients arriving in the kitchen via the restaurant's own boat. Cocktails can be enjoyed at dockside tables or on the deck of the 146-ft (50-m) *Schooner America*.

DOYLESTOWN Paganini Ristorante 🧒 ♿ 🍸 $$$

81 West State St, Doylestown, PA, 18901 ***Tel*** *(215) 348-5922*

A local favorite for fine Italian cuisine, this restaurant is in the heart of downtown Doylestown. It has several small dining rooms where patrons can ask for custom cooking such as fresh pastas and a variety of sauces. No dinner service on Saturday and no lunch service on Sunday.

GETTYSBURG Dobbin House Tavern 🧒 ♿ 🍸 $$$

89 Steinwehr Ave, Gettysburg, PA, 17325 ***Tel*** *(717) 334-2100*

This cozy and quaint colonial tavern and restaurant *(see p140)* date to 1776. Full of antiques, it has costumed servers and a historic ambience. The menu consists of old-fashioned hearty dishes such as charbroiled meats and fowl. It is located across from where Abraham Lincoln delivered the Gettysburg Address *(see p121)*.

GETTYSBURG Farnsworth House Inn 🧒 ♿ 🎵 🍸 $$$

401 Baltimore Ave, Gettysburg, PA, 17325 ***Tel*** *(717) 334-8838*

Quaint dining rooms housed in a historic 1810 Gettysburg in *(see p140)*, where over 100 bullet holes from the Civil War can still be seen. Period specialties include game pie, pumpkin fritters, peanut soup, and sweet potato pudding. It features dinner theater every Friday and Saturday evening from December through February.

GETTYSBURG Herr Tavern and Public House 🧒 ♿ 🍸 $$$$

900 Chambersburg Rd, Gettysburg, PA, 17325 ***Tel*** *(717) 334-4332*

Once used as the first Confederate hospital during the Battle of Gettysburg, this 1815 country inn is now a B&B with five elegantly decorated dining rooms. The menu offers carefully prepared meat and seafood entrées served with tasteful garnishes and sauces. Reservations are required on weekends. No lunch service on Sunday.

HARRISBURG Appalachian Brewing Company 🌙 🍸 $$

50 N Cameron St, Harrisburg, PA, 17010 ***Tel*** *(717) 221-1080*

The first brewpub in Pennsylvania's state capital is located in an impressive, historic three-story brick-and-timber building. Along with a large selection of handcrafted ales and lagers there is also an innovative menu, with plenty of tasty choices to complement your drinks.

Key to Price Guide *see p145* **Key to Symbols** *see back cover flap*

HERSHEY Lebbie Lebkicher's at Hershey Lodge $$

West Chocolate Ave and University Dr, Hershey, PA, 17033 **Tel** *(717) 533-3311, (800) 437-7439*

This casual and friendly restaurant, located in the Hershey Lodge, offers full hot and cold buffets ranging from salads and soups to seafood and prime rib selections. A special buffet is set up for children with pizzas, chicken nuggets, macaroni and cheese, and other kid favorites. Near Hershey Park and other attractions.

KING OF PRUSSIA California Café Bar & Grill $$$

The Plaza at King of Prussia Mall, 160 N Gulph Road, King of Prussia, PA, 19406 **Tel** *(610) 354-8686*

Buttercup yellow walls and funky sea-green architectural details set the tone for this cool California-style restaurant, part of a countrywide dining chain. Eclectic and themed menu offering "savory" American fare, all of which is prepared with fresh, regional foods of the season. An upbeat dining experience while at the King of Prussia Mall.

NEW HOPE Havana $$$

105 S Main St, New Hope, PA, 18938 **Tel** *(215) 862-9897*

Casual, fun dining and drinking on the main street. The large patio is great for people-watching in good weather. Outdoor heaters, live bands, and DJs make it a vibrant spot all year long. The food is not the draw here, but simple nachos, sandwiches, and salads are good fillers. Everything's overpriced, but in New Hope, it's expected.

NEW HOPE The Landing $$$

22 N Main St, New Hope, PA, 18938 **Tel** *(215) 862-5711*

Elegant dining with dramatic views of the Delaware River. In the summer the deck is the place to be, but the dining room is also welcoming and comfortable. Simple snacks, salads, and sandwiches are given the same attention as the more sophisticated pastas, steaks, and seafood dishes. Kids' menu available. Open seven days a week.

NEW HOPE Logan Inn Restaurant $$$$

10 W Ferry St, New Hope, PA, 18938 **Tel** *(215) 862-2300*

A fine-dining restaurant in a historic inn dating back to 1727, Logan Inn is one of the five oldest in the US. Located in the heart of New Hope, it features a lovely dining room and a porch that offers views of the bustling town center. Carefully prepared duck, seafood, beef, and pasta specialties available.

PENNSYLVANIA DUTCH COUNTRY Plain and Fancy Farm Restaurant $

3121 Old Philadelphia Pike, Bird-In-Hand, PA, 17505 **Tel** *(717) 768-4400*

Everyday is like grandmother's home cooking at this popular family-style restaurant near the Amishview Inns *(see p141)* in the Pennsylvania Dutch Country. Friendly pass-the-platter dining features roast beef, golden fried chicken, baked Lancaster County sausage, mashed potatoes, shoofly pie, apple dumplings, and more.

PENNSYLVANIA DUTCH COUNTRY The Family Cupboard Restaurant $

3029 Old Philadelphia Pike, Bird-in-Hand, PA, 17534 **Tel** *(717) 768-8886*

Amish and Mennonite home cooking does not get much better than this. Daily specials and full lunch and dinner buffets feature made-from-scratch pies and dishes from fresh farm vegetables such as green beans and carrots, mashed potatoes, and ham, chicken, and beef. Great for family dining.

PENNSYLVANIA DUTCH COUNTRY Kling House Restaurant $$

Rt 340, Intercourse, PA, 17534 **Tel** *(717) 768-8261*

This popular restaurant offers unique Pennsylvania Dutch Country and American fare with home-made jellies and relishes made at the adjoining Kitchen Kettle Village. House specials include portabella mushroom focaccia and grilled pita-pizza, among others. Closed Sunday.

PENNSYLVANIA DUTCH COUNTRY Miller's Smorgasbord $$

2811 Lincoln Hwy E (Rt 30), Ronks, PA, 17572 **Tel** *(717) 687-6621*

Sample a wide range of Pennsylvania Dutch treats and eat as much as you want at this buffet-style eatery – a tradition since 1929. Chilled steamed shrimp and carved top sirloin, turkey, chicken pot pie, and fresh bakery desserts are favorites. No lunch service. Breakfast is served only on Sunday mornings starting at 8am. Located on busy Route 30.

PENNSYLVANIA DUTCH COUNTRY 1764 Restaurant $$$

14 E Main St, Lititz, PA, 17543 **Tel** *(717) 626-2115*

An elegant dining room with colonial decor adds to the charm of this restaurant within the landmark 18th-century General Sutter Inn. Black Angus beef, oversized chops, seafood, fowl, and pasta highlight the menu's fine food selections. Breakfast specialties include farm fresh eggs and grilled cinnamon buns.

PENNSYLVANIA DUTCH COUNTRY Historic Revere Tavern $$$

3063 Lincoln Hwy E, Paradise, PA, 17562 **Tel** *(717) 687-8601*

Built in 1740, this tavern was once owned by the 15th US president, James Buchanan. Casual dining in a colonial atmosphere with fireplaces. Seafood, steaks, and unique snapper turtle soup highlight the menu. Along busy Route 30 in the Pennsylvania Dutch Country. No lunch service on Sunday and Monday.

WASHINGTON CROSSING Washington Crossing Inn $$$$

1295 Washington Memorial Rd, Washington Crossing, PA, 18977 **Tel** *(215) 493-3634*

Dating to 1817, this restaurant sits near where General Washington crossed the Delaware River in 1776. New-style American cuisine is served in a colonial ambience. Chops, steaks, and seafood are very well prepared. Lunch menu includes radicchio and arugala salad, grilled rib-eye steak, and smoked turkey breast arugala.

SHOPS AND MARKETS

The Philadelphia area is a stronghold for shopping with stores and outlets ranging from specialty boutiques, grand shopping centers, and malls to discount retailers and factory stores. Key shopping areas mentioned on the following pages include Center City's boutiques and shops on Market and Walnut Streets, and the shops and galleries in Old City and in the chic district

Precious gems at Jewelers' Row

of South Street. Situated in downtown Philadelphia are Antique Row and Jewelers' Row, while a variety of upscale and trendy shops are the highlights on the main streets of Manayunk and Chestnut Hill. The King of Prussia Mall is one of the nation's largest retail shopping complexes, while the cities of Reading and Lancaster have perhaps the largest number of factory outlet stores in the country.

SHOPPING HOURS

Most retailers in central Philadelphia are open seven days a week, from 10am to 6pm on Mondays through Saturdays with some varying hours, and from noon until 5pm or 6pm on Sundays. Many Center City stores are open for an extra hour or two on Wednesday nights and sometimes on Friday nights.

Outside the city, individual retail stores usually have similar hours from 10am to 6pm. Malls, however, are often open until 9pm or 9:30pm Monday through Saturday, and noon until 6pm or 7pm on Sundays. Some specialty stores have reduced hours on weekends, or may close one or two days during the week.

The popular VF Outlet Village in Reading, Pennsylvania

Storefronts on a street in Chestnut Hill, Philadelphia

TAXES

There is no sales tax on clothing and shoes in Pennsylvania. For all other items, there is a 6 percent state sales tax and an additional 1 percent tax within Philadelphia, adding up to a 7 percent sales tax when shopping in the city. However, no sales tax is levied if your purchases are shipped to an address outside Pennsylvania, but additional shipping fees may apply. Foreign visitors may have to pay duties on larger purchases they wish to take home.

SALES

Finding a sale in the US is as easy as picking up a local newspaper – especially on weekends. Most large retailers compete on a daily basis, with many regularly slashing prices. Smaller stores may have clearance racks with reduced items, while sales are often more limited in trendy shops and high-end boutiques. The nation's "biggest shopping day of the year" occurs on the day after Thanksgiving and is called "Black Friday," when prices are cut by 70 percent or more. Similar sales take place after Christmas.

PAYMENT

Except for the smallest stores, major credit cards are accepted at most shops, boutiques, and retail outlets. In fact, department stores usually issue their own credit cards for return shoppers, though these are often issued at higher interest rates. In the US, the major credit cards accepted are Visa, Master Card, American Express, Discover Card, and Diners Club.

Cash is always accepted, and identification is necessary when using traveler's checks. Personal checks are discouraged, unless drawn from a local or well-known US bank. Stores do not accept foreign currency.

RETURNING MERCHANDISE

Most shops and stores will-willingly issue refunds and credits for returns, providing the merchandise is in good condition and not used or damaged. Sales receipts must accompany goods. Time limits for returns vary from store to store, with most allowing between 10 to 30 days. Be aware, however, that certain items purchased during special sales or promotions are non-returnable, and that some stores will issue in-store-credit returns only and not cash.

A couple enjoying shopping

DEPARTMENT STORES

There is no shortage of world-class department stores in the Philadelphia area, with most concentrated in the **King of Prussia Mall** *(see p156)*, Center City, and a few other area malls.

The historic Wanamaker Building *(see p70)* at 13th and Market Streets was named after Pennsylvanian John Wanamaker, a businessman who is considered to be the father of the department store. This Italian Renaissance-style building has housed many of the best department stores since its completion in 1910. Today, **Macy's** Center City occupies this impressive space. This flagship store features high-end designers and affordable brand names. It also has a full-service Visitors' Center where shoppers can make dinner reservations and get information on the city's attractions. Another upmarket retail giant to open its doors in Center City is **Barney's** and in the King of Prussia Mall, the high-end department store **Neiman Marcus** offers the ultimate shopping experience with some of the best names in fashion in women's apparel, accessories, shoes, and jewelry. The same is true for children's and men's clothing. The store also offers quality bed and bath items, novelty rugs, and furniture.

Nordstrom, another leading fashion specialty store, offers high-quality gifts, apparel, shoes, and beauty products from several hundred brand names. High fashion, stylish accessories, and the latest fragrances can be found at **Bloomingdale's**, which also stocks a wide range of house gifts, luggage, and more. **JCPenney** has a broad range of apparel, shoes, and gifts for men, women, and children. **Sears** is also one of the nation's best-known department stores, known for its large appliances, tools, lawn and garden gear, automobile repair services, and household services. The King of Prussia Mall also has another branch of Macy's.

Interior of King of Prussia Mall, a retail shopping complex

Interior of Shops at Liberty Place, a shopping mall in Center City

MALLS

There are several indoor malls in and around Philadelphia, allowing people to enjoy and indulge in year-round shopping, dining, and entertainment.
The Gallery at Market East, the city's largest mall, is located in Center City along Market Street between 8th and 12th Streets. The four-level mall connects with both the Pennsylvania Convention Center and Market East Station. It houses another 130 shops and eateries, and more than 30 pushcarts stocked with merchandise ranging from sunglasses and artworks to household wares and all manner of eclectic items.

The **King of Prussia Mall**, located in a suburb to the northwest of the city, is accessible via the Schulykill Expressway and is a 30-minute drive from Center City. With seven department stores (see p155) and vast parking lots and garages, it is one of the nation's largest retail shopping complexes comprising two separate sections: The Plaza and The Court. Expansive buildings with elaborate glass-ceiling atriums house more than 360 specialty

shops, and an array of 40 restaurants and eateries. Nearby, Mall Boulevard has a good selection of retail and wholesale stores, and a multi-screen movie complex. North of the city, along Route 1 in Bensalem, is the **Neshaminy Mall**, which includes 125 stores, restaurants, and a colossal 24-screen cinema complex.

SPECIALTY SHOPPING CENTERS

Groups of specialty shops are housed in large central Philadelphia buildings, offering visitors and office workers easy access to shopping – especially during the lunch hour or after work.

With offices and the luxury Park Hyatt hotel above it, the century-old **Bellevue Building** in Center City has a host of upscale boutiques, world-class restaurants, a spa, a food court with the classic American steakhouse, The Palm, and more to offer. Also in Center City, the **Shops at Liberty Place** features 60 shops that sell fine apparel, shoes, jewelry, specialty foods, and beauty products.

An impressive glass dome sits atop a circular rotunda – all part of the complex that makes up Liberty Place (see p79).
The Bourse Food Court and Specialty Shops is in the heart of Independence Mall, directly across from the Liberty Bell Center. The Bourse offers tourists in Old City a break from sightseeing itineraries with gift and souvenir shops and a food court.

SHOPPING DISTRICTS

Clusters of shops and restaurants in popular neighborhoods are known as shopping districts. One of Center City's most chic areas, **Rittenhouse Row**, includes upscale establishments along Walnut Street leading up to Rittenhouse Square (see p78). Several restaurants have storefronts facing the square, with outdoor seating in summer.

Anchored by New Market and Head House Square, **South Street** (see p67) offers a diversity of stores, shops, restaurants, eateries, and bars. Many of these cater to the avant-garde and eclectic trends of the younger crowds that often cram the area along South Street from Front to 11th Streets.
Main Street Manayunk (see p97) is very popular on weekends for its many restaurants, pubs, and nightlife. Clothes and shoe shops, salons, antique shops, and a

Shops and boutique windows at Main Street Manayunk

Shop sign at Manayunk

host of boutiques and galleries also line Main Street.

In **Chestnut Hill** *(see p96)*, more than 100 boutiques, galleries, antiques stores, restaurants, and cafés take up nearly a dozen blocks along Germantown Avenue. **Jewelers' Row** and **Antique Row** span several blocks in Center City.

MARKETS

The city's central farmers' market is the popular **Reading Terminal Market** *(see p73)*, where vendors sell farm-fresh produce, meats, poultry and seafood, flowers, pastries, and baked goods. Amish specialties and ethnic dishes representing the city's diverse population are particularly popular.

The nation's oldest and largest outdoor market, the **Italian Market** *(see p99)*, features several blocks of vendors who sell seafood, fresh produce, meats, Italian specialties, and desserts. The area is home to some of the city's best Italian restaurants.

To savor some delicious, home-style cooking of the Pennsylvania Dutch Country,

Vendors at the Italian Market, one of the city's oldest outdoor markets

take some time to drive out to the small villages of Bird-In-Hand and Intercourse. **The Amish Barn Restaurant and Gift Shop**, for instance, offers authentic local food as well as handicrafts and souvenirs.

DISCOUNT AND OUTLET MALLS

Located in an area northeast of Philadelphia is the **Franklin Mills Mall**, home to more than 200 retail and factory stores such as Last Call, Neiman Marcus, Ann Taylor, and Factory Store. Its outlets include those for Casual Corner, Saks Fifth

Avenue, Polo Ralph Lauren, JCPenney, and many others.

A complex of restored old factory buildings, **VF Outlet Village** in Reading is one of the county's largest groupings of factory store outlets. Several multistory buildings house discounted clothing, shoes, and household wares from Vanity Fair, Wrangler, Lee, Liz Claiborne, London Fog, Tommy Hilfiger, and Reebok.

Atlantic City Outlets, The Walk, in New Jersey, has merchandise from manufacturers, including Van Heusen, Guess, Geoffrey Beene, Casual Corner, and Brooks Brothers, at reduced prices.

DIRECTORY

MALLS

The Gallery at Market East
Market St between 9th & 11th Sts. **Map** 3 C2.
Tel (215) 625-4962.

King of Prussia Mall
Rt 202 & Mall Blvd, King of Prussia.
Tel (610) 337-1210.

Neshaminy Mall
1 & Bristol Rd, Bensalem.
Tel (215) 357-6100.

SPECIALTY SHOPPING CENTERS

The Bourse Food Court and Specialty Shops
111 S. Independence Mall East. **Map** 4 D3.
Tel (215) 625-0300.

The Shops at the Bellevue
200 S Broad St. **Map** 2 F5.
Tel (215) 875-8350.

Shops at Liberty Place
16th & Chestnut Sts.
Map 2 E4.
Tel (215) 851-9055.

SHOPPING DISTRICTS

Antique Row
Pine St between 9th & 17th Sts. **Map** 3 B4.

Chestnut Hill
7600–8700 Germantown Ave, Chestnut Hill.
Tel (215) 247-6696.

Jewelers' Row
Sansom St between 7th & 8th Sts; and 8th St from Chestnut to Walnut Sts.
Map 3 C3.
Tel (215) 627-1834.

Main Street Manayunk
Main Street, Manayunk.
Tel (215) 482-9565.

Rittenhouse Row
Area around Rittenhouse Square. **Map** 2 D5.
Tel (215) 972-0101.

South Street
South St from Front to 11th Sts. **Map** 3 B4.
Tel (215) 413-3713.

MARKETS

The Amish Barn Restaurant and Gift Shop
3029, Old Philadelphia Pike, Rte 340, Bird-in-Hand, PA.
Tel (717) 768-3220.

Italian Market
9th St between Christian & Wharton Sts. **Map** 3 C5.
Tel (215) 922-5557.

Reading Terminal Market
12th & Arch Sts.
Map 3 B2.
Tel (215) 922-2317.

DISCOUNT AND OUTLET MALLS

Atlantic City Outlets, The Walk
Michigan Ave between Pacific & Baltic Aves, Atlantic City, NJ.
Tel (609) 872-7002.

Franklin Mills Mall
1455 Franklin Mills Circle, PA.
Tel (215) 632-1500.

VF Outlet Village
801 Hill Avenue, Reading, PA.
Tel (610) 378-0408.

Fashion and Accessories

Center City is Philadelphia's main shopping district with more than 2,100 retail stores. Many offer the finest in clothes, shoes, accessories, and jewelry. Key fashion shops and boutiques are located along Walnut Street on Rittenhouse Row. Designer clothing stores are also found at the Gallery at Market East mall, as well as within the small shopping centers at the Bellevue Building and Liberty Place. When looking for the latest in high fashion, do not forget the department stores and specialty stores at the King of Prussia Mall.

Entrance to the upmarket shops in Liberty Place

WOMEN'S FASHION

With so many stores and boutiques to choose from, women will be delighted with a shopping spree in Center City. Located just one block from Rittenhouse Square on Walnut Street, **Jones New York** offers a range of fine apparel. Nearby, the **Knit Wit** boutique carries a variety of elegant black cocktail dresses as well as cruise-wear. **Ann Taylor**, on the same block, has upbeat and high-fashion designs for both business and pleasure. **Ann Taylor Loft**, **Express**, and lingerie store **Victoria's Secret** are also at Liberty Place.

The number of women's apparel stores in the King of Prussia Mall is extensive and you will need plenty of time to get round them all. In addition to Victoria's Secret and Ann Taylor, there are upscale stores from top international designers, the latest classic and trendy fashions from **New York and Company** and **Lane Bryant**, and the risqué designs of **Frederick's of Hollywood**.

Main Street Manayunk features several women's clothing boutiques. **Showing with Style** offers fashionable maternity clothes, while Nicole Miller and **Paula Hian Designs** stock upscale evening wear for women.

MEN'S FASHION

Men looking for the perfect suit or designer clothing will not leave the city empty handed. **Boyds Philadelphia** has been around for over 60 years and is one of Center City's premier stores. One of the most elegant shops at the Bellevue, **Polo Ralph Lauren** has a full line of clothing from the world-renowned designer. Men will also find a variety of stores at the Shops at Liberty Place, including **Jos. A. Bank**, **Les Richard's Mensware**, and **Andrew's Ties**.

In the King of Prussia Mall, **Hugo Boss Store** features the label's clothing, sportswear, and accessories. Other popular men's stores include **Bachrach**, which is one of the nation's largest privately owned retailers, and **Talbots Mens** with its line of casual wear and outerwear.

MEN'S AND WOMEN'S FASHION

With shops in the Bellevue Building and Manayunk, **Nicole Miller** features men's and women's formalwear, as well as accessories. A line of both casual and dressy apparel can be found at **J. Crew** and **Express** at the Shops at Liberty Place, while casual wear is the highlight of **Old Navy** and **Gap** at the Gallery at Market East. **Guess** features more trendsetting clothing at the same mall. At King of Prussia, **Brooks Brothers** sells traditional, fine-quality apparel. **Eddie Bauer** features winter clothes, while **Banana Republic** offers casual jeans and dressy jackets. Other popular outlets include **Abercrombie & Fitch**, and the hip styles of **Diesel**.

Casual sneakers

SHOES AND ACCESSORIES

Featuring a line of fur, shearling, leather, and cloth, **Jacques Ferber** on Walnut Street offers unique outerwear. **Touches**, in Center City, has many one-of-a-kind varieties of jewelry, picture frames, and scarves.

For men's shoes, **Sherman Brothers** offers a wide selection of top brands and hard-to-find sizes. Both men's and women's choices for shoes abound in the King of Prussia Mall, with stores including **Bakers**, **Kenneth Cole**, **Rockport**, **Timberland**, **Bostonian**, and **Johnston Murphy**.

Window shopping at one of Center City's numerous upscale boutiques

JEWELRY

Philadelphia's Jewelers' Row was established in 1851, and is the nation's oldest and one of the largest diamond districts. Stores on the row include a seemingly unlimited selection of diamonds, rubies, sapphires, and emeralds. Owned by the same family for four generations, **Barsky Diamonds** specializes in diamonds. **Safian and Rudolph Jewelers**, in business for over 50 years, deals in precious stones, while **Tiffany & Co.**, in Center City, has offered the finest in jewelry, crystal, and accessories for more than 150 years. Other prominent Center City jewelers include **Govberg Jewelers** and **LAGOS The Store**.

DIRECTORY

WOMEN'S FASHION

Ann Taylor
1713 Walnut St.
Map 2 E5.
Tel (215) 977-9336.
King of Prussia Mall.
Tel (610) 354-9380.

Ann Taylor Loft
Liberty Place. **Map** 2 E4.
Tel (215) 557-9181.
King of Prussia Mall.
Tel (610) 337-1550.

Daffy's
1700 Chestnut St.
Map 2 E4.
Tel (215) 963-9996.

Frederick's of Hollywood
King of Prussia Mall.
Tel (610) 265-1499.

Jones New York
1711 Walnut St.
Map 2 E5.
Tel (215) 864-0110.

Knit Wit
1718 Walnut St.
Map 2 E5.
Tel (215) 564-4760.

Lane Bryant
King of Prussia Mall.
Tel (610) 265-6106.

New York and Company
King of Prussia Mall.
Tel (610) 354-0560.

Paula Hian Designs
106 Gay St, Manayunk.
Tel (215) 487-2762.

Showing with Style
4321 Main St, Manayunk.
Tel (267) 297-7035.

Victoria's Secret
Liberty Place. **Map** 2 E4.
Tel (215) 564-1142.
King of Prussia Mall.
Tel (610) 337-0788.

MEN'S FASHION

Andrew's Ties
1625 Chestnut St. **Map** 2 E4. *Tel (215) 988-1260.*

Bachrach
King of Prussia Mall.
Tel (610) 265-0159.

Hugo Boss Store
King of Prussia Mall.
Tel (610) 992-1400.

Boyds Philadelphia
1818 Chestnut St.
Map 2 D4.
Tel (215) 564-9000.

Jos. A. Bank
Liberty Place. **Map** 2 E4.
Tel (215) 563-5990.
King of Prussia Mall.
Tel (610) 337-2131.

Les Richard's Mensware
1625 Chestnut St. **Map** 2 E4. *Tel (215) 751-1155.*

Polo Ralph Lauren
200 S Broad St. **Map** 2 F5.
Tel (215) 985-2800.

Senor
4390 Main St, Manayunk.
Tel (215) 487-3667.

Talbots Mens
King of Prussia Mall.
Tel (610) 962-0881.

MEN'S AND WOMEN'S FASHION

Abercrombie & Fitch
King of Prussia Mall.
Tel (610) 265-5650.

Banana Republic
1401 Walnut St. **Map** 2 F5. *Tel (215) 751-0292.*
King of Prussia Mall.
Tel (610) 768-9007.

Brooks Brothers
1513 Walnut St. **Map** 2 E5. *Tel (215) 564-4100.*
King of Prussia Mall.
Tel (610) 337-9888.

Diesel
King of Prussia Mall.
Tel (610) 768-5855.

Express
Liberty Place. **Map** 2 E4.
Tel (215) 851-0699.
King of Prussia Mall.
Tel (610) 337-8912.

Gap
1510 Walnut St.
Map 3 C2.
Tel (215) 732-3391.

Guess
The Gallery at Market East, Market St between 9th & 11th Sts. **Map** 3 C2.
Tel (215) 627-2229.
1520 Walnut St. **Map** 3 A3. *Tel (215) 875-8525.*

J. Crew
Liberty Place. **Map** 2 E4.
Tel (215) 940-2711.

Nicole Miller
200 S Broad St. **Map** 2 F5.
Tel (215) 546-5007.
4249 Main Street, Manayunk.
Tel (215) 930-0307.

Old Navy
The Gallery at Market East, Market St between 9th & 11th Sts. **Map** 3 C2.
Tel (215) 413-7012.

SHOES AND ACCESSORIES

Bostonian
King of Prussia Mall.
Tel (610) 265-4323.

Jacques Ferber
1708 Walnut St.
Map 2 E5.
Tel (215) 735-4173.

Johnston Murphy
King of Prussia Mall.
Tel (610) 265-0165.

Kenneth Cole
1420 Walnut St. **Map** 2 E5. *Tel (215) 790-1690.*
King of Prussia Mall.
Tel (610) 337-2650.

Nine West
Liberty Place.
Map 2 E4.
Tel (215) 851-8570.

Rockport
King of Prussia Mall.
Tel (610) 265-5800.

Sherman Brothers Shoes
1520 Sansom St.
Map 2 E4.
Tel (215) 561-4550.

Timberland
King of Prussia Mall.
Tel (610) 265-2193.

JEWELRY

Barsky Diamonds
724 Sansom St.
Map 4 D3.
Tel (215) 925-8639.

Govberg Jewelers
1818 Chestnut St.
Map 2 E5.
Tel (215) 546-6505.

LAGOS The Store
1735 Walnut St.
Map 2 E4.
Tel (215) 567-0770.

Safian & Rudolph Jewelers
701 Sansom St.
Map 4 D3.
Tel (215) 627-1834.

Tiffany & Co.
1414 Walnut St.
Map 2 E5.
Tel (215) 735-1919.

Specialty Shops

With shopping districts, upscale shops, and one-of-a-kind stores, central Philadelphia has a wide range of merchandise that would satisfy even the hard-to-please shopper. Many specialty shops and gift stores specialize in finding the perfect gift or souvenir. Antique Row has numerous stores along an eight-block stretch in Center City, while in Old City sits a large cluster of art galleries. Other key shopping areas with unique crafts, books, and flower stores include Manayunk and Chestnut Hill. The colossal King of Prussia Mall has a seemingly unending choice of everything, from home furnishings and electronics to sporting goods.

![Shops located in the Chestnut Hill market area]

Shops located in the Chestnut Hill market area

ANTIQUES

Spread over eight blocks on Pine Street between 7th and 11th Streets, Antique Row *(see p157)* features boutiques and shops offering a selection of fine furniture, period antiques, collectibles, estate jewelry, and vintage clothing. One such store is **M. Finkel & Daughter**, which sells period furniture, 17th- to 19th-century needlework, and decorative accessories. The nearby **Classic Antiques** offers a large selection of country French furniture, mirrors, and accessories as well as 18th- and 19th-century European antiques. The **South Street Antiques Market** is the city's only indoor antiques market with 27 dealers selling pieces from vintage Victorian to modern, including estate jewelry, furniture, pottery, and accessories.

ART GALLERIES

The Old City Arts Association has 50 members, including art galleries, which are open until 9pm on the first Friday of every month – an event

that is appropriately called "First Friday." The **Berman Gallery** and the **Moderne Gallery** feature contemporary furniture, pottery, fine arts, and metalwork. The **Artists' House Gallery** offers works rendered by local artists and available for sale at affordable prices.

Located on Antique Row, **Seraphin Gallery** has art from international contemporary painters, sculptors, and photographers, including 18th- through 20th-century works by artists from America and Europe. In Center City, **Newman Galleries** specializes in 19th-century American and European paintings, and early 20th-century American art from the New Hope School.

The Clay Studio recently celebrated 30 years in Old City. This studio exhibits works by emerging and established artists and also offers a range of classes.

BOOKS

An excellent choice for mainstream books and magazines is **Barnes & Noble** at Rittenhouse Square. Also in that square is the independent **Joseph Fox Bookshop**, while **Books a Million**, has a more commercial store in Gallery at Market East mall.

For hard-to-find books, the **Philadelphia Rare Books and Manuscript Company** features early printed books dating from the 16th century, and manuscripts, old bibles, and other books from around the world that cover a wide realm of topics. Opened in 1936, **Robin's Bookstore** is the oldest independent bookstore in the city with a vast collection of African-American books, literature, poetry, New Age, and children's books.

FOOD AND COOKERY

Within the Italian Market are specialty food stores. Family owned for more than 50 years, **DiBruno Bros. House of Cheese** sells more than 400 types of cheese and gourmet foods. **Termini Brothers Gold Medal Pastry Bakery** is a local favorite with hand-made Italian confections made from recipes that date to the 1800s. Serving chefs and home cooks since 1906, **Fante's Kitchen Wares Shop** offers an extensive selection of cooking wares and utensils.

Gourmet cheese

GIFTS, CRAFTS, AND SOUVENIRS

As a result of its varied traditions and its status as one of America's oldest cities, Philadelphia offers a range of gifts and mementos. **Xenos Candy'n Gifts** has classic souvenirs showcasing Old City sights, including replicas of Liberty Bell, flags, and other collectables. Similar items are found in **The Bourse** nearby, while the **Pennsylvania General Store** has locally-made foods and crafts. **Scarlett Alley** offers art, furnishings, jewelry, leather goods, books, and children's items. **Sweet Violet** features fine gifts for personal care as well as for homes. Fine-rolled, handmade cigars can be bought at the **Black Cat Cigar Company** and **Holt's Cigar Company** in Center City.

FLORISTS

A wide-ranging choice of flowers is available from Philadelphia's florists. Some, such as **Nature's Gallery Florist** in Center City, are also able to assist with the floral side of party planning. **Ten Pennies Florist**, a staple in Philadelphia for more than 20 years, offers exquisite arrangements for any occasion.

MUSIC

For the latest in music CDs and recordings, **f.y.e.** has extensive music selections featuring rock, pop, hip-hop, jazz, folk, classical, and more. Visit **Repo Records** on South Street to thumb through a wide range of import singles, and rows of used records and

CDs. **Philadelphia Record Exchange** is the city's spot to find second-hand vinyl and CDs.

Music CDs

SPORTING GOODS

The nation's largest family-owned sports goods chain, **Modell's Sporting Goods**, has stores in Center City and King of Prussia Mall, and also sells home-team apparel and footwear. For camping gear, kayaks, and other outdoor items, shop at **Eastern Mountain Sports**, also at King of Prussia Mall.

DIRECTORY

ANTIQUES

Classic Antiques
922 Pine St. **Map** 3 C4.
Tel (215) 629-0211.

M. Finkel & Daughter
936 Pine St. **Map** 3 C4.
Tel (215) 627-7797.

South Street Antiques Market
615 S 6th St. **Map** 3 D5.
Tel (215) 592-0256.

ART GALLERIES

Artists' House Gallery
57 N 2nd St. **Map** 4 E2.
Tel (215) 923-8440.

Berman Gallery
136 N 2nd St. **Map** 4 E2.
Tel (215) 733-0707.

The Clay Studio
139 N Second St.
Map 4 E2.
Tel (215) 925-3453.

Moderne Gallery
111 N 3rd St. **Map** 4 E2.
Tel (215) 923-8536.

Newman Galleries
1425 Walnut St. **Map** 2 E5.
Tel (215) 563-1779.

Seraphin Gallery
1108 Pine St. **Map** 3 B4.
Tel (215) 923-7000.

BOOKS

Barnes & Noble
1805 Walnut St.
Map 2 D4.
Tel (215) 665-0716.

Books a Million
The Gallery at Market East,
Market St. **Map** 3 C2.
Tel (215) 923-1912.

Joseph Fox Bookshop
1724 Sansom Street.
Map 3 A2.
Tel (215) 563-4184.

Philadelphia Rare Books and Manuscript Company
Tel (215) 744-6734.

Robin's Bookstore
108 S 13th St. **Map** 3 B3.
Tel (215) 735-9600.

FOOD AND COOKERY

DiBruno Bros. House of Cheese
Italian Market, 930 S
9th St. **Map** 3 C5.
Tel (215) 922-2876.
109 S 18th St. **Map** 2 E4.
Tel (215) 665-9220.

Fante's Kitchen Wares Shop
Italian Market, 1006 S
9th St. **Map** 3 C5.
Tel (215) 922-5557.

Termini Brothers Gold Medal Pastry Bakery
1523 S 8th St.
Tel (215) 334-1816.

GIFTS, CRAFTS, AND SOUVENIRS

Black Cat Cigar Company
1518 Sansom Street.
Map 2 E4.
Tel (800) 220-9850.

The Bourse
5th between Market &
Chestnut Sts. **Map** 4 D3.
Tel (215) 625-0300.

Holt's Cigar Company
1522 Walnut St.
Map 2 E5.
Tel (215) 732-8500.

Pennsylvania General Store
Reading Terminal Market.
Map 3 C2.
Tel (215) 592-0455.

Scarlett Alley
241 Race St. **Map** 4E2.
Tel (215) 592-7898.

Sweet Violet
4361 Main St, Manayunk.
Tel (215) 483-2826.

Xenos Candy'n Gifts
231 Chestnut St. **Map** 4
E3. *Tel (215) 922-1445.*

FLORISTS

Nature's Gallery Florist
Map 2 D4.
Tel (215) 563-5554.

Ten Pennies Florist
1921 S Broad St. **Map** 3
C2. *Tel (215) 336-3557.*

MUSIC

f.y.e.
100 South Broad Street.
Map 3 B2.
Tel (215) 496-8338.

Repo Records
538 South St. **Map** 4 D4.
Tel (215) 627-3775.

Philadelphia Record Exchange
618 South St. **Map** 4 D4.
Tel (215) 922-2752.

SPORTING GOODS

Eastern Mountain Sports
King of Prussia Mall.
Tel (610) 337-4210.

Modell's Sporting Goods
934 Market St. **Map** 3 C2.
Tel (215) 629-0900.
King of Prussia Mall.
Tel (610) 337-4522.

ENTERTAINMENT IN PHILADELPHIA

Stretching along the "Avenue of the Arts," Broad Street is home to a plethora of renowned performing arts facilities. Heading the list are the Kimmel Center for the Performing Arts and the Academy of Music, home to the world-class Philly POPS, Philadelphia Orchestra, Opera Company of Philadelphia, and the Pennsylvania Ballet. Numerous other venues feature

Detail of façade at the Forrest Theater

live chamber music, theater productions and musicals, rock, hip hop and jazz-fusion concerts, and varied programs of gospel. Universities also put on several music, theater, and dance shows. Nightclubs hosting live bands abound in Old City and South Street, while a drive or train ride of an hour or so brings you to Atlantic City's glittering casinos on the New Jersey shoreline.

Visitors wait for a show at Kimmel Center for the Performing Arts

INFORMATION

There are several websites and newspapers that carry the latest information on musical concerts, theatrical performances, nightlife, and other entertainment options in and around the city.

The *Weekend* section of the **Philadelphia Inquirer**, published every Friday, details the goings-on in town, from the latest movies to gallery exhibitions to extensive listings of live performances, including ballet, chamber and classical music, opera, theater, and jazz. The art district has its own website, Avenue of the Arts.

The **Philadelphia City Paper** and **Philadelphia Weekly** also showcase arts, music, and cinema listings. They also have extended information on daily nightclub acts and performances. These two publications are weeklies and are available free at many cafés, pubs, and bookstores throughout the city. They also have websites with up-to-date listings.

Philadelphia's most comprehensive news website is **www.phillyfunguide.com**. It has information on all types of activities in the city and also has a number of saver deals.

TICKETS

Seats for most of the major symphony, opera, chamber music, ballet, and pop performances in Philadelphia can be booked through **Ticket Philadelphia**. The main box office is in the **Kimmel Center for the Performing Arts**. Tickets can be bought in person, on the phone or online. Tickets for various events and theatrical performances can also be bought at the box office of each venue, or over the phone, online or in person via **Ticketmaster**. Be aware, however, that ticketing services often add a fee to the total cost. Ticketmaster is one of the world's largest e-commerce sites, in addition to having more than 3,300 retail outlets and 19 worldwide telephone call centers. It acts as the exclusive ticketing service for various performing arts venues and theaters.

Some hotels may also sell show tickets, especially those in Center City or near the theater district. Check with the concierge in your hotel for the best ticketing options.

The Philadelphia Orchestra at Verizon Hall in the Kimmel Center

"Avenue of the Arts" lights up for a night of theater and culture

ENTERTAINMENT DISTRICTS

The hub of Philadelphia's performing arts and theater district is the so-called **Avenue of the Arts**, which extends south of City Hall on South Broad Street. This two-block area is anchored by the Kimmel Center for the Performing Arts and the world-renowned **Academy of Music** *(see p76)*. Also located in this area is the Merriam Theater, hosting professional touring productions, as well as the 300-seat Wilma Theater *(see p164)*, whose productions address current political and social issues. Three blocks east of the area is the Forrest Theatre *(see p164)*, while the Prince Music Theater is on Chestnut Street.

Besides theater and cultural activities, Philadelphia has a thriving nightlife with scores of restaurants, nightclubs, smaller theater venues, and comedy clubs concentrated along South Street. A vibrant nightlife scene also abounds in the Old City area around Chestnut, Market, Front, and 2nd Streets with a wide variety of restaurants, cozy pubs, and martini bars.

Along the Delaware River, Columbus Avenue is home to some of Philadelphia's up-and-coming nightspots north and south of Penn's Landing – some are on piers stretching into the river, while others are seasonal outdoor clubs. Much of the city's lesbian and gay nightlife is centered in the neighborhood between Pine and Chestnut Streets north to south and Broad and 11th Streets west to east.

Across the Delaware, meanwhile, the Susquehanna Bank Center at the Camden Waterfront *(see p101)* hosts concerts through the year, drawing big-name musical acts, as does the Wells Fargo Complex in south Philadelphia *(see p166)*.

Going beyond Philadelphia, Atlantic City *(see p127)* is just a short drive or train ride from Center City, and an entertainment destination in itself, with more than a dozen sprawling casino hotels and resorts, most of which have popular nightclubs, concert venues, and pulsing and glitzy discos.

South Street – an entertainment hub for the younger crowd

DISABLED ACCESS

Most of the major concert halls and theaters in Philadelphia accommodate disabled patrons and wheelchairs. The Kimmel Center for the Performing Arts and the Academy of Music have accessible wheelchair seating locations for performances, captioning for the hearing impaired, and assisted listening devices available on a first-come, first-served basis. Call ahead for details.

Some smaller venues and clubs may be less than adequate in accommodating disabled patrons. Check with the venue or the **Mayor's Commission on People with Disabilities** for more information. The commission provides a forum for the disabled to express opinions on programs and services in Philadelphia.

DIRECTORY

TICKETING

Ticketmaster
Various Outlets.
Tel (215) 336-2000.
www.ticketmaster.com

Ticket Philadelphia
Tel (215) 893-1999.
www.ticketphiladelphia.org

DISABLED ACCESS

Kimmel Center & Academy of Music
Department of Audience & Visitor Services. **Map** 2 E5.
Tel (215) 670-2327.
www.kimmelcenter.org

Mayor's Commission on People with Disabilities
1401 JFK Blvd. **Map** 2 F4.
Tel (215) 686-2798.
www.phila.gov/aco/index.html

USEFUL WEBSITES

Avenue of the Arts
www.avenueofthearts.org

Philadelphia Citypaper.net
www.citypaper.net

Philadelphia Fun Guide
www.phillyfunguide.com

Philadelphia Weekly Online
www.philadelphiaweekly.com

Philly.com (Philadelphia Inquirer)
www.philly.com

The Arts in Philadelphia

A cultural Mecca for the performing arts, Philadelphia has world-class venues that host excellent chamber and symphony music, and some of the finest performances in opera, ballet, and theater. Topping the list are concerts by the renowned Philadelphia Orchestra and Philly POPS, which are performed in the city's premier venue, the multitheater Kimmel Center for the Performing Arts. Chamber music ensembles play before smaller crowds, while grand opera and ballet productions take the stage in the Victorian-era Academy of Music. Several theaters in and around Center City host performances that range from Broadway productions and musicals to African-American theater. Entertainment is also provided by choral groups and the area's top music schools, which hold classical concerts and dance performances by students.

Forrest Theater, host to touring dance and theater companies

CLASSICAL MUSIC AND SYMPHONY

One of the city's best, the **Philadelphia Orchestra** has shared the stage with some of the world's most influential classical musicians for more than 100 years. The orchestra's home was the **Academy of Music**, but it now performs at the Verizon Hall in the **Kimmel Center for the Performing Arts**.

Also performing at Verizon Hall is one of the nation's most-renowned POPS orchestras playing big band, classics, Broadway hits, and rock'n roll tunes. Grammy Award-winning pianist and band leader Peter Nero has been leading the **Philly POPS** since 1979. In summer, both orchestras perform at an outdoor venue, **The Mann Center**, also home to jazz, dance, opera, and musical theater programs.

Chamber music can be enjoyed on Sunday afternoons and Monday evenings at the Kimmel Center's Perelman Theater. The **Chamber Orchestra of Philadelphia** performs here, playing a musical repertoire from the 18th century to the present day. The **Philadelphia Chamber Music Society** presents more than 60 chamber music, piano, vocal, and choral concerts a year, which are performed by internationally known groups as well as emerging artists. Presenting a unique classical experience is the **Philomel Baroque Orchestra** – a small ensemble of accomplished musicians who play early classical and Baroque music on period instruments.

THEATERS AND THEATER COMPANIES

Stage productions run the gamut from national touring shows to politically inspired acts produced locally. The

Philadelphia Theatre Company is the city's leading producer of contemporary American theater, while the **Arden Theatre Company** brings to life dramatic and theatrical stories by the greatest storytellers of all time.

The **Forrest Theatre** hosts Broadway shows and is the city's premier theatrical arts venue. The **Walnut Street Theatre** – America's oldest – is home to musicals and plays.

The **Wilma Theater** has productions with contemporary themes, while the smaller **Society Hill Playhouse** features offbeat and "off-Broad Street" productions. The **Freedom Theatre**, located on the northern stretch of the Avenue of the Arts, is one of the country's leading venues for African-American performances.

OPERA AND BALLET

Local lovers of grand opera have been enjoying performances by the Opera Company of Philadelphia for more than 30 years. The Pennsylvania Ballet, which has been thrilling audiences for over 40 years, performs at the Academy of Music and the Merriam Theater. Its season has six productions, including the old Yuletide favorite, The Nutcracker *(see p35)*, which has become an annual Philadelphia tradition.

Pennsylvania Ballet dancer performing *Swan Lake*

Academy of Music, oldest opera house in the US still used for its original purpose

VOCAL ARTS AND CHOIRS

There are several choral groups in the city such as the renowned **Philadelphia Boys Choir and Chorale**. The 100-member choir performs patriotic music and Broadway show tunes. The group holds more than 40 performances each year, and travels on international tours.

The **Philadelphia Singers**, an ensemble of 24 professional vocalists, performs with leading national and local orchestras and other perform-ing arts organizations such as the Philadelphia Orchestra, the Pennsylvania Ballet, and the Curtis Institute of Music. A 100-voice symphonic chorus, the **Choral Arts Society of Philadelphia** also appears often with the Philadelphia Orchestra. The **Academy of Vocal Arts**, around since 1934, produces operas with the **Chamber Orchestra of Philadelphia**. The academy's resident artists also hold recitals and concerts.

MUSIC SCHOOLS' PERFORMANCES

Often considered one of the most prestigious conserv-atories, the **Curtis Institute of Music** trains some of the best young musicians from around the world. The students hold free public recitals and concerts in the institute's Field Concert Hall located opposite Rittenhouse Square, and play in various venues around the city when they are not touring.

Local musicians and students training in classical, jazz, dance, and theater arts also hold recitals and concerts at the **University of the Arts**, Temple University's **Esther Boyer College of Music and Dance**, and through **PENN Presents** at the University of Pennsylvania's Annenberg Center for the Performing Arts.

DIRECTORY

CLASSICAL MUSIC AND SYMPHONY

Academy of Music
1420 Locust St.
Map 2 E5.
Tel *(215) 790-5800;*
box office: (215) 893-1999.

Chamber Orchestra of Philadelphia
Perelman Theater,
Kimmel Center.
Map 2 E5.
Tel *(215) 545-5451;*
box office: (215) 893-1709.

Kimmel Center for the Performing Arts
Broad & Spruce Sts.
Map 2 E5.
Tel *(215) 790-5800;*
box office: (215) 893-1999.

The Mann Center
52nd St & Parkside Ave.
Tel *(215) 546-7900; box office: (215) 893-1999.*

Peter Nero & the Philly POPS
Verizon Hall,
Kimmel Center.
Map 2 E5.
Tel *(215) 546-6400;*
box office: (215) 893-1999.

Philadelphia Chamber Music Society
Various venues.
Tel *(215) 569-8587;*
box office: (215) 569-8080.

Philadelphia Orchestra
Verizon Hall, Kimmel Center. **Map** 2 E5.
Tel *(215) 893-1900; box office: (215) 893-1999.*

Philomel Baroque Orchestra
Various venues.
Tel *(215) 487–2344;*
box office: (215) 569-9700.

THEATERS AND THEATER COMPANIES

Arden Theatre Company
40 N 2nd St. **Map** 4 E2.
Tel *(215) 922-1122.*

Forrest Theatre
1114 Walnut St.
Map 3 B3.
Tel *(215) 923-1515.*

Freedom Theatre
1346 N Broad St.
Tel *(215) 765-2793.*

Philadelphia Theatre Company
480 S Broad St.
Map 2 D5.
Tel *(215) 985-1400; box office: (215) 985-0420.*

Society Hill Playhouse
507 S 8th St. **Map** 3 C4.
Tel *(215) 923-0210.*

Walnut Street Theatre
825 Walnut St. **Map** 3 C3. **Tel** *(215) 574-3550.*

Wilma Theater
265 S Broad St.
Map 2 F5.
Tel *box office: (215) 546-7824.*

OPERA AND BALLET

Opera Company of Philadelphia
Academy of Music.
Map 2 E5.
Tel *(215) 893-3600; box office: (215) 732-8400.*

Pennsylvania Ballet
Merriam Theater,
Academy of Music.
Map 2 E5.
Tel *(215) 551-7000.*

VOCAL ARTS AND CHOIRS

Academy of Vocal Arts
Various venues.
Tel *(215) 735-1685.*

Choral Arts Society of Philadelphia
Various venues.
Tel *box office: (215) 545-8634.*

Philadelphia Boys Choir and Chorale
225 N 32nd St.
Map 1 B2.
Tel *(215) 222-3500.*

Philadelphia Singers
Kimmel Center
& various venues.
Map 2 E5.
Tel *(215) 751-9494.*

MUSIC SCHOOLS' PERFORMANCES

Curtis Institute of Music
Field Concert Hall
& various venues.
1726 Locust St.
Map 2 E5.
Tel *(215) 893-7902; box office: (215) 893-1999.*

Esther Boyer College of Music and Dance
Temple University,
1715 N Broad St.
Tel *(215) 204-8301.*

PENN Presents
Annenberg Center for the Performing Arts, University of Pennsylvania.
Tel *(215) 898-6701;*
box office: (215) 898-3900.

University of the Arts
Broad & Pine Sts.
Map 2 E5.
Tel *(215) 545-1664.*

Music and Nightlife

Philadelphia fills its after-dark hours with the latest sounds in rock, folk, pop, jazz-fusion, hip-hop, and salsa. These rhythms can be heard at venues offering live music, sometimes seven days a week. Many are clustered within the prominent entertainment districts of South Street, Old City, Main Street Manayunk, and the areas along the Delaware Avenue waterfront. Philadelphia is often a regular stop for major bands and musical acts on world tours, including top rock, jazz, hip-hop, and country and pop musicians. Those opting for a less energized night out can enjoy conversation and cocktails at friendly neighborhood taverns and bars located throughout the city.

ROCK AND FOLK MUSIC

For the top touring rock bands, check listings in local newspapers *(see p162)* for concerts at the **Wells Fargo Complex** and other major venues, including the **Tower Theater, Keswick Theatre**, and the **Susquehanna Bank Center**, located on the waterfront. Also check listings for concerts held in Atlantic City.

For a taste of local rock music, **Khyber** in Old City has shows several nights a week and is a mainstay for Philadelphia's rock scene. Live performances by local rock groups also take place at the **Pontiac Grille** on South Street and the **Grape Street Pub** in Manayunk.

Folk musicians and fans frequent the **Tin Angel** in Old City. One of the region's newest venues that attracts folk artists, gospel choirs and alternative rock acts is **World Café Live**, located on the campus in University City.

BLUES, JAZZ, AND WORLD MUSIC

Blues and jazz clubs range from upbeat nightspots and restaurants, where top artists

Alma de Cuba, famous for its Cuban cuisine and live music

perform, to smaller and cozier lounges. **Warmdaddy's** is a popular southern blues club and restaurant offering live jazz. Its 100-seat dining room overlooks the main stage where artists perform nightly; Tuesdays are reserved for open jam sessions made up of local musicians. **Ortlieb's Jazzhaus** is another hot venue that offers world-class jazz music six nights a week. **Chris' Jazz Club**, on Samson Street, has become something of an institution amongst the city's jazz lovers. The line-up includes a good mix of up-and-coming and established talent. Some clubs offer a range of international music,

such as salsa, flamenco, and more. For instance, musicians at **Alma de Cuba** belt out live Cuban music performances every week.

NIGHTCLUBS AND DISCOS

Philadelphia offers a wide range of late-night venues to suit all musical persuasions. The city's younger crowd parties late into the night with clubs churning out music until 2am. The cutting-edge dance club **Shampoo** features dance halls and lounges with multiple bars and DJs. On Delaware Avenue, restaurant and nightclub **Cavanaugh's River Deck** features concerts and DJs in an all-outdoors venue along the Delaware River, with views of the Benjamin Franklin Bridge.

A trendy nightspot for the city's chic elite is the **32° Luxe Lounge** in Old City. It includes two premium bars and a lush VIP lounge with European bottle service. The Polynesian-themed **Tiki Bob's Cantina** has a signature drink, the Tiki Nut. For classic funk to old-school hip-hop and reggae, to the latest DJ mixes, **Bleu Martini** in Old City is the place to be seen in Philadelphia.

BARS AND TAVERNS

Many Center City hotels and restaurants have comfortable bars that are ideal for relaxing and for conversation. Philadelphia also has a number of neighborhood bars and pubs that play live music. **Monk's Café** in south Philadelphia is a bistro with more than 200 beer brands from around the world and 20 Belgian draught ales. If you are not sure what to go for, their *Beer Bible* gives a description of each beer available.

Irish pubs with great food and Guinness beer on tap include **Fergie's Pub**, which has live music most evenings and a traditional Irish menu, and the **Irish Pub** that serves Irish-American food in a casual dining ambience.

Draught Guinness

Performers at the popular Chris' Jazz club

McGillin's Olde Ale House is the oldest operating tavern in the city, offering a great selection of beer. The **Bishop's Collar** has a friendly atmosphere with a selection of microbrews, and creative but inexpensive pub fare. It is a great place to unwind after visiting the Museum of Art or Boathouse Row.

GAY CLUBS AND BARS

Several nightclubs and bars are centered in the city's main gay and lesbian district, located between Broad and 11th Streets, and Chestnut to Pine Streets. The **Bump Lounge** is the city's premier gay lounge serving food and cocktails seven days a week. With three floors of energizing house music, disco, and hip-hop, **Voyeur Nightclub** has a bit of everything and is worth a visit. Nearby is **Sisters**, the city's largest lesbian bar with dining and dancing. For more information, visit the Greater Philadelphia Tourism and Marketing Corporation's website (*see p133*) or look at the Philadelphia Convention and Visitors Bureau's *Gay and Lesbian Travel Guide*, available at the Independence Visitors Center.

Voyeur Nightclub, a prominent gay nightspot

COMEDY CLUBS

Many clubs in town and across the river in New Jersey feature stand-up comedy acts. The city's "Original Comedy Club," the **Laff House** on South Street, brings in comedians from all over the country, with open mike nights, and main acts on Friday and Saturday nights. The **Helium Comedy Club** draws the nation's top acts to this 250-seat theater. Two lounges inside the club offer food and specialty drinks. Punters buying a drink before 7pm on Wednesdays can see that night's show for free.

DIRECTORY

ROCK AND FOLK MUSIC

Grape Street Pub
4100 Main St, Manayunk.
Tel (215) 483-7084.

Keswick Theatre
Easton Rd & Keswick Ave,
Glenside, PA.
Tel (215) 572-7650.

Khyber
56 S 2nd St. **Map** 4 E3.
Tel (215) 238-5888.

Pontiac Grille
304 South St.
Map 4 D5.
Tel (215) 925-4053.

Susquehanna Bank Center
1 Harbour Blvd,
Camden Waterfront,
New Jersey.
Tel (856) 365-1300.

Tin Angel
20 S 2nd St.
Map 4 E3.
Tel (215) 928-0978.

Tower Theater
69th & Ludlow Sts,
Upper Darby, PA.
Tel (215) 568-3222.
www.tower-theater.com

Wells Fargo Complex
Broad St & Pattison Ave.
Tel (215) 336-3600.
www.comcast-
spectator.com

World Café Live
3025 Walnut St.
Tel (215) 222-1400.
www.worldcafelive.com

BLUES, JAZZ, AND WORLD MUSIC

Alma de Cuba
1623 Walnut St.
Map 2 E4.
Tel (215) 988-1799.

Chris' Jazz Club
1421 Samson St.
Map 3 A3.
Tel (215) 568-3131.
www.chrisjazzcafe.com

Ortlieb's Jazzhaus
847 N 3rd St.
Tel (215) 922-1035.

Warmdaddy's
1400 Colombus Blvd.
Map 4 E5.
Tel (215) 462-2000.
www.warmdaddys.com

NIGHTCLUBS AND DISCOS

32° Luxe Lounge
416 S 2nd St. **Map** 4 E4.
Tel (215) 627-3132.

Bleu Martini
245 2nd St. **Map** 4 E2.
Tel (215) 940-7900.

Cavanaugh's River Deck
417 N Columbus Blvd.
Map 4 F1.
Tel (215) 629-7400.

Shampoo
417 N 8th St. **Map** 4 D1.
Tel (215) 922-7500.

Tiki Bob's Cantina
461 N 3rd St. **Map** 4 E1.
Tel (215) 928-9200.

BARS AND TAVERNS

Bishop's Collar
Map 2 D1.
Tel (215) 765-1616.

Fergie's Pub
Map 2 F5. *Tel (215) 928-
8118.*
www.fergies.com

Irish Pub
Map 2 D4.
Tel (215) 568-5603.

McGillins Olde Ale House
1310 Drury St. **Map** 3 B2.
Tel (215) 735-5562.

Monk's Café
264 S 16th St. **Map** 2 E5.
Tel (215) 545-7005.
www.monkscafe.com

GAY CLUBS AND BARS

Bump Lounge
1234 Locust St. **Map** 2 F5.
Tel (215) 732-1800.

Sisters
1320 Chancellor St. **Map**
3 A3. **Tel** (215) 735-0735.

Voyeur Nightclub
1221 St James Place. **Map**
2 F5. **Tel** (215) 735-5772.

COMEDY CLUBS

Helium Comedy Club
2031 Sansom St. **Map** 2
D4. **Tel** (215) 496-9001.
www.heliumcomedy.com

Laff House
221 South St. **Map** 4 E5.
Tel (215) 440-4242.

Outdoor Activities and Sports

Whether you are an active participant or simply a spectator, there is no shortage of sporting activities in Philadelphia all year round. In the warmer months, the region's many recreational areas and parks are packed with hikers, bicyclists, joggers, and golfers. In the winter months, outdoor enthusiasts opt for ice-skating or head for the nearby ski slopes in the Pocono Mountains. Local sports fans are passionate about their many professional home teams that play throughout the year. They flock to the city's stadiums and arenas to watch baseball, football, basketball, and hockey. The area's colleges and universities compete in the above sports and others such as volleyball, swimming, and gymnastics.

Inline skater

BICYCLING, JOGGING, AND SKATING

Philadelphia has an extensive greenbelt running through it with miles of walking and biking trails, most of which are found in Fairmount Park *(see p97)*. On warmer days of the year, hundreds of enthusiasts take to the city's most popular trail, the 8.4-mile (13.5-km) paved inline skating, walking, and biking path that runs parallel to Kelly and Martin Luther King Jr Boulevard *(see p98)* along both sides of the Schuylkill River. The **Bicycle Club of Philadelphia** has information about the various bike paths within the area, and schedules bike rides each weekend for cyclists of all experience levels.

Other popular hiking and biking trails can be found along Wissahickon Gorge in Fairmount Park. There are also 6 miles (9.6 km) of trails within **Valley Forge National Historic Park** *(see p129)*. Valley Forge is a starting point for the 22-mile (35-km) bike path ending in Fairmount Park. The path runs on a former railroad track route along the Schuylkill River.

GOLF AND TENNIS

The Philadelphia area has numerous 18-hole golf courses that challenge players at all levels. Courses situated in the city include the **Cobbs Creek Golf Club** and the **Walnut Lane Golf Club**, located within Wissahickon Valley Park. The professionally ranked **Tattersall Golf Club** sits in scenic West Chester countryside, while **Makefield Highlands** is the only true links-style golf course in the Tri-State area.

Public tennis courts in many parks are free on a first-come, first-served basis. Local tennis clubs that charge a fee include **Friends of Chamounix Tennis** situated in Fairmount Park and **Aqua Hab** in nearby Bala Cynwyd.

WINTER ACTIVITIES

As Christmas approaches, many outdoor enthusiasts bundle up and trade their inline blades for ice skates. Philadelphia and its surrounding areas have several ice-skating rinks, but the most popular is the **Blue Cross RiverRink** at Penn's Landing, where skaters enjoy an Olympic-sized rink with views of the Ben Franklin Bridge and the Delaware River.

Skiers head to the Pocono Mountains. This usually involves a day trip, and most ski slopes are within a two-hour drive. The **Pocono Mountains Vacation Bureau, Inc.** has information about ski slopes and snow conditions.

PROFESSIONAL SPECTATOR SPORTS

South Philadelphia's modern stadiums are the venue for most professional sports competitions held in the city. The **Philadelphia Phillies** play throughout the summer season at the Citizens Bank Park. The 43,000-seat stadium is one of the most fan-friendly ballparks to host major league baseball games. Rough-and-tumble football action kicks off in August as the

Paved walking and biking path in Fairmount Park *(see p95)*

Philadelphia Eagles start their season with games at Lincoln Financial Field, a 68,000-seat stadium.

During the cold winter months, sports fans head back indoors to watch basketball played by the **Philadelphia 76ers** at the Wells Fargo Center, which seats 21,000. Hockey fans flock to the Wells Fargo Center as well for spirited games on ice with the **Philadelphia Flyers**. The area's minor league baseball team, the **Camden Riversharks**, plays ball at Campbell's Field at the Camden Waterfront. Other popular home teams play soccer and lacrosse.

For horse racing fans, the **Philadelphia Park Casino & Racetrack** has live thorough-bred racing all year round every Saturday through Tuesday. The racetrack is home to the GII Pennsylvania Derby on Labor Day.

Camden Riversharks in baseball action at Campbell's Field

COLLEGE SPORTS

Over a dozen colleges and universities in the Philadelphia area take part in intercollegiate sports programs and competitions, a tradition that dates back more than 200 years. Some of the nation's best college basketball is played by what is called the Big Five – **St. Joseph's University**, **University of Pennsylvania**, **Temple University**, **Villanova University**, and **LaSalle University**. Schools in the area have both men's and women's activities in a full range of other sports, and competitions in football, soccer, field hockey, volley-ball, swimming, gymnastics, and more are held regularly.

DIRECTORY

BICYCLING, JOGGING, AND SKATING

Bicycle Club of Philadelphia
Tel (215) 735-2453.
www.phillybikeclub.org

Valley Forge National Historic Park
Rt 23 & N Gulph Rd.
Tel (610) 783-1077.
www.nps.gov/vafo

GOLF AND TENNIS

Aqua Hab
600 Righters Ferry Rd, Bala Cynwyd, PA.
Tel (610) 664-6475.
www.aquahab.com

Cobbs Creek Golf Club
72nd & Lansdowne Aves.
Tel (215) 877-8707.

Friends of Chamounix Tennis
50 Chamounix Dr,
Fairmount Park.
Tel (215) 877-6845.

Makefield Highlands Golf Club
1418 Woodside Road,
Yardly, PA.
Tel (215) 321-7000.
www.makefield highlands.com

Tattersall Golf Club
1520 Tattersall Way, West Chester, PA.
Tel (610) 738-4410.
www.tattersallgolfclub.com

Walnut Lane Golf Club
800 Walnut Lane.
Tel (215) 482-3370.
www.fairmountpark.org/ walnutlanegolfclub

WINTER ACTIVITIES

Blue Cross RiverRink
Penn's Landing. **Map** 4 F3. *Tel (215) 925-7465.*
www.riverrink.com

Pocono Mountains Vacation Bureau, Inc.
1004 Main St,
Stroudsburg, PA 18360.
Tel (800) 762-6667.
www.800poconos.com

PROFESSIONAL SPECTATOR SPORTS

Camden Riversharks
Campbell's Field, 401 N Delaware Ave, Camden.
Tel (856) 963-2600.
www.riversharks.com

Philadelphia 76ers
Wells Fargo Center,
3601 S Broad St.
Tel (215) 339-7600.
www.nba.com/sixers

Philadelphia Eagles
Lincoln Financial Field,
1020 Pattison Ave.
Tel (267) 570-4510.
www.philadelphia eagles.com

Philadelphia Flyers
Wells Fargo Center,
3601 S Broad St.
Tel (215) 465-4500.
www.philadelphiaflyers.com

Philadelphia Park Casino & Racetrack
3001 Street Rd, Bensalem.
Tel (215) 639-9000,
(800) 523-6886. www. philadelphiapark.com

Philadelphia Phillies
Citizens Bank Park, 1 Citizen Bank Way.
Tel (215) 463-1000.
www.phillies.com

COLLEGE SPORTS

LaSalle University
1900 W Olney Ave.
Tel (215) 951-1000.
www.lasalle.edu

St. Joseph's University
5600 City Ave.
Tel (610) 660-1712.
www.sju.edu

Temple University
801 N Broad St.
Map 2 F1.
Tel (215) 204-8499.
www.temple.edu

University of Pennsylvania
3451 Walnut St.
Map 1 A4.
Tel (215) 898-6151.
www.upenn.edu

Villanova University
Tel (610) 519-4500.
www.villanova.edu

CHILDREN'S PHILADELPHIA

Parents will find a plethora of activities that will keep their children amused when in Philadelphia and the surrounding area. Museums, such as The Franklin and the Academy of Natural Sciences, thrill kids with hands-on exhibits and workshops, while the Adventure Aquarium and the Philadelphia Zoo

Actor dressed as George Washington

entertain with an array of sea creatures and animals. Educational tours can be taken at historic buildings, where actors dress up as colonial figures and perform skits. In the Dutch Country, kids can enjoy Amish-style buggy rides and much more at the Dutch Wonderland Family Amusement Park in Lancaster.

Ride the Ducks pleasure craft going around Philadelphia

HISTORIC SIGHTS AND TOURS

Tour guides at key historic buildings provide informative tours to young and old alike; however, some sights will interest children more than others. The **National Constitution Center** (see pp48–9) features interactive exhibits explaining the US Constitution, where children, for example, might try on a judge's robe at a replica of the Supreme Court bench, or cast their ballot for their all-time favorite president. Many tours

Historic Lights of Liberty show at Independence Hall

cater to families, such as the popular **Ride the Ducks** (see p175). Using amphibious vehicles, the tour whisks visitors through Old City and Society Hill and Penn's Landing before taking a dip in the Delaware River for an exhilarating cruise. Children and parents show their enthusiasm by raucously blowing colorful "duck whistles."

Kids also enjoy the multimedia **Lights of Liberty Show** (see p175), a brisk walking tour through Old Town at dusk. Participants don headphones and watch images – which tell the story of the American Revolution – projected on historic buildings. For younger children, ask for a special version for ages 6 to 12.

MUSEUMS

Philadelphia's premier museum for children is the **Please Touch Museum**. Aimed at kids aged under eight, it has several

exhibits that enhance a child's ability to learn discovery and play. For instance, the Alice's Adventures in Wonderland exhibit is based on the popular classic story and includes many settings from the book to encourage problem solving and language skills. The SuperMarket has checkouts, shopping carts, and toy food items, while Barnyard Babies teaches about life on a farm. Other activities include interactive theater performances with musicians, dancers, and storytellers. The museum is located in Memorial Hall in the Fairmount Park District.

Banner at the Academy of Natural Sciences

The Franklin Institute (see p85) has hands-on exhibits, with some such as Electricity Hall reflecting Benjamin Franklin's inventions. Children learn about the human heart and bioscience at the Giant Walk-Through Heart. Other exhibits include the Train Factory, which has an actual 350-ton (770,000-lb) locomotive, and the Franklin Air Show, which has a flight simulator. The Fels Planetarium features virtual tours through space. At the **Academy of Natural Sciences** (see p85), children can see the fossils of a Tyrannosaurus rex and other species in Dinosaur Hall. Youngsters can also check out the Live Animal Center, which houses over 100 animals, and live butterflies stored in a tropical rainforest habitat that has been replicated at the museum. In addition to model boats and deep-sea diving apparatus, kids enjoy squeezing through the small hatches and passageways of the submarine *Becuna* at the **Independence Seaport Museum** *(see pp64–5).* Boys, in particular, enjoy the old fire engines and pumpers at **Fireman's Hall** *(see p51).* At the **Fairmount Water Works** *(see p88),* interactive exhibits challenge children to learn about city water resources. The center also has a virtual helicopter tour of the watershed.

The **National Liberty Museum** *(see p53)* takes a more serious approach to entertaining children by helping combat violence and bigotry through interactive exhibits, glass artworks, and more. One display is Kids Vote, which asks youngsters to take a stand on such issues as handgun law and the death penalty. Another exhibit, Jellybean People, features two life-sized models made of multicolored jellybeans to show that people are the same inside, regardless of skin color.

For children with an artistic flair, the **Philadelphia Museum of Art** *(see pp90–93)* offers drawing classes and gallery tours on Sundays. The **Pennsylvania Academy of the Fine Arts** *(see pp74–5)* has workshops on most Saturday mornings.

Beyond Philadelphia, in the Pennsylvania Dutch Country, Strasburg offers kids train

Philadelphia Zoo, home to many animal species

displays, a train museum, and rides on the **Strasburg Railroad** *(see p119).* In Hershey, children will love the simulated chocolate factory at **Chocolate World** *(see p124),* and the roller coaster rides and attractions at Hershey Park.

GARDENS, ZOOS, AND WATERFRONT ACTIVITIES

An instant hit with children is the **Philadelphia Zoo** *(see p98).* While close-up views of wild animals such as lions and rare white tigers are a big draw, kids also enjoy the Tastykake Children's Zoo, where they can pet docile sheep, rabbits, and newly hatched chicks.

Tarantulas at the Insectarium

At the **Philadelphia Insectarium**, youngsters can safely observe the workings of a beehive from behind a glass partition, touch the likes of tarantulas and giant beetles, and see thousands of other live and mounted insects. Kids can also play in a man-made spider web.

The **Adventure Aquarium** at the Camden Waterfront *(see p101)* has a huge tank with hundreds of aquatic species, including sharks, sea turtles, and more than 1,000 kinds of fish. Kids can touch harmless species in the Touch-a-Shark exhibit and see seals frolic in outdoor pools. Also at the waterfront, the **Camden Children's Garden** is an interactive park with different areas, including the Butterfly Garden, Railroad Garden, Dinosaur Garden, and the Storybook Gardens. The latter has themes from classic children's books such as Frances Hodgson Burnett's *The Secret Garden* and Lewis Carroll's *Alice in Wonderland.*

DIRECTORY

MUSEUMS

Please Touch Museum
4231 Avenue of the Republic.
Tel (215) 963-0667.
www.pleasetouchmuseum.
org

GARDENS, ZOOS, AND WATERFRONT ACTIVITIES

Adventure Aquarium
1 Aquarium Dr, Camden, NJ.
Tel (856) 365-3300.
www.adventurequarium.
com

Camden Children's Garden
3 Riverside Drive, Camden, NJ.
Tel (856) 365-8733.
www.camdenchildrensgarden.
org

Philadelphia Insectarium
8046 Frankford Ave.
Tel (215) 335-9500.
www.myinsectarium.com

Interactive exhibits inside Fairmount Water Works

SURVIVAL GUIDE

PRACTICAL INFORMATION

Philadelphia thrives on tourism thanks to its rich colonial history and culture, and its world-class museums and restaurants. An efficient infrastructure – including clearly marked signs, a state-of-the-art visitor center, and a well-planned transit system – has been created by the city authorities and the National Park Service to give visitors a memorable vacation. Most of Philadelphia's central neighborhoods can be explored on foot and many areas in the city are safe, but visitors should take sensible precautions as in any major city. The following pages include tips on a wide range of practical matters to ensure a trouble-free stay.

Independence
VISITOR CENTER ★

Independence Visitor Center sign

VISAS AND PASSPORTS

All visitors to the US must have a valid passport and, in some cases, a visa. The US is 1 of 36 countries, including the UK, France and Australia, participating in the Visa Waiver Program (VWP), which permits those who qualify to enter without a visa and stay up to 90 days.

The US operates an Electronic System for Travel Authorization (ESTA) for VWP travelers. Visitors must register and pay online at https://esta.cbp.dhs.gov at least 72 hours in advance of departure; authorization will be valid for two years when issued. Alternatively, your national passport-issuing agency can provide information. VWP travelers who have not obtained approval through ESTA will be denied boarding any plane to the US.

It is always best to check the US State Department's website (www.state.gov/travel) before travel for the most up-to-date information and entry requirements.

TOURIST INFORMATION

The **Independence Visitor Center** *(see p45)*, located in the heart of Independence National Historical Park, is within walking distance of many sights in Philadelphia's central historic core. In addition to brochure racks and self-service information booths, visitor concierges assist with ticket sales and provide information on shopping, attractions, hotels, restaurants, and other visitor needs. The free, timed tickets which are required for entrance

Tour guide in colonial attire leading tourists in Old City

to Independence Hall are also available here.

The **Greater Philadelphia Tourism Marketing Corporation** offers comprehensive information about the Philadelphia region on its website.

The **Philadelphia Convention & Visitors Bureau** provides information for tour groups, conventions, and international visitors on their website.

Smoking is prohibited in most buildings and stores, except in designated areas, and it is strictly banned from all restaurants, taverns, and pubs throughout the city.

ADMISSION PRICES

Attractions within Independence National Historical Park are free of charge, which makes Philadelphia a budget-friendly place to visit. A number of others, including the Rodin Museum, request nominal donations of $3–5. Admission fees for most major sights, such as the National Constitution Center and Franklin Institute, generally range between $10 and $16. Many offer discounts or free admission for children. The

Philadelphia CityPass offers entry to six sights for $59 and is valid for nine consecutive days.

OPENING HOURS

Most museums and historic buildings open from 9 or 10am to 5pm daily, with extended summer hours. Business and banking hours are 9am–5pm Monday to Friday *(see p178)*. Central Philadelphia shops open 10am to 7pm *(see p154)*.

PUBLIC CONVENIENCES

Free public and wheelchair-accessible restrooms can be found at the Independence Visitor Center and in the Bourse at 5th Street between Market and Chestnut Streets. In other parts of Center City, the Reading Terminal Market, the Shops at the Bellevue, department stores, and malls have facilities.

TAXES AND TIPPING

Pennsylvania's state sales tax is 6 percent, with an extra 1 percent city tax in Philadelphia (7 percent total). There is no tax on clothing or shoes. Hotel taxes are 15.5 percent, and car rental taxes and fees can add 20 percent or more to the rental price.

It is usual to tip wait staff 15 percent of the final bill, and 20 percent or more for great service; for bar staff $1 per drink. Tip hotel or airport porters $1 per bag and at least as much for the room maid per night ($2 at upscale hotels), and up to $10 or more for a helpful concierge. Valet parking attendants expect $1–2, while cab drivers should be tipped 10–15 percent of the fare.

TRAVELERS WITH SPECIAL NEEDS

Most city buildings and sidewalks accommodate disabled persons as required by US law, but some historic colonial structures do not have adequate provisions. SEPTA buses *(see p186)* are equipped with lifts while **SEPTA CCT** and **ADA Paratransit** offer transportation for disabled passengers unable to use standard services. The **Mayor's Commission on People with Disabilities** provides information for disabled visitors to Philadelphia.

International Student Identity Card

STUDENTS AND SENIOR TRAVELERS

The Philadelphia area has numerous colleges and universities, so an **International Student Identification Card (ISIC)** or **Student Advantage Card** is recommended as these are accepted for discounts. Senior citizens also receive discounts, including reduced admission to many sights.

GAY AND LESBIAN TRAVELERS

Philadelphia is a gay-friendly destination known for its lively GLBT scene. Midtown Village (between 11th and Broad Streets and Chestnut and Pine Streets) is nicknamed "the Gayborhood" for its many gay-owned and gay-friendly shops, restaurants, accommodations, and clubs. The **William Way Community Center** hosts tours, activities, and programs geared toward the gay community. The weekly *Philadelphia Gay News* lists events, as does www.visitphilly.com.

RESPONSIBLE TOURISM

Greenworks Philadelphia, an initiative focusing on expanding environmentally friendly policies and programs, has had a major effect on the city's commitment to sustainability.

There are now several neighborhood farmers' markets from May through November. One of the most popular is the Saturday morning market at Head House Square in the Society Hill district. The **Clark Park Farmers' Market** in the University City area operates year-round (May–Oct: Thu and Sat, Dec–Apr: Sat). From Thursday to Saturday, Amish farmers bring their home-baked goods and produce to **Reading Terminal Market**, where other purveyors sell their foodstuffs all week long.

Many city restaurants, such as Matyson *(see p149)*, build their menus around locally sourced produce.

Several Philadelphia hotels, including Hotel Palomar *(see p136)*, have earned LEED status (Leadership in Energy and Environmental Design) for their energy-efficient design.

Locally grown, organic produce at a neighborhood farmers' market

DIRECTORY

CONSULATES

British Consulate
1818 Market St. **Map** 2 D4.
Tel (215) 557 7665.

Canadian Consulate
1650 Market St. **Map** 2 D4.
Tel (267) 207-2721.

TOURIST INFORMATION

Greater Philadelphia Tourism Marketing Corporation
www.visitphilly.com

Independence Visitor Center
6th & Market Sts. **Map** 4 D2.
Tel (215) 965-7676. **www.**
independencevisitorcenter.com

Philadelphia CityPass
www.citypass.com/philadelphia

Philadelphia Convention & Visitors Bureau
1700 Market St. **Map** 2 E4.
Tel (215) 636-3300.
www.philadelphiausa.travel

TRAVELERS WITH SPECIAL NEEDS

ADA Paratransit
Tel (215) 580-7145.

Mayor's Commission on People with Disabilities
Tel (215) 686-2798.
www.phila.gov/aco/index.html

SEPTA CCT
1234 Market St. **Map** 2 F4.
Tel (215) 580-7145.

STUDENT TRAVELERS

International Student Identification Card
www.isic.org

Student Advantage Card
www.studentadvantage.com

GAY AND LESBIAN TRAVELERS

William Way Community Center
1315 Spruce St. **Map** 1 C5.
Tel (215) 732-2220.

RESPONSIBLE TOURISM

Clark Park Farmers' Market
43rd St & Baltimore Ave.

Reading Terminal Market
12th & Arch Sts. **Map** 3 C2.

Personal Security and Health

Philadelphia police insignia

For the most part, central Philadelphia is generally safe and the majority of visitors touring the sights do not have any problems with crime. Nonetheless, as in any big American city, taking common-sense precautions will ensure a trouble-free visit. Although major crime is rare in high-density tourist areas, it is advisable to be aware of your surroundings at all times. Public transportation and walking in much of the central area is usually safe during the day, but visitors should opt for a taxi at night or for staying in prominent nightlife areas such as those in Old City, Center City, and Society Hill and Penn's Landing.

Philadelphia police officers on bicycles

POLICE

The Philadelphia Police Department provides round-the-clock car patrols as well as bicycle, horseback, and foot patrols. Police presence is plentiful throughout Center City, and there is often 24-hour surveillance by police and National Park Service rangers around key sights in Independence National Historical Park. The city's public transportation service, SEPTA, has its own police force that patrols the underground transit systems. Traffic and parking enforcement officers also make rounds on foot. Most are friendly when approached and will offer directions. Park rangers are usually helpful with answering questions about city sights and attractions. In Center City, police stations are located at 8th and Race Streets (Map D2), 9th and South Streets (Map C4), and 1201 S. 20th Street.

IN AN EMERGENCY

Call 911 to report life-or-death emergency situations or matters requiring an immediate response from medical, police, or fire department personnel. Most hospital emergency rooms in and around the city are open 24 hours daily and take walk-in patients or those delivered by ambulance. Emergency rooms are busiest during weekend evenings so there might be a long wait. Hotel personnel can locate the nearest hospital, or arrange a doctor's appointment for non-life threatening medical conditions. To get specialized assistance for people with disabilities, call **Relay Services**. Philadelphia International has its own **Airport Medical Emergencies** center. The **University of Pennsylvania Dental School Clinic** is one of a number of city clinics offering emergency dental care services. Ask your hotel staff for assistance.

WHAT TO BE AWARE OF

The popular tourist areas in Center City and around Independence National Historical Park are generally safe, but it is wise to follow basic safety precautions. Watch out for purse-snatchers and pickpockets, and do not leave personal items such as handbags or cameras unattended. Avoid wandering into dark alleys and deserted streets, especially in West Philadelphia. Local police and park rangers can offer directions and answer questions.

Do not carry a large amount of cash or wear excessive jewelry. Carry just one credit card and enough cash for the day's activities; leave other cards, traveler's checks, and your passport locked in your hotel room safe. Passports should be carried only when exchanging currency or traveler's checks. It is wise to make copies of your passport and record your credit card numbers in case of theft.

You may see homeless people on the city streets. If approached, it is best to ignore requests for a cash handout.

A 24-hour CVS pharmacy in a Philadelphia neighborhood

Police car

Police SUV

Fire engine

The legal drinking age in Pennsylvania and New Jersey is 21. Young people need to show photo ID as proof of age when ordering alcohol. Liquor and wine can be bought only at state-run stores, while beer is sold at special distribution centers or by the six-pack in bars.

LOST AND STOLEN PROPERTY

If your property is lost or stolen, chances of recovery are slim. Nonetheless, contact local authorities through the **Philadelphia Police (Non-Emergency)** line to file a report and keep a copy of the same for insurance purposes. It may be helpful to contact the Lost and Found in department stores, the Independence Visitor Center (see p174), or **Philadelphia International Airport**. Also, contact taxi companies or the public transit system in case missing items are turned in.

Call your debit or credit card company to report a lost or stolen credit card, and contact your currency exchange provider for lost traveler's checks (see p179). If your passport is lost or stolen, contact your country's consulate or embassy immediately (see p175).

HOSPITALS AND PHARMACIES

Philadelphia has excellent medical facilities should you become ill during your visit. There are a number of walk-in clinics that will treat minor ailments, while all main hospitals in the city offer accident and emergency care.

Visitors should be advised, however, that medical care can be expensive. Even if carrying medical insurance, you may still have to pay upfront and claim reimbursement from your insurance company later, so do not forget to ask for all necessary forms and receipts. Most medical facilities in the city accept credit cards.

Pack enough prescription drugs, and it is advisable to keep two sets of the same medicines in different travel bags, in the unlikely event that one is lost or stolen. There are several pharmacies open 24 hours daily in Central and Greater Philadelphia, including **CVS** and **Rite Aid**. Some pharmacies have medical personnel for minor, non-critical health issues (such as **Convenient Care Center**). Ask hotel personnel for directions.

TRAVEL AND HEALTH INSURANCE

Because the cost of medical care in the US is so high, it is essential to purchase travel insurance before you visit. Packages should include medical and dental coverage, as well as trip cancellation, flight delay, lost or stolen baggage, and even death and dismemberment insurance.

DIRECTORY

POLICE

All Emergencies
Tel 911 for police, fire, and emergency medical attention.

Philadelphia Police (Non-Emergency)
Tel (215) 686-1776.

IN AN EMERGENCY

Airport Medical Emergencies
Tel (215) 937-3111.

Dental Emergencies
Tel (215) 925-6050.

Special Assistance (Relay Services)
Tel (800) 654-5984.

University of Pennsylvania Dental School Clinic
240 South 40th St.
Tel (215) 898-4615.

LOST AND STOLEN PROPERTY

Philadelphia International Airport Lost and Found
Communications Center located between Terminals C and D.
Tel (215) 937-6888.

HOSPITALS AND PHARMACIES

Convenient Care Center
16th Street between Chestnut and Market Sts. **Map** 2 E4.
Tel (215) 399-5890.

CVS
1826 Chestnut St. **Map** 2 D4.
Tel (215) 972-0909.

Finding a Doctor (Non-Emergency)
Tel (215) 563-5343.

Rite Aid
2301 Walnut St. **Map** 1 C4.
Tel (215) 636-9634.
5040 City Line Ave.
Tel (215) 877-2116.

Thomas Jefferson University Hospital
111 S. 11th St. **Map** 3 C3.
Tel (215) 966-6000.

Banking and Currency

There is no shortage of local and international banks in Philadelphia, especially in Center City. Cash can be easily withdrawn through the city's numerous ATMs, which accept most major credit and debit cards. Foreign notes can be exchanged for American dollars in hotels and at currency exchange offices. However, be advised that most currency exchange offices and banks are closed on Sundays and hotels charge high commission. Also, it is prudent not to carry all your money and cards at the same time.

Wawa, a local convenience store chain, that offers ATMs with no service fees. Check with your bank which transaction fees apply. Also, notify your credit or debit card provider of your travel plans so your card does not get blocked while you are away.

The lobby of a PNC Bank branch with multiple ATMs

BANKS AND CURRENCY EXCHANGE

Major banks found in Philadelphia include **PNC Bank**, **Citizens Bank**, **Citibank**, and **Wells Fargo Bank**, which are usually open from 9am to 5pm weekdays (later on Fridays), and 9am until noon on Saturdays. **TD Bank** is open daily and most branches are open until 8pm during the week. Currency exchange services are available at airport kiosks, **American Express Travel Services Office**, and several banks. Hours vary but most currency exchange offices are open from 9am to 5:30pm. Some hotels offer an exchange service but fees are higher. It is a good idea to bring around $100 into the US in case exchange services are not immediately available.

ATMS

Cash is easily accessible through the numerous ATMs in the Philadelphia area. They are found at bank entrances, in office complexes, at shopping malls, grocery stores, and restaurants, and even in convenience stores. Cash is distributed in $10 and $20 bills, and can be withdrawn with a debit or credit card, including VISA or MasterCard. ATMs often charge a fee for withdrawals by non-bank members, while the user's bank might also charge a fee. Generally, fees are significantly higher, sometimes up to $4, at freestanding ATMs not attached to a bank. One exception is

Automated teller machine (ATM) for convenient withdrawals

CREDIT CARDS AND TRAVELER'S CHECKS

Most restaurants and shops accept major credit cards such as **Visa**, **MasterCard**, **American Express**, **Discover Card**, and **Diners Club**. Credit cards are not only safer than carrying lots of cash, some credit cards also offer insurance benefits on retail goods while providing reward points or airline miles. For travelers, credit cards are essential in the event of a medical emergency, as they are honored as payment at most US hospitals. A valid credit card is required for car rentals, and most hotels request credit card numbers to make a room reservation. Many businesses accept traveler's checks in US dollars as payment without charging a fee. You can cash them at local banks with identification such as a passport, driver's license, or student ID. Personal foreign currency checks are rarely accepted.

WIRING MONEY

Money can be wired internationally through **Western Union**, which has locations in supermarkets, convenience stores, travel agencies, business centers, and other locations including **Travelex Currency** in Center City. In addition to sending and receiving money within minutes, Western Union also offers overnight delivery of checks to private residences or offices as well as a three-day service whereby cash can be deposited directly into a designated bank account. The amount you may send and hours of operation vary by location. Fees generally start at about $40 and increase based on the amount being wired and expedited delivery options.

Coins

American coins (actual size shown) come in 1-, 5-, 10- and 25-cent, as well as $1 denominations; 50-cent pieces are minted but rarely used. Each coin has its own name: 1-cent coins are known as pennies; 5-cent coins as nickels; 10-cent coins as dimes; and 1-dollar coins (and bills) are sometimes called "bucks."

**25-cent coin
(a quarter)**

**10-cent coin
(a dime)**

**5-cent coin
(a nickel)**

**1-cent coin
(a penny)**

Bills (Bank Notes)

The units of currency in the United States are dollars and cents. There are 100 cents to the dollar. Bank notes come in the following denominations: $1, $5, $10, $20, $50, and $100. There is also a $2 bill, but it is rarely used and is more of a collector's item. Security features include subtle color hues and improved color-shifting ink in the lower right hand corner of the face of each note.

1-dollar bill ($1)

5-dollar bill ($5)

10-dollar bill ($10)

20-dollar bill ($20)

50-dollar bill ($50)

100-dollar bill ($100)

DIRECTORY

BANKS AND CURRENCY EXCHANGE

American Express Travel Services Office
16th St & JFK Blvd. **Map** 2 E4.

Citibank
1211 Walnut St. **Map** 1 A4.

Citizens Bank
1515 Market St. **Map** 2 D4.

PNC Bank
19th & Walnut Sts. **Map** 2 D4.

Wells Fargo Bank
123 S Broad St. **Map** 3 B3.

ATMS

Wawa
912-16 Walnut St. **Map** 3 C3.

CREDIT CARDS AND TRAVELER'S CHECKS

American Express
Tel (800) 528-4800.

Diners Club
Tel (800) 847-2911.

Discover Card
Tel (800) 347-2683.

MasterCard
Tel (800) 307-7309.

Visa
Tel (800) 847-2911.

WIRING MONEY

Travelex Currency
1800 JFK Blvd. **Map** 1 B3.
Tel (215) 563-7348.

Western Union
628 South Broad St. **Map** 2 F2.
Tel (215) 735-5154.

Communications and Media

A colorful US postage stamp

Like most major cities, Philadelphia has excellent communication systems. The US Postal Service is reliable and efficient, with regular pickups from mailboxes throughout the city. There are numerous local television and radio stations, as well as two major daily newspapers. Internet cafes and wireless hotspots are located throughout the city, and for those who need them, fax services are also available. With the advent of cell phones, card- or coin-operated pay phones are less common but can be found in hotels, malls, restaurants, and on some street corners.

CELL PHONES

The major cell phone services in Philadelphia are **Sprint**, **Verizon**, **AT&T**, and **T-Mobile**. The US uses a different frequency for cell services than that used overseas, so you need a quad-band phone to connect to the US network. Tri-band phones are usually compatible, too. You may also need to activate the "roaming" facility.

Alternatively, you can rent a cell phone, available at **AllCell Rental**, or buy a disposable phone at local pharmacies or convenience stores.

PUBLIC TELEPHONES

The increase in cell phone usage has resulted in fewer coin- and credit card-operated pay phones, but some are still available in hotel lobbies, shopping malls, restaurants, gas stations, bars, and some city streets. Pay phone rates vary by carrier but most local call charges start at about 50 cents for the first three minutes. Prices for long-distance or calls abroad can vary as different telephone companies set their own rates. Operator-assisted calls are more costly than calling direct. Prepare to have lots of dimes, nickels, and quarters on hand for coin-operated phones. Local and international phone cards can be bought from convenience stores.

INTERNET

Internet access is available at Internet cafés, public libraries, bookstores, and at some office supply and photocopy/fax centers, such as **FedEx Office**.

Most hotels have business centers where guests can check their emails. These services are often charged by the minute or by 15-minute blocks, which can become costly so check the hotel's prices before making a reservation.

Library Internet services are often free but may have time limits.

Many book stores and the **ING Direct Cafe** in Center City are free Wi-Fi hotspots, as are **Philadelphia Java Company** in the Society Hill neighborhood and **Old City Coffee** in the Old City arts district.

For connectivity on the go, many Amtrak trains offer Wi-Fi on some intercity routes out of Philadelphia.

One of many cafés offering Wi-Fi to its customers

POSTAL SERVICES

Philadelphia's **Main Post Office** at Market and 30th Streets, directly across from the 30th Street Station, is open 8am to 9pm Monday through Saturday and 11am to 7pm on Sunday. Most other branches are open weekdays from 9am to 5pm and Saturday from 9am to noon.

Letters and parcels weighing less than 16 ounces (454 g) require only stamps and can be mailed in the blue mailboxes on street corners, or in letter slots in hotels and office buildings.

Standard blue US mailbox

The cost of a stamp for first-class delivery of a standard letter is 44 cents. The US Postal Service, **FedEx**, and **DHL** offer a variety of overnight letter and parcel services, while **UPS** delivers large boxes and packages. FedEx offices are located in major office buildings in Center City and in Kinko's business services stores.

TELEVISION AND RADIO

Philadelphia carries the major US broadcast networks. Channel numbers vary depending on the service provider but generally you can find CBS on channel 3, ABC on channel 6, NBC on channel 10, PBS on channel 12, FOX on channel 29, CW on channel 57, and Telemundo on channel 62. Cable companies carry popular sports, news, entertainment, and movie networks, such as ESPN, HBO, and CNN.

Radio stations, on both the AM and FM frequencies, include a variety of music, talk, and news shows. Radio station KYW 1060 AM provides round-the-clock news, weather, sports, and finance reports. Some public radio stations offer commercial-free programming. WHYY-FM (90.9) focuses on call-in shows, political reports, and cultural news, while WXPN-FM (88.5) airs world, alternative, and new music. WRTI (90.1) focuses on jazz and blues as well as reporting on cultural events. Satellite radio is available through subscription and offers dozens of channels dedicated to a particular format.

NEWSPAPERS AND MAGAZINES

The city's two main daily newspapers are the *Philadelphia Inquirer (see p162)* and the *Philadelphia Daily News*. Both can be found in newsstands or in news boxes on street corners. Both weekday editions are 75 cents each. The *Inquirer*'s Sunday edition is $1.50; the *Daily News* does not publish a Sunday edition.

The *Philadelphia Business Journal* is published weekly and focuses on local business news as it relates to national trends. Other special-interest publications include the *Philadelphia Tribune* focusing on the African-American community, the *Philadelphia Gay News*, and *Al Dia*, the city's Latino newspaper. Two weekly alternative publications, *Philadelphia City Paper* and the *Philadelphia Weekly* provide political commentary and entertainment coverage. They are available for free and can be found in news boxes on street corners.

Monthly magazines *Philadelphia Magazine* and *Philadelphia Style* focus on trends, fashion, dining, and cultural activities.

Selection of local Philadelphia newspapers at a newsstand

TRAVEL INFORMATION

Whether traveling from within or outside the country, Philadelphia is easily accessible by air, train, bus, and car. Philadelphia International Airport is served by many international and regional airlines. Amtrak's 30th Street Station is a busy rail hub on the Northeast Corridor line that runs between Washington, D.C. and Boston.

US Airways plane

The station is also a stop for trains arriving from other regions of the country. A number of interstate highways, that crisscross most of the Philadelphia metropolitan area, cater to motorists and long-distance bus services. The city also has a cruise ship terminal along the Delaware River that serves as a stop on some liners' itineraries.

View of Terminal A at Philadelphia International Airport

ARRIVING BY AIR

Philadelphia is conveniently located in the middle of the US Northeast Corridor, situated about halfway between New York and Washington, D.C. Flying times are about 5 hours from the US West Coast, 1 to 3 hours from the Midwest, 3 to 5 hours from the Caribbean, and 7 to 10 hours from Europe.

Philadelphia is a hub for **US Airways** and **Southwest Airlines**. It is also served by many other airlines, including **Air Canada**, **Air Jamaica**, **British Airways**, **Delta Airlines**, **Lufthansa**, **Midwest Airlines**, **Northwest Airlines**, and **United Airlines**.

PHILADELPHIA INTERNATIONAL AIRPORT

Philadelphia's airport is located 7 miles (11 km) south of Center City. Seven terminals accommodate more than 1,200 flights daily to and from 120 cities, with direct flights to 36 destinations in Europe, Canada, and the Caribbean, and connecting flights to Asia.

The International Terminal A-West has 13 gates and 60 ticket counters, over 20 retail shops and restaurants, and currency exchange centers.

Domestic service is located in Terminals A-East through F.

The airport also has more than 100 shops, restaurants, and fast food stands scattered throughout the terminals, with more than 30 contained in the Philadelphia Marketplace located between Terminals B and C.

Drivers who are picking up arriving passengers can wait in the nearby Cell Phone Lot. Located 1 minute from the passenger pick-up zone, the lot has space for 150 cars and monitors that provide real-time flight arrival information.

ON ARRIVAL

International flights arrive at Terminal A-West. The modern terminal has plenty of US immigration booths to ensure you get through security checks as soon as possible. There are also food halls, gift shops, and currency exchange desks in the terminal. A staff member fluent in the language of the plane's country of origin meets each plane to answer questions and direct visitors to the Immigration Hall (INS).

Upon arrival at INS, staff will check the customs and

Arrivals Hall at Philadelphia International Airport, featuring words from the Declaration of Independence

SEPTA bus ferrying passengers to Philadelphia

I-94 forms distributed during the flight. Both ask questions such as name, birth date, country of citizenship, passport number, and current address. The customs form asks further questions, including do you have any vegetables, fruit, or commercial merchandise in your baggage. The I-94 form consists of two parts; one part will be returned to you as you will need it on your return journey.

Non-US citizens are directed to CBP (Customs and Border Protection), where officers check passports, customs and I-94 forms, and will also fingerprint and photograph foreign visitors.

Passengers who warrant further inspection are directed to a secondary screening area.

Once cleared, everyone may collect their baggage in the Customs area; customs forms must be returned before exiting.

Upon exiting, passagers can proceed to the International Arrivals Hall.

TICKETS AND FARES

A little research can bring big savings on airfares. Generally, the lowest fares are available 14 to 21 days before the departure date, although reasonably priced tickets can still be bought 7 days in advance. Before booking, check the airlines' policies as changing travel arrangements can incur penalties.

While airlines and travel agents often offer good fares, it is worth examining popular travel Internet sites as well, such as **Comparefare**, **Expedia**, **Priceline**, **Travelocity**, **Kayak**, **Lowestfare**, and **lastminute. com**. These websites often

sell consolidated tickets, which are also available through travel agents.

Several airlines offer special discounts through their websites, and while many of those offers require departures within a short time frame, the savings can be significant.

Other options include booking with smaller carriers and flying during the off-season, which can also reduce rates.

Philadelphia's high season peaks in the summer, then around Thanksgiving (late November), and the week before Christmas through New Year's Day. Book well in advance if you plan to travel during those times and don't expect to find any discounts.

TRANSPORT INTO THE CITY

SEPTA's Airport Regional Rail Line operates every 30 minutes and connects all terminals with Center City and Amtrak's 30th Street Station, which has rail connections to other points in the city and beyond. Train station for each terminal lie between the ticketing and baggage claim areas – visitors should look for the relevant signs. Tickets are $7.

SEPTA buses 37 and 108 also ferry passengers into the city for a $2 fare. Look for the red-white-and-blue SEPTA bus signs.

For shuttle van services, look for **Centralized Ground Transportation** and **Philadelphia Airport Shuttle** counters in all baggage claim areas.

Taxis are plentiful at each terminal. They charge a flat rate of $28.50 for a trip into Center City, with an additional fee of $1 per passenger.

Major rental car companies also operate at the airport; they include **AVIS**, **Enterprise**, **Hertz**, and **National Car Rental**. Most have information phones at all baggage claim areas. There are limo companies specializing in airport transit, too.

ARRIVING BY CAR

Several major roadways and interstate highways lead to Philadelphia from surrounding states and major cities in the northeast. Driving times to Philadelphia from some of these cities are as follows: 6 hours from Boston, 2 hours from Baltimore and New York, and 3 hours from Washington, D.C. The resort beach towns of New Jersey are about 1 to 1 hour and 30 minutes away.

The major north–south highway is I-95, which leads into the city center as it parallels the Delaware River. From the east, motorists driving on the New Jersey Turnpike should take Exit 4 and then follow signs to the Benjamin Franklin Bridge or the Walt Whitman Bridge into Philadelphia.

An alternative from the New Jersey Turnpike is taking Exit 6 to connect with the Pennsylvania Turnpike that runs north of the city. This is the major highway leading into Philadelphia from the west. Take the Valley Forge exit and then proceed east on I-76, the Schuylkill Expressway.

Interstate 676 cuts through the middle of Center City, connecting I-95 with I-76.

It's a good idea to carry a road atlas map and a city street map for all trips by car.

The Benjamin Franklin Bridge across the Delaware River

Philadelphia's 30th Street Station on Amtrak's Northeast Corridor, the second busiest of the Amtrak system

ARRIVING BY TRAIN

Philadelphia is served by **Amtrak**, the country's passenger rail service, which links the city to the entire nation and to Canada. Most trains serving the city operate along the Northeast Corridor from Boston to Washington, D.C., with stops in Baltimore, New York, and a number of locations in New Jersey, Delaware, Connecticut, and Rhode Island. Amtrak's lines also provide express services such as the premium, high-speed Acela Express that runs from Boston to Washington, D.C.

Tickets can be booked online or by calling Amtrak. It is best to reserve well in advance and be as flexible as possible to ensure good seating and prices. Note that certain discounts may apply, including those for students and senior citizens. If booked in advance, tickets can be picked up on the day of travel at either an

Amtrak service window or through kiosks at train stations.

Due to increased security measures, when conductors ask to see tickets, passengers from the US, Canada, and Mexico are required to show photo identification, which may be a driver's license or passport, while other foreign visitors must show a passport.

Passenger cars are comfortable and have snack bar services as well as dining cars on longer routes. Coach class seats for most journeys are reserved, except for shorter trips. Sleeping quarters are available on trains for long-distance destinations; some of the first class sleeping accommodations have showers and toilets in the compartments.

Philadelphia's main train hub is Amtrak's 30th Street Station – an impressive Beaux-Arts building with a columned façade and large atrium. Inside are ticket booths for both Amtrak and SEPTA regional

rail lines, restaurants, fast food eateries, gift shops, and newsstands. "Red cap" porters are available to help with luggage.

There are many taxis outside, and if you are carrying baggage, it is best to get a cab for the short hop to a central Philadelphia hotel.

ARRIVING BY BUS

Greyhound Lines, which serves destinations across the US, operates a **bus terminal** in Center City on Filbert Street, between 10th and 11th Streets, one block north of Market Street. Buses arrive daily from New England, New York, and points south and southwest of Philadelphia. Transcontinental buses also arrive from routes through St. Louis and Chicago. Stops include Amtrak's 30th Street Station, and others in north and south Philadelphia.

Compared with other modes of transportation, such as trains or planes, Greyhound's fares are more economical. The company offers wide-ranging discounts, including those for students, senior citizens, children, military personnel, and veterans, as well as cheaper fares if tickets are bought online. While advance purchases might save you money, walk-up tickets are available at reasonable prices.

Greyhound's buses are modern and efficient. Much of its fleet is either equipped with lifts or other equipment to accommodate disabled passengers or those in need of help. Under certain conditions,

An Amtrak train – backbone of America's passenger rail system

Greyhound bus, an economical way to reach destinations across America

personal care attendants may travel with disabled passengers at a reduced fare. For more information, call the **Greyhound Customers with Disabilities Travel Assistance Line** at least 48 hours before departure.

Discount bus operators **Bolt Bus** and **MegaBus** provide budget transportation to Philadelphia from New York and Washington, D.C. Both companies offer free Wi-Fi, plug-ins for electronic equipment, and fares starting as low as $1.

Bolt Bus stops across the street from the western entrance to 30th Street Station and tickets for the journey can be purchased in advance online, by phone, or on the bus at the time of your departure.

MegaBus tickets are only available online. Be prepared to give the driver your reservation number or show a printout of the confirmation form. MegaBus stops at both the Independence Visitor Center and 30th Street station.

ARRIVING BY SEA

Located in the former Philadelphia Navy Yard, the city's cruise ship berth along the Delaware River is the **Philadelphia Cruise Terminal at Pier 1** which serves approximately 30 ships per year. All cruise liners offer on-board luxury facilities and entertainment as well as beautiful views of the city.

Cruise ship passengers can visit Philadelphia's tourist sights via their cruise line's shuttle service or public transportation. SEPTA bus 17 from Broad and Flagship Streets, one block north of Pier 1, takes about 30 minutes to reach the Independence Visitor Center and Independence Mall.

Among other services, Pier 1 has ATM machines and cafés nearby. The Cruise Terminal is a 10-minute drive from Philadelphia International Airport and 15 minutes from 30th Street Station.

DIRECTORY

ARRIVING BY AIR

Philadelphia International Airport
Tel (215) 937-6937, (800) 745-4283.
www.phl.org

Air Canada
Tel (888) 247-2262.

Air Jamaica
Tel (800) 523-5585.

British Airways
Tel (800) 247-9297.

Delta Airlines
Tel (800) 221-1212.

Lufthansa
Tel (800) 645–3880.

Midwest Airlines
Tel (800) 452-2022.

Northwest Airlines
Tel (800) 225-2525.

Southwest Airlines
Tel (800) 435-9792.

United Airlines
Tel (800) 241-6522.

US Airways
Tel (800) 428-4322.

TICKETS AND FARES

CompareFare
www.comparefare.com

Expedia
www.expedia.com

Kayak
www.kayak.com

lastminute.com
http://us.lastminute.com

Lowestfare.com
www.lowestfare.com

Priceline
www.priceline.com

Travelocity
www.travelocity.com

TRANSPORT INTO THE CITY

Airport Parking
Tel (215) 683-9842, (215) 683-9825.

AVIS
Tel (800) 331-1212.
www.avis.com

Centralized Ground Transportation
Tel (215) 937-6958.

Enterprise
Tel (800) RENT-A-CAR.
www.enterprise.com

Hertz
Tel (800) 654-3131.
www.hertz.com

National Car Rental
Tel (800) 227-7368.
www.nationalcar.com

Philadelphia Airport Shuttle
Tel (215) 969-1818.

ARRIVING BY CAR

Pennsylvania Department of Transportation
Travel information & interstate road conditions.
Tel (717) 783-5186.
www.dot.state.pa.us

Pennsylvania Turnpike Commission
Tel (717) 939-9551.
www.paturnpike.com

ARRIVING BY TRAIN

Amtrak
Tel (800) 872-7245.
www.amtrak.com

ARRIVING BY BUS

BoltBus
Tel (877) 265-8287.
www.boltbus.com

Greyhound Customers with Disabilities Travel Assistance Line
Tel (800) 752-4841.

Greyhound Lines
Tel (800) 229-9424.
www.greyhound.com

Greyhound Bus Terminal
1001 Filbert St.
Map 3 C2.
Tel (215) 931-4000.

Megabus
Tel (877) 462-6342.
www.megabus.com

ARRIVING BY SEA

Philadelphia Cruise Terminal at Pier 1
5100 S Broad St.
Tel (215) 462-6790, (856) 968-2048.

Getting Around Philadelphia

Taxi sign

Most of Philadelphia's famous sights are in Independence National Historical Park, also known as "America's most historic square mile." These sights, including Independence Hall and the Liberty Bell, are within walking distance of each other in Old City, and just a short walk from attractions in Society Hill and Penn's Landing. A quick ride or stroll from the historic area brings visitors to Center City and the Museum District. The Philly Phlash bus service runs through the heart of the city during the warmer months, while buses and subways, operated by the Southeastern Pennsylvania Transit Authority (SEPTA), run year-round. Taxis are also an easy and generally affordable option.

GREEN TRAVEL

Philadelphia is increasingly committed to eco-friendly initiatives as demonstrated by its Greenworks Philadelphia scheme *(see p175)*. SEPTA have one of the largest hybrid bus fleets in the US. By 2012, one in three buses will be powered by a diesel-electric engine. Two car-sharing programs, **ZipCar** and **Philly CarShare**, have dozens of locations throughout Philadelphia that help alleviate traffic and emissions. There are also some designated bike lanes, and the core of the city is pedestrian-friendly.

FINDING YOUR WAY IN PHILADELPHIA

Thanks to the foresight of the city's founder William Penn, getting around central Philadelphia is easy with its simple grid pattern *(see p18)*.

Numbered streets begin at the city's easternmost boundary along the Delaware River at Front Street (technically "1st street") and progress westward in an ascending order. Note that what would be "14th street" is called Broad Street (or Avenue of the Arts at its southern end).

These streets intersect Market Street, the demarcation for whether they're proceeded by "north" or "south" in the address. You'll notice that building numbers become larger the more distant they are from Market Street.

Many streets running east and west are named after trees, especially in Center City.

WALKING

With a compact, user-friendly downtown, the best way to explore Center City, Independence National Historical Park, and nearby sights is on foot.

Mounted on street poles throughout Center City are "Walk! Philadelphia" signs with colorful maps of the downtown area. Community service representatives in teal uniforms are also available throughout Center City to help visitors with directions.

TRAVELING BY SUBWAY

SEPTA operates subway routes throughout Philadelphia, making connections to regional rail lines at the Market East, Suburban, and 30th Street stations *(see transport map at back)*. Maps are also posted in each station.

There are two lines, the Market-Frankford Line (blue line) and the Broad Street Subway (orange line).

Subway fares are $2 and exact change is required. Transfers cost $1 for trips that necessitate more than one transit in the same direction. Independence passes, Family passes, and tokens are available at SEPTA sales offices, newsstands, or the Independence Visitor Center *(see p45)*. An Independence pass is a day ticket that allows travel on all forms of SEPTA transport in zone 1 and costs $11. A Family pass is similar to an Independence pass but is $28 and vaild for a family of up to five. Tokens are $1.55; they

are cheaper than purchasing individual tickets.

TRAVELING BY BUS

SEPTA also operates bus routes throughout the city. Fares are the same as for subways *(see Traveling by Subway)*, and schedules are posted on the SEPTA website. Tickets and tokens can be bought on board, from newsstands or from SEPTA sales booths.

Useful routes include bus 38, which runs from Independence Mall to the Philadelphia Museum of Art and beyond. Bus 21 travels passed Penn's Landing to the University of Pennsylvania. Bus 42 circles neighborhoods in Society Hill along Spruce Street before heading west along Walnut Street to the University of Pennsylvania campus, returning via Chestnut Street.

Seats at the front are prioritized for elderly or disabled riders, who can board via lifts. Buses also have bike racks.

BICYCLES

Central Philadelphia has designated bike lanes on Spruce Street heading east and Pine Street heading west. Cycling is also permitted on Benjamin Franklin Parkway, which leads to the Philadelphia Museum of Art. This track continues onto the city's most popular cycling route that runs along Kelly Drive and West River Drive. Bicycles can be rented along here during the summer *(see p168)*.

Children under 12 years old must wear a helmet when

Bicycling – an enjoyable way to get out and see some sights

Colorful Philly Phlash tourist bus

riding a bike. Cyclists are required to obey all traffic signals and stay off sidewalks.

RIVERLINK FERRY

Operating from Memorial Day weekend in May through to the Labor Day weekend in September, **RiverLink Ferry** provides a scenic 12-minute ride across the Delaware River to the Adventure Aquarium and the *Battleship New Jersey.*

The ferry departs every 30 minutes from both the Camden Waterfront and Penn's Landing in Philadelphia. Visitors can purchase tickets at dockside terminals outside the Independence Seaport Museum for the outbound trip from Philadelphia.

Landlubbers can cross the river via the Waterfront Connection bus service ($2), which departs every 30 minutes from the Independence Visitor Center and stops at the same sights. Like the Riverlink Ferry, it operates only during the summer months.

GUIDED TOURS

Most city tours, ranging from guided walks to trips by horse-drawn carriage, are centered around the Independence National Historical Park district. The **Big Bus Company** offers tours on double-decker, open-roof buses with hop-ons and hop-offs at 20 sights. The **Constitutional Walking Tour of Philadelphia** provides several historic district guide options, including by MP3 player. **Ride the Ducks** is an excursion in an amphibious vehicle that ends with a big splash into the Delaware River. **Ghost Tours of Philadelphia** includes

a candlelit walk with haunting tales through Old City and Society Hill. The night-time **Lights of Liberty Show** winds through Historic Philadelphia with narrators recounting America's struggle for independence. Between May and October, the **Philly Phlash** bus loops from Penn's Landing to Fairmount Park, making stops at more than 25 attractions.

TAXIS

Taxis can be hailed in the street, though the best place to find one is at a hotel. Several cab companies serve the city, and if you must reserve a taxi for a specific time, call at least 30 minutes in advance *(see Useful Numbers on Sheet map).* Fares vary, with at least a $2.70 base fare and $2.30 for each additional mile. All taxis accept credit card payments.

DRIVING IN CENTRAL PHILADELPHIA

Except during rush hour, driving in town is not particularly difficult. The main Center City thoroughfares, Broad and Market Streets, have two-way traffic, while most other streets have one-way traffic. Vehicles are driven on the right side, and right-hand turns can be made at a red light after a full stop, unless a sign prohibits it. Seatbelts are required by law and using cell phones while driving is prohibited. Violators will be fined. With some exceptions, overseas visitors can drive with a valid driver's license issued by their home country. If the license is not in English, an international driving permit is required.

PARKING

Street parking is usually hard to find. It costs $2 per hour, payable by cash, credit card, or SmartCards (available from convenience stores) at green parking kiosks throughout Center City and Independence Mall. Put your receipt inside the windshield and keep track of the time; enforcement officers will write a ticket for expired receipts.

Parking on residential streets is often permitted for non-permit holders but read the signs carefully. Parking lots are numerous; rates can run from $15 to $30 plus per day.

DIRECTORY

GREEN TRAVEL

Philly CarShare
www.phillycarshare.org

ZipCar
www.zipcar.com

PUBLIC TRANSPORTATION

RiverLink Ferry
Penn's Landing. *Tel* (215) 968-5465. **www**.riverlinkferry.org

SEPTA
Tel (215) 580-7800.
www.septa.org

GUIDED TOURS

Big Bus Company
111 S. Independence Mall East.
Map 4 D3. *Tel* (215) 923-5008.
ww.bigbustours.com

Constitutional Walking Tour of Philadelphia
Tel (215) 525-1776.
www.theconstitutional.com

Ghost Tours of Philadelphia
Tel (215) 413-1997.
www.ghosttour.com

Lights of Liberty Show
6th & Chestnut Sts. **Map** 4 D3.
Tel (215) 629-4026.
www.historicphiladelphia.org

Philly Phlash
www.phillyphlash.com

Ride the Ducks
Tel (215) 227-3825, (877) 877-8225. **www**.phillyducks.com

Traveling Outside Philadelphia

Philadelphia has an excellent regional rail service with SEPTA trains running from Center City to far western suburbs, parts of nearby New Jersey, and northern Delaware. Amtrak provides a daily train service to Lancaster, Harrisburg, and towns west of Philadelphia. New Jersey Transit takes passengers to Atlantic City and other areas along the Jersey shore. However, it is advisable and more practical to rent a car when traveling to remote sights in the Pennsylvania Dutch Country and Gettysburg.

SEPTA train – an ideal way to go beyond Philadelphia

MAIN TRAIN STATIONS

Amtrak's **30th Street Station** is a hub for train services along the East Coast with frequent transits to New York, Boston, and Washington, D.C. as well as daily departures to Lancaster, Harrisburg, and towns west of Philadelphia. "Red cap" staff offer free baggage assistance, but be sure to accept assistance only from uniformed staff, and request a claim ticket for each bag.

Interior of 30th Street Station, one of the biggest in Pennsylvania

Other facilities include free Wi-Fi and a selection of shops. **Suburban Station** at 16th Street in Center City is a central point for regional rail service with connections to SEPTA's Market-Frankford Line. Here, dozens of underground shops offer a variety of wares.

Market East Station, at 11th Street, is adjacent to the Gallery at Market East mall and also intersects with the Market-Frankford Line.

REGIONAL RAIL SERVICE

SEPTA provides outstanding rail services to many of Philadelphia's outermost suburbs to the north, south, and west of the city. Trips to the outermost stops sometimes take over an hour.

SEPTA's Airport Line connects the city and outer suburbs with Philadelphia International Airport *(see p182)*. The Wilmington–Newark Line travels south, with a stop in Wilmington, Delaware. The Paoli–Thorndale Line travels west and north from Center City, with Doylestown *(see p125)* as the last stop. The

Manayunk–Norristown Line runs through Manayunk *(see p97)*, while the Chestnut Hill East and Chestnut Hill West Lines end their routes in Chestnut Hill, stopping along the way in Germantown *(see pp96–7)*.

Train are comfortable, air-conditioned, and have lots of seats. However, they fill up quickly during the morning and afternoon rush hour.

Tickets can be purchased at the three Center City stations, at suburban stations, and on board.

SERVICES TO NEW JERSEY

New Jersey is a short drive or train ride from Center City, Philadelphia. In summer the best way to reach the Camden Waterfront, just across the Delaware River from Penn's Landing, is by RiverLink Ferry *(see p187)*. You can also take the **PATCO** High Speedline over the Benjamin Franklin Bridge and get off at the Broadway stop for waterfront attractions. Collingswood and Westmont stops are also well placed for exploration on foot.

To reach New Jersey beach resort towns, you can take a 1 hour and 30 minute journey on **New Jersey Transit's Atlantic City Rail Line** departing from 30th Street Station.

SERVICES TO PENNSYLVANIA DUTCH COUNTRY AND GETTYSBURG

Renting a car is the best way to explore most of the towns and villages that lie beyond Philadelphia, but it is also possible to take organized bus tours or public transportation.

Amtrak provides train services from Philadelphia's bustling 30th Street Station to towns west of Philadelphia, including Lancaster and Harrisburg.

In Lancaster, the **Red Rose Transit Authority (RRTA)** operates bus schedules in the city and for surrounding towns, including Pennsylvania Dutch communities. These buses have busy timetables and tend to have limited services to the outlying smaller communities, including Paradise, Lititz, Intercourse, Bird-In-Hand,

Toll booths on Interstate 76, Philadelphia

and Ephrata. Buses to these areas usually stop after the afternoon rush hour. On weekends, service is reduced.

To reach Gettysburg, you will need to rent a car as no public transport travels there.

ROADS AND TOLLS

Turnpikes are interstate highways that charge tolls. The Pennsylvania Turnpike and the New Jersey Turnpike both require motorists to pick up a toll ticket before entering the highway, and then pay the toll when exiting.

The Pennsylvania Turnpike (I-76/276) is the fastest route from Philadelphia to Harrisburg, and a one-way toll costs approximately $5. Although not an interstate, the Atlantic City Expressway is also a toll road. Some expressways have both numbers and names, such as the Vine Street Expressway (I-676/30).

Some toll booths accept only cash or exact change while others use an electronic system known as "E-Z Pass" which scans vehicles and deducts the toll from the driver's account.

CAR RENTALS

To rent a car, US and Canadian residents must have a valid driver's license, while foreign visitors need an international driver's license and valid passport. The minimum rental age is usually 25, and a major credit card in your name is required.

Personal auto insurance often covers rental cars, but check the limitations of coverage with your insurance company. If you're not covered, it

is a good idea to purchase liability and collision insurance.

ZipCar (*see p186*) offers by-the-hour car rental. Fees include a modest membership, and hourly rates can start from $7 per hour. A valid driver's license is required and, depending on country of origin, additional documentation might be requested.

GASOLINE

Most gas stations in Philadelphia have self-service pumps. However, in New Jersey, state law mandates that attendants pump the gas. Rented cars should be returned with a full tank to avoid extra charges.

RULES OF THE ROAD

The speed limit on interstates is usually 65 mph (105 km/h), and 55 mph (88 km/h) on highways in and around Philadelphia. City streets usually have a 25 to 35 mph (40 to 56 km/h) limit. It's wise to heed speed limits, since a speeding ticket can result in a hefty fine. In Philadelphia it is illegal to drive while talking on a cell phone.

Unless otherwise noted by a sign, making a right turn is permitted at a red light. Watch for pedestrians since they have the right of way.

Drive carefully during bad weather, as semi-trucks often spew mist during heavy rainstorms, resulting in poor visibility. Also, bridges and overpasses can become ice-slicked during winter.

Wearing a seatbelt is required by law. It is also a good idea to keep all doors locked, stay

on main roads, avoid unfamiliar neighborhoods, and abstain from drinking alcohol. Be aware that drink-driving offenses are vigorously prosecuted in the US.

Members of affiliated international automobile clubs are entitled to take advantage of reciprocal benefits offered by the **American Automobile Association** (AAA).

PHILADELPHIA STREET FINDER

Map references given in this guide for sights, hotels, restaurants, shops, and entertainment venues refer to the Street Finder maps on the following pages (see How the Map References Work). Map references are also given for Philadelphia's hotels (see pp134–41) and restaurants (see pp145–53). A complete index of the street names and places of interest marked on the maps can be found on the following pages. The map below shows the area of Philadelphia covered by the four Street Finder maps. This includes the sightseeing areas (which are color-coded) as well as the rest of central Philadelphia. The symbols used to represent sights and useful information on the Street Finder maps are listed in the key below.

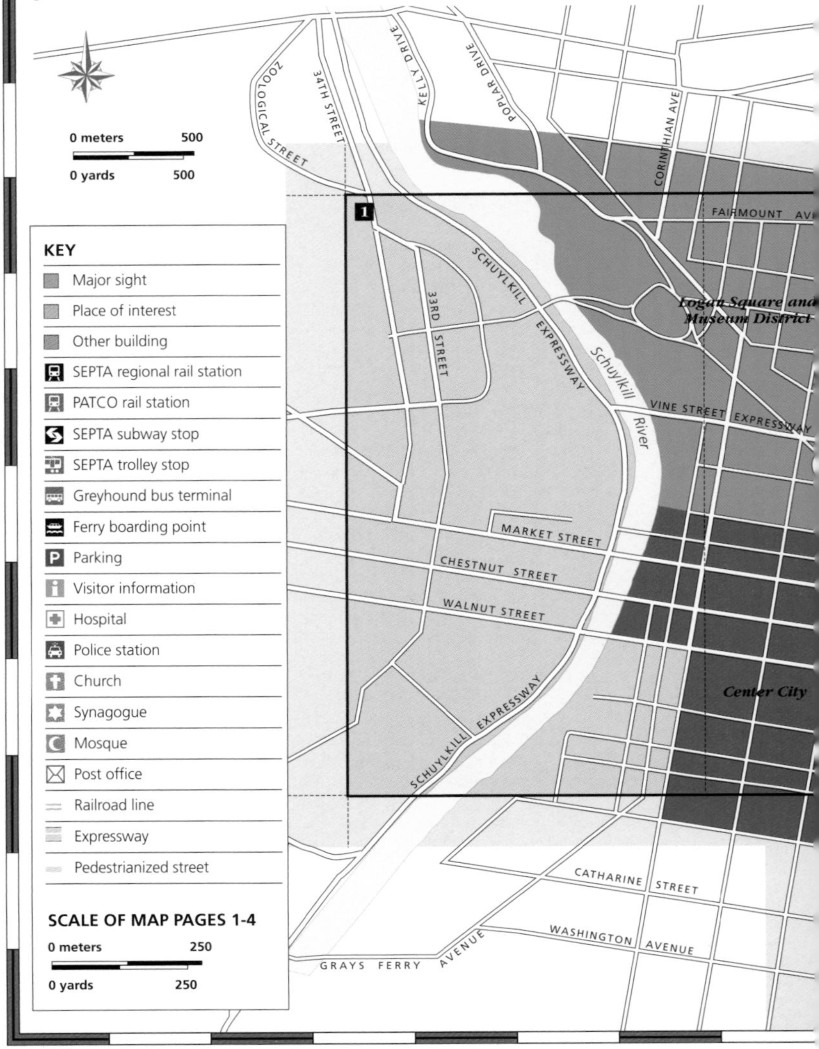

0 meters 500

0 yards 500

KEY

- Major sight
- Place of interest
- Other building
- 🚃 SEPTA regional rail station
- 🚃 PATCO rail station
- Ⓢ SEPTA subway stop
- 🚋 SEPTA trolley stop
- 🚌 Greyhound bus terminal
- ⛴ Ferry boarding point
- P Parking
- i Visitor information
- ✚ Hospital
- 🚓 Police station
- ✝ Church
- ✡ Synagogue
- ☪ Mosque
- ⊠ Post office
- ⸗ Railroad line
- ≡ Expressway
- ▭ Pedestrianized street

SCALE OF MAP PAGES 1-4

0 meters 250

0 yards 250

ZOOLOGICAL STREET

34TH STREET

KELLY DRIVE

POPLAR DRIVE

CORINTHIAN AVE

FAIRMOUNT AVE

SCHUYLKILL EXPRESSWAY

33RD STREET

Logan Square and Museum District

VINE STREET EXPRESSWAY

Schuylkill River

MARKET STREET

CHESTNUT STREET

WALNUT STREET

Center City

SCHUYLKILL EXPRESSWAY

CATHARINE STREET

WASHINGTON AVENUE

GRAYS FERRY AVENUE

HOW THE MAP REFERENCES WORK

The first figure tells you which Street Finder map to turn to.

Eakins Oval ⑧

Benjamin Franklin Parkway. **Map** 1 C1.
🚆 *30th St Station.* Ⓢ *Spring Garden.* 🚌 *38, Philly Phlash.*

The letters and numbers form the map coordinates. Letters are along the top of the map, while numbers are along the sides.

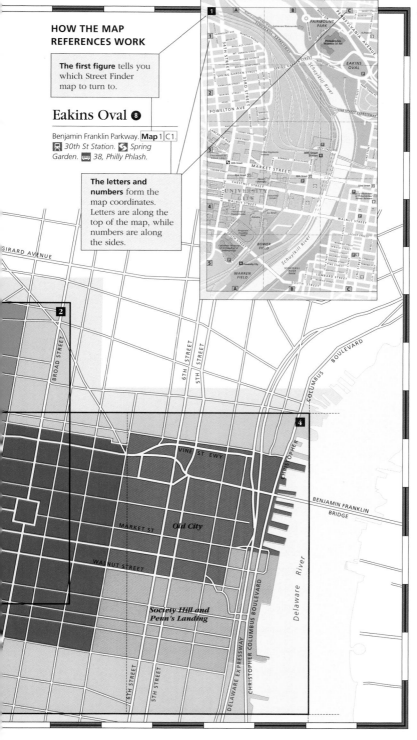

Street Finder Index

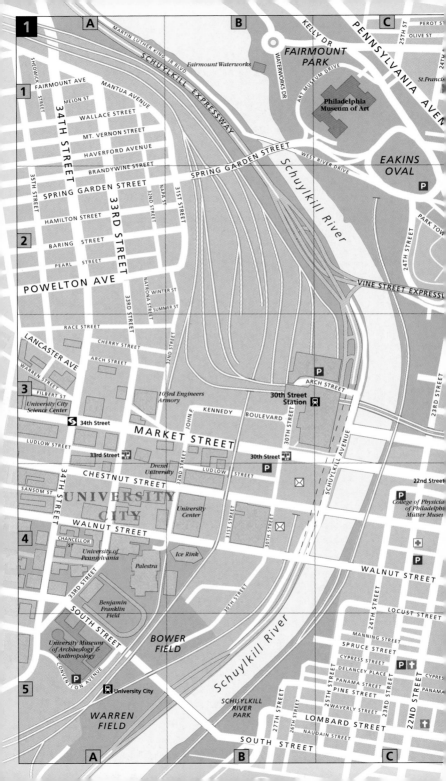

General Index

Acknowledgments

Main Contributor

Richard Varr spent a part of his childhood in Philadelphia and returned to the area in 1999. A former television and newspaper reporter, he now writes for newspapers, magazines, and websites, including Porthole Cruise Magazine and onboard publications of several cruise lines.

Factchecker

Scott Walker

Proofreader

Word-by-Word

Indexer

Jyoti Dhar

DK London

Publisher Douglas Amrine
Publishing Manager Lucinda Cooke
Managing Art Editor Kate Poole
Senior Designer Tessa Bindloss
Senior Cartographic Editor
Casper Morris
Senior DTP Designer Jason Little
Dk Picture Library Martin Copeland, Romaine Werblow
Production Controller Louise Daly
Revisions Beverley Ager, Emma Anacootee, Julie Bond, Andi Coyle, Anna Freiberger, Rhiannon Furbear, Camilla Gersh, Vinod Harish, Phil Hunt, Hayley Maher, Sonal Modha, Helen Peters, Marianne Petrou, Jeanette Pierce, Ellen Root, Azeem A. Siddiqui, Jeanette Tallant, Jeffrey Towne, Helen Townsend, Ros Walford.

Additional Photography

Shaen Adey, Paul Bricknell, Geoff Dann, Steve Gorton, Dave King, Andrew Leyerle, Tim Mann, Ray Moller, Stephen Oliver, Ian O'Leary, Tim Ridley, Clive Streeter, Scott Suchman, Matthew Ward, Jerry Young.

Dorling Kindersley would like to thank the following people whose contributions and assistance have made the preparation of this book possible.

Cartography

Back Endpaper reproduced with permission from SEPTA.

Special Assistance

The Barnes Foundation: Henry Butler; Independence National Historical Park: Superintendent; Gettysburg Convention & Visitors Bureau: Stacey Fox; Greater Philadelphia Tourism Marketing Corporation: Paula Butler, Kristen Ciappa, Meryl Levitz, Cara Schneider, Donna Schorr; National Liberty Museum: Amanda Hall; Pennsylvania Convention Center Authority: Patti Spaniak; Pennsylvania Dutch Convention & Visitors Bureau: Cara O'Donnell; Philadelphia Academy of the Fine Arts: Laura Blumenthal, Gene Castellano, Robert Cozzolino, Barbara Katus, Michelle McCaffrey; Philadelphia Convention & Visitors Bureau: Ellen Kornfield, Marissa Phillip; Philadelphia Museum of Art: Holly Frisbee, Rachel Udell; Philadelphia Water Department: Ed Grusheski; Rodin Museum: John Zarobell.

Photography Permissions

Dorling Kindersley would like to thank the following for their assistance and permission to photograph at their establishments:

Academy of Natural Sciences, Atwater Kent Museum, Bishop White House, City Tavern, College of Physicians of Philadelphia/Mütter Museum, Civil War & Underground Railroad Museum of Philadelphia, Eastern State Penitentiary, Ebenezer Maxwell House, Confederate Memorial Hall, New Orleans, Gettysburg National Military Park Visitor Center and Cyclorama Center, Independence Hall, Independence Seaport Museum, Landis Valley Museum, National Constitutional Center, Pennyslvania Academy of the Fine Arts, People's Place Quilt Museum, Reading Terminal Market as well as all the state and national parks, churches, hotels, restaurants, shops, museums, galleries, and other sights too numerous to thank individually.

Picture Credits

a – above; b – below/bottom; c – center; f – far; l – left; r – right; t – top

Works of art have been reproduced with the permission of the following copyright holders:

© ARS, NY and DACS, London 2005 84b, *Irish Memorial* by Glenna Goodacre 104cr, *Frank Rizzo* by Diane Keller 99br, *Horticulture Mural* by David McShane 89bc, *L'Ouverture* by Ulrick Jean Pierre 51tc, Cover of *The Saturday Evening Post* (June 28, 1958) by Norman Rockwell 27ca.

The publishers would like to thank the following individuals, companies, and picture libraries for their kind permission to reproduce their photographs:

ALAMY IMAGES: Bernie Epstein 115t; Jeff Greenberg 115bl; Andre Jenny 42tl, 100b; Dennis MacDonald 144cla; Mira 183br; vario images GmbH & Co. KG/ Hady Khandani 177cl.
Photograph ©2010 reproduced with the Permisson of THE BARNES FOUNDATION: 25cra, 86bc, 86tr, 87bl, 87tl.
BRIDGEMAN ART LIBRARY: © The Barnes Foundation, Merion, Pennsylvania, USA *Postman* 1889 (oil on canvas) by Vincent van Gogh (1853–90) 86tr; *Gardanne* 1885–86 (oil on canvas) by Paul Cezanne (1839–1906) 86cl; *After the Concert* 1877 (oil on canvas) by Pierre-Auguste Renoir (1841–1919) 87cra; *Card Players and Girl* 1890–92 (oil on canvas) by Paul Cezanne (1839–1906) 87crb.
CENTER CITY DISTRICT: 187tl; CLIVEDEN (A NATIONAL TRUST PROPERTY): 21cra, 107br. CHRIS'S JAZZ CAFÉ: 166bl; CORBIS: 9(inset), 13tl, 18t, 20tr, 21cr, 22crb, 23t, 33bc,

37 (inset), 38, 83cra, 111(inset), 173(inset), 185b, 189tl; The Barnes Foundation, Merion Station, Pennsylvania 83c; Dave Bartuff 39t, 40tr; Bettmann 8–9, 17ca, 17bl, 19ca, 19crb, 19bc, 21tl, 21br, 22t, 22bl, 22br, 23bc, 40cla, 53br, 131(inset); Kevin Fleming 94; Rose Hartman 61br; Robert Holmes 36–37; Kelly-Mooney Photography 127b; Bob Krist 2tr, 80; 68, 172-3, 188bl; Francis G. Mayer 16, 20-21c, 63br, Mary Ann McDonald 115crb; Charles O'Rear 46b; Philadelphia Museum of Art: *Peaceable Kingdom* by Edward Hicks (1780–1849) 18crb, 90tr, *Sunflowers* by Vincent van Gogh (1853–90) 90cl, 91cla, *Dormition of the Virgin (*1427) by Fra Angelico (1387-1455) 92cl, *Jester Vase* (1894) by Marc-Louis-Emmanuel Solon (1835-1913) Joseph E. Temple Fund 92bc, *The Staircase Group* (1795) by Charles Willson Peale (1741-1827) The George W. Elkins Collection 92br; 93tl, *Bird Tree* (1800–1830) Bequest of Lisa Norris Elkins (Mrs. William M. Elkins) 93c, *Gala Ensemble* Italy (late 19th to early 20th century) Bequest of Helen P. McMullen 93b; PictureNet 113 tr; Poodles-Rock 20cl, 20br; Bill Ross 2–3, 127t; Joseph Sohm: Visions of America 21crb, 42bl, 48c; Joseph Sohm- ChromoSohm Inc. 43cla; David H. Wells 83br, 102. CORBIS SABA: Erik Freeland 23crb; CVS/ PHARMACY: 176br.

FAIRMOUNT WATERWORKS & INTERPRETIVE CENTER: 171bl FLEISCHMAN GERBER AND ASSOCIATES: Esto/Peter Aaron 77br; THE FOOD TRUST: 175bc; FRANKLIN INSTITUTE SCIENCE MUSEUM : 26cb FREE LIBRARY OF PHILADELPHIA: 18bl, 19br, 21bc.

GETTYSBURG CONVENTION & VISITORS BUREAU: Paul Witt 123cl, 123br. GREATER PHILADELPHIA TOURISM MARKETING CORPORATION: 133bl, 174tc; R.Kennedy 44cra; C. Ridgeway 25ca; GREYHOUND LINES, INC.: 185tl. ING DIRECT – PHILDELPHIA CAFÉ: 180bl.

LEONARDO MEDIA LTD.: 133tl

MASTERFILE: David Zimmerman 110–111.

NATIONAL CONSTITUTION CENTER: 48tr. NATIONAL MUSEUM OF AMERICAN JEWISH HISTORY: 27cr, 41t.

PENNSYLVANIA ACADEMY OF THE FINE ARTS: 27tl, 74tr, 75cra, 75crb, *The Cello Player* (1896) by Thomas Eakins Oil on canvas. 64 1/4 x 48 1/8 inches. Accession no:1897.3. Joseph E. Temple Fund 74cl, *The Fox Hunt* by Winslow Homer Oil on canvas. 38 x 68 1/2 inches. Accession no: 1894.4. Joseph E. Temple Fund 74br, *Pantocrator* (2002) Oil on linen (triptych) 87 7/8 x 193 3/4 inches. Accession no: 2033.7.a-c by Vincent Desiderio 75tl. PENNSYLVANIA DUTCH CONVENTION & VISITORS BUREAU: 11br, 34cla, 112b, 118b; K. Baum 113b; THE PENNSYLVANIA TURNPIKE COMMISSION: 189tl; PHILADELPHIA CONVENTION & VISITORS BUREAU: ©Alma de Cuba PR 166c; ©Barnes Foundation 25cra; ©Bob Krist 14tr; ©Camden Riversharks Baseball/David Brady 169t; ©Cuba Libre Restaurant & Rum Bar/Mimi Janosy 142br; Melvin Epps 58cl; © Independence Seaport Museum/Rusty Kennedy 65cra; ©The Inn at the Union League of Philadelphia 70tr; ©National Constitution Center/Scott Frances Ltd. 25cb, 40cl, 48bl, 49tl, 49cr; Jim McWilliams 32cla, 34br, 168b, 170b, 184t; ©Pennyslavania Academy of the Fine Arts/Rick Echelmeyer 24; ©Pennyslavania Ballet/Steve Belkowitz 164c; ©Pennyslavania Horticultural Society/Rob Ikeler 32br; Jon Perlmutter 30cla; ©Philadelphia International Airport/ Richard McMullin 182b; ©Philadelphia Office of the City Representative 33cra; ©Philadelphia Orchestra/Eric Sellen 162b; ©The Plaza and The Court at King of Prussia 155b; ©PR Le Bec-Fin 143b; ©Ritz Carlton, Philadelphia 132b; Edward Savaria Jr. 10tc, 25bl, 35cla, 35br, 46c, 70cl, 70b, 71crb, 101b, 142cl, 143tl, 158tr, 160cla, 163tl, 170cla; 190tc Anthony Sinagoga 41crb, 44cl, 158bl ©Valley Forge Convention & Visitors Bureau 170t; ©Westin Philadelphia 132t; PHILADELPHIA MUSEUM OF ART, PENNSYLVANIA: Portrait of Dr. Samuel D. Gross (The Gross Clinic) (1875) by Thomas Eakins. Gift of the Alumni Association to Jefferson Medical College in 1878 and purchased by the Pennsylvania Academy of the Fine Arts and The Philadelphia Museum of Art in 2007 with the generous support of some 3,600 donors 91bl; Noah's Ark (1846) by Edward Hicks, Bequest of Lisa Norris Elkins, 1950 91crb; PHILADELPHIA POLICE DEPARTMENT OFFICE OF MEDIA RELATIONS: 177cla, 177tl; PHILLIES: 32tc; PHOTOLIBRARY: Mark & Audrey Gibson 186br; PNC FINANCIAL SERVICES GROUP: 178cla; PURE: 167tr.

STA TRAVEL GROUP: 175clb.

U.S. AIRWAYS: 182tc.

RICHARD VARR: 43cr.

WYK HOUSE AND GARDEN: 106t.

Front endpaper: All special photography except CORBIS : cr, Kevin Fleming tr, Bob Krist tl; MASTERFILE: David Zimmerman cl.

JACKET:
Front - PHOTOLIBRARY: JTB Photo.
Back - ALAMY IMAGES: Mike Booth bl; Lee Foster cl; Andre Jenny cla; CORBIS: Bob Krist tl.
Spine - PHOTOLIBRARY: JTB Photo t.

All other images © Dorling Kindersley. For more information see www.dkimages.com

SPECIAL EDITIONS OF DK TRAVEL GUIDES

DK Travel Guides can be purchased in bulk quantities at discounted prices for use in promotions or as premiums. We are also able to offer special editions and personalized jackets, corporate imprints, and excerpts from all of our books, tailored specifically to meet your own needs.

To find out more, please contact:
(in the United States) **SpecialSales@dk.com**
(in the UK) **TravelSpecialSales@uk.dk.com**
(in Canada) DK Special Sales at
general@tourmaline.ca
(in Australia)
business.development@pearson.com.au